The Wisdom Bridge

ADVANCE PRAISE FOR *THE WISDOM BRIDGE*

'Being a parent today is extremely challenging. *The Wisdom Bridge* by Daaji is a book that parents will find very helpful. It is both an inspiring and practical resource that parents will refer to often as they care for their children'—**Jack Miller, professor, University of Toronto and author of *The Holistic Curriculum* and *Whole Child Education***

'This is a practical and much-needed book that helps parents in guiding their children. As a father, a professor and a student of spirituality, I find the wisdom in this book enlightening. So grateful that we have this book handy in today's times'—**Clancy Martin, professor of philosophy, University of Missouri, Kansas City, award-winning author and contributing editor, *Harper's Magazine***

'Daaji's teachings are deeply human and spiritual. How to live a life that lifts the hearts of our children and how to come together as a family, Daaji gives us a poignant message from his heart through this profound book'—**Kabir Bedi, award-winning actor, television presenter and author**

'What a delight! This book removes the difficulty from topics like discipline and character-building that most teachers and parents struggle with. Daaji's idea of wisdom bridges and cherishing them is an ode to the values and ideals of our country. This is a timely book that families will benefit from, including my own'—**Pullela Gopichand, chief national coach, Indian badminton team and recipient of the Padma Bhushan**

'As a mother of two college students, I have certainly juggled taking care of my children and preparing them for their future, at the same time. I encourage parents to use the tools in *The Wisdom Bridge*, to guide them through the complexities of parenthood. It is often said, "There is no textbook for parenting." Daaji has now created one

The Wisdom Bridge

*Nine Principles to a Life that
Echoes in the Hearts of Your Loved Ones*

DAAJI

Kamlesh D. Patel

From the bestselling author of
The Heartfulness Way and *Designing Destiny*

PENGUIN
ANANDA

An imprint of Penguin Random House

PENGUIN ANANDA

USA | Canada | UK | Ireland | Australia
New Zealand | India | South Africa | China

Penguin Ananda is part of the Penguin Random House group of companies
whose addresses can be found at global.penguinrandomhouse.com

Published by Penguin Random House India Pvt. Ltd
4th Floor, Capital Tower 1, MG Road,
Gurugram 122 002, Haryana, India

First published in Penguin Ananda by Penguin Random House India 2022

ISBN 9780143459064

For sale in the Indian Subcontinent only

Typeset in Adobe Garamond Pro by Manipal Technologies Limited, Manipal
Printed at Thomson Press India Ltd, New Delhi

www.penguin.co.in

Wisdom (noun)

wis·dom | \ ˈwiz-dəm

Synonyms:
good sense, discernment, accumulated philosophic or scientific
learning

Antonyms:
density, brainlessness, irrationality, imbecility, lunacy

Source: Merriam-Webster Dictionary

to help you on your journey. As the old African proverb states, "It takes a village to raise a child." You can now consider Daaji part of your family's village'—LaShaun Martin, national vice president, operations, Mocha Moms, Inc., and gospel recording artist

'We are living in unprecedented times. Daaji's book, *The Wisdom Bridge*, provides parents with a clear and tested path to help our children face the future head-on, with solutions and answers that come deeply from the heart. Based on years of wisdom and experience, this pragmatic and insightful guide for parents is essential reading'—Harriet Shugarman, award-winning author of *How to Talk to Your Kids about Climate Change: Turning Angst into Action*, university professor and policy analyst

'I teach students how to develop an intuitive connection with music through feeling (*bhaav*). It is through feeling and introspection that self-awareness develops. Whether it's the journey of music or life, what matters is growing self-awareness. I impart this lesson through the flute, and Daaji does this by pouring the wisdom of spirituality into hearts through meditation'—Pt Hariprasad Chaurasia, internationally acclaimed flautist, teacher and winner of multiple global awards and recognitions

'Wise words from a wise man. I have children, and I plan to put Daaji's words into action'—Omi Vaidya, award-winning actor and comedian

'*The Wisdom Bridge* by Daaji is a gift for all families. The stories and insights in the book can be shared and applied across generations' — Ricky Kej, multi-Grammy-winning Indian music composer

Contents

Principle 7
Youth Are the Future. Guide Them, Don't Break Them.

Principle 8
Lifestyle Is an Expression of One's Attitudes

Principle 9
Discipline Your Love, Not Love Your Discipline

Dear Parents

I once read a story of a master and a disciple who lived with him. After years of training, one day the master told the disciple that he was now ready to go out in the world and make a mark of his own. On the day of parting, the master's wife kept delaying the disciple's departure, giving some excuse or the other. Finally, in the evening, after running out of excuses to keep him from leaving, she reluctantly handed the disciple a lantern and some of his favourite food for his travels. A long journey lay ahead for him, and part of it wove through dirt tracks and wilderness. The disciple had walked only a short distance when he heard the voice of his master calling him back. He turned around and dutifully walked back. Upon arriving, the master took away the lantern from the disciple and then said, 'Dear son, now you may go home. May you grow and grow.'

Why would the master take the lantern away? Did the disciple reach home safely? Why was the disciple allowed to leave while it was dark? Through these questions, the story encapsulates what every parent goes through while raising a child. In the story, the master is a metaphor for discipline, the master's wife is a metaphor for love and taking back the lantern symbolizes children guided by their inner light.

As parents, we care for our children, love them, nurture them and a day comes when they step outside the protective bubble of home. *The Wisdom Bridge* will help parents guide their children on the path of wisdom as they grow up in life. When children are exposed to the good and the not-so-good of life, wisdom will help them in making the right decisions. My experience as a meditation teacher, concern as a grandfather, learnings as a father and observations as a student of life all came together in writing *The Wisdom Bridge*.

This book is for parents. I use the word 'parent' as an umbrella term to address anyone caring for a child in some capacity. It includes parents, grandparents, uncles, aunts, teachers and caregivers. Also, I use the word 'family', to address the many flavours that families come in—large joint families, nuclear families, families with co-parents, single parents and so on.

In the past forty years, I've had the privilege of meeting thousands of families from all over the world. I have meditated with them, dined with them, travelled with them and counselled them. I have also done a fair bit of matchmaking and officiated at hundreds of weddings. Many of the children who grew up around me are now married and raising beautiful families of their own.

Daily I receive emails from parents who share their joys and sorrows. In their 'happily ever after' messages, parents send me pictures of their newborns. They tell me about their children's hobbies, graduations and college admissions. I also get a steady stream of 'we tried everything, but nothing changes' emails. Being a victim of bullying, struggling with gender identity, suffering from low self-esteem, relationship troubles and grappling with substance abuse are some of the challenges parents say their children face. And when things go wrong, parents blame themselves. They blame themselves for not acting in time, for not having instilled the correct values and for not being available when they were needed.

How can families face challenges with more resilience? What can a family do to avoid some heartache? What can parents learn from wisdom and science? I have pondered over these questions for many years. I have meditated for answers. I have had enlightening conversations with psychologists and educators. And ever since I became a grandfather three years ago, the motivation to share what I have learned has only become stronger.

It all came to a head during the pandemic. As the virus hunted down humanity, families lost loved ones. Two adolescents I know were orphaned overnight. Their parents and elders succumbed to COVID-19 and died in different hospitals within days. The children now live with me and study at the Heartful learning centre.

During the early months of the pandemic, the question that kept coming up in my mind was, 'How do I help parents through this new normal?' While the COVID-19 pandemic will end, I am concerned about its after-effects on families, especially children. For the past many years, I have been speaking about the well-being of families, the nurturing of children and the need to take care of our elders. Against the backdrop of the pandemic, with an increased sense of urgency, I started writing this book.

Parents Are Doing Their Best and They Need Support

For most parents today, the scene at home is different from when they grew up. If you are forty and older, you may have spent more time enraptured by stories from grandparents and elders than your children did. Families today lack support and are somehow DIY-ing parenting. The DIY-ing starts well before the baby arrives. From breathing classes and setting up the nursery, to mind-numbing research on car seats, strollers and cribs, parents have to figure out everything on their own.

But most parents, especially mothers, have no help or prior experience in taking care of children. The first time they burp a baby or put one to bed is when their little one arrives. A few decades ago, the situation was different. In those days, families were large and lived together or in proximity. There were uncles and aunts to help them out. Elder siblings doubled up as caregivers and homemakers. Life skills flowed serenely from the elders to the children. In contrast to the past, today's parents are toiling to make up for the support many no longer have.

As a result, these days, parents are present in their children's lives with more attention and intensity than ever before. 'Tiger', 'helicopter', 'lawnmower', 'free-range' and 'dolphin' are some of the terms used to describe styles of parenting. All the attention of the parents are well-intentioned. It shows the eagerness of parents to prepare their children: prepare them for STEM; prepare them for change; prepare them for leadership; and prepare them for success.

Prepare is the new care.

The prepare frenzy has swapped carefree summers with advanced math and science classes. Soccer mothers and chess fathers shapeshift into schedule managers and chauffeurs driving children from one activity to another. Many children start computer programming as early as grade 5, but I wonder how many are taught about their emotional programming with the same enthusiasm. Parents strive to send their children to leafy private schools that can cost their savings and then some to improve their chances of joining an IIT or IIM in the future.

Again, it's all well-intentioned, but I don't think it's working as planned. Data shows that pre-teens and teens from affluent, well-educated families are an *at-risk* group. They are identified with the *highest rates* of depression, substance abuse, anxiety disorders and other emotional issues such as unhappiness when compared with *any other group of children* across the USA.[1] While I don't have similar data for India and other countries, my conversations with parents from these countries give me a grim feeling that they're trending the same way. We are feeding our children a super-sized diet of desire and ambition. The question is, are we doing enough to nurture a child's inner growth?

Parents are doing what they can. Given their stress and the lack of support, parenting can at times feel like a hopeless effort. Not to mention expensive. The baby product industry in the USA alone is around $30 billion, and it shows the eagerness of parents to do a good job. They enrol in parenting classes, read books (including this one), learn from other cultures and make personal sacrifices, because deep inside, they want to be the best parents they possibly can.

The Wisdom Bridge will channel the parents' energies away from anxiety to appreciation. It will give them a new appreciation of how to tap into their heart's wisdom and raise happy and resilient children. *The Wisdom Bridge* will take the focus away from *prepare* and put the spotlight back on *care*.

Preparing children is like teaching them the block and tackle of surviving in the world—don't talk to strangers, follow a routine, study hard, don't eat junk food and so on. One may call it the transactional side of parenting. No doubt it's essential, and it's a lot of work. But on its own, 'prepare' is an incomplete idea. 'Care', on the other hand, includes nurturing the child spiritually, mentally, emotionally and physically. Prepare pushes the parents to 'do more, do more', while care guides the parents to 'do what matters'. Prepare is a transaction, while care is a deep relationship. Care comes from a place of 'What is good for my child's development?' Care is a long-term view of the child's flourishing in life. Care is a sacred activity and it begins at home.

In its essence, caring is the *real* preparing.

Guided by Wisdom, Parenting Becomes Heartful

To learn how wisdom helps in caring, we must first understand the heart. Across cultures, the heart is the seat of wisdom. It is a source of feeling and intuition. We have all experienced the heart's inspiration. It cannot be contested, only heeded; for inspiration is the language of the heart. When parenting is guided by the heart, we actively channel inspiration to guide us in our role. In reassuring silence and timely vigilance, the heart speaks. When we heed the heart's wisdom, there are only confident decisions instead of disabling doubt.

Does it mean that following the heart's wisdom is the antidote for all parenting problems? Does it mean our children will always do the right thing? That's not how it works. Children are affected by many things—the environment at home, the neighbourhood they live in, the school they attend, their friends, the books they read, the media they are exposed to and so on. Wisdom takes away the anxiety that comes from trying to control everything and helps the parents focus on laying a strong foundation for the child.

Parenting is many things, but the one thing it's not is a perfection pageant. There are no perfect parents. *We all learn on the job.* Children see their parents as the best in the world, not because they won the best parent competition. They are the best because they are *their* parents. The unconditional, innocent love from the children keeps the parents going. We all make mistakes. Each day we'll find something, no matter how tiny, that we might have handled differently. It's okay. Hug it out, resolve not to repeat it and move on.

Wisdom says the soul chooses the parents. We chose our parents, and our children chose us. In turn, as parents, we choose the best virtues and qualities that help our children design their destinies. *The Wisdom Bridge* is a guidebook for this noble journey.

The Principles

The Wisdom Bridge offers a simple framework of principles that are easy to apply. When you're in the dark and you reach for a matchbox, it doesn't matter which match you choose to strike. They all give light. These principles are like those matches. They come from a place of wisdom, and it doesn't matter which one you pick; they light up the road ahead.

In all, there are nine principles. The book is divided into nine sections, each of which covers one principle. Here are the principles:

1. Raising a child still takes a village.
2. Be guided by wisdom. Seek it. Cultivate it. Share it.
3. Preparation begins long before the children arrive.
4. Happy mothers make happy families.
5. Early childhood is the foundation of wisdom.
6. Character builds personality.

7. Youth are the future. Guide them, don't break them.
8. Lifestyle is an expression of one's attitudes.
9. Discipline your love, not love your discipline.

Parents are busy and most of them don't get more than twenty minutes of uninterrupted time before a chore, a task or a notification pulls them away. That's why most chapters in this book will take twenty minutes or less to read. Each chapter is also divided into subsections to help parents better navigate this book.

Parents can read the book in one go or can read the parts relevant for them. I would encourage the parents to scribble notes and highlight the lines they like. When they revisit the book, the notes will enhance their reading experience.

Within each chapter, there are tips and suggestions. Best of all, we have built a website—www.wisdombridge.in. The QR code below takes you to the website. Here you can download the 'Readers Guide'. It will help you identify the parts of the book most relevant to you, saving you further time.

Thank you for choosing this book.

It comes straight from my heart, and I hope it touches yours. Sometimes when the journey seems tiring and the skies turn dark, when you find yourself at the crossroads of indecision and doubt, I pray this book lights the path towards 'happily ever after' and away from the dark lanes of 'we've tried everything, but nothing changes'.

Visit www.wisdombridge.in
Download the Readers Guide and
access the bonus materials.

Principle 1

Raising a Child Still Takes a Village

1

A Village Is the People, Not the Place

Raising a child is a team effort. Mother, father, grandfather, grandmother, uncles, aunts, teachers and caregivers all play an essential role in a child's life. And when the village comes *together*, the child thrives.

The village is not the place, it's the people.

A few generations ago, whether one was rich or poor, educated or illiterate, everyone had a village to count on. But not anymore. Today, most of us live far away from our parents and grandparents. Even if we wish to live close by, it's not easy. Our homes are smaller, lifestyles are different and our jobs can take us from one city to another. Moreover, the COVID-19 pandemic has upended our travelling habits. So, in these changing times, how do we recreate the *togetherness* of the village?

By 'togetherness', I mean the togetherness of hearts. It's the kindred feeling of closeness we experience with loved ones. Togetherness is the soul of this book and it's expressed in the idea that *humanity thrives when we nurture the bonds that connect us*. And this nurturing begins in the family and continues in the village.

The African proverb, 'It takes a village to raise a child' conveys the idea of togetherness. Throughout this book, I share ideas and practices to rekindle that sense of connection, togetherness, of community in the modern setting. So whether you're an urban couple with bouncy toddlers, an iPad-ninja grandfather or a diligent caregiver, this book helps you bring your heart into your relationships. And where there is heart, there is love; and love strengthens togetherness. I was blessed to experience such love in the village that raised me.

The Village Offered Togetherness and Support

I was born in the autumn of 1956, in a village named Kalla in Gujarat, India. Kalla was dusty brown in the summers, fresh green during the monsoons and always golden in my heart. We had fewer than fifty families in the village, and most of our homes were along one main street. The two places for people to gather were the temple and the mosque.

My father was an ayurvedic doctor, and he treated various ailments of the people in the village. His practice was mostly pro bono. We had some farmland near the river and my father worked in the fields too. The produce from the farms put the food on the table.

We didn't have a table though. We sat on the ground and ate. Even though our house was sparse, what gave it a special grace was my grandmother's presence. Her genteel nature dignified everything, even our modest means. She was a source of moral support for my mother, who toiled away to take care of the home and raise five children. We were two brothers and three sisters. I was the fourth child, and my younger sister was the fifth. There were many children in Kalla, and we all played together. I was too naughty for my own good and often got into trouble.

When I compare my childhood and that of my grandchildren, what stands out the most is the freedom that we enjoyed. My childhood was carefree, free-spirited and had a sense of openness that is missing today. These days, children who live close enough to do so rarely walk to school. When I was growing up, we walked to school and, even better, ran home. Today, while children play outside, parents are expected to hover nearby. When we used to play, we would run around in open spaces like wild horses until sundown, and the surveillance network of grandmothers watched over all of us giving the parents much-needed reassurance that someone had their eyes on the children. As a child, life in Kalla was much freer. For instance, I could eat at anyone's house, and it was a normal thing to do. On most days, some friend or the other would eat with us. And it wasn't uncommon for me to down two lunches, one at home and the other at someone else's house, because they made what I liked. Also in those days, we children never carried a water bottle around. If you felt thirsty, you knocked at someone's door and drank some water. Same went for using the restroom. If you had to go, you simply knocked on the door, asked for permission and that was that. The children felt a sense of belonging to a community. They didn't face a sense of rejection. Children were welcome everywhere, and as a result their confidence and sense of self developed well.

The other noticeable difference is in making children feel *special* versus *making them feel secure*. During my childhood, we grew up with the sense of security that came from the love and care of the family and community. But I don't remember that I was made to feel *special* or *gifted* in any way. Nowadays,

I see an increased emphasis on making our children feel special and talented. When the spotlight shifts from providing a sense of security to making the child feel special for their talents, it breeds insecurity, first in the parents and then the children.

When the children are made to feel special, then the focus is on their accomplishments and the result is an overcrowded shelf of medals and trophies. Encouragement is good, but persistent recognition does a disservice by putting the children under pressure to perform. We can't change the society at large, but in our families, we can focus more on loving the child and making the child feel secure.

Don't praise children too much. For children, praise is a sound whose echo registers as a warning in a subtle way. They may get ideas like, 'What if next time I am not able?', 'What if I can't?' and so on.

Besides this, persistent praise leads children to correlate your love and attention to their accomplishments. They begin feeling that 'If I do well, Mother and Father will love me even more.' As parents, acknowledge the child's efforts over the results. Whether children win or lose, celebrate their efforts with small gestures—a weekend ice cream, maybe a movie night or a note at their table—and then move on. The focus should be on the future. Such an approach will help them take both wins and losses in stride, because neither means the loss of love.

Praise can also be expressed by throwing over-the-top birthdays and sweet-sixteen bashes, which are common nowadays. When we were young, we never celebrated birthdays. In most cases, families would make a note of the time and alignment of stars as per the calendar to draw up a horoscope of the child. Sometimes mothers would make a sweet dish, but other than that, birthdays were not a thing. Children were loved, cared for and no spotlight attention was given to make the child feel special and gifted.

The way we socialized back then was also different. There was no show-off culture, perhaps because there were no televisions in Kalla (that we had no electricity might have something to do with it). My father encouraged me to read aloud chapters from the Mahabharata every night. This reading became my primary activity during the monsoon of 1965. I was nine years old then. Old and young from nearby homes would finish their dinner and come to our house. I would begin reading under the warm glow of the hanging lantern, and it went on for about an hour. I loved those sessions!

Evenings like those were a welcome reprieve for my parents, who had many things to worry about. Life was simple, but it was not easy. After all, raising five children and taking care of my grandmother on our modest means was not easy. But there was one thing my parents didn't have to worry about. And that was *support*.

While my mother was working at home and my father was in the fields, they didn't have to worry about the children. My parents were not alone in raising us. The village was our family. All five of us siblings grew up under the loving care of our parents, grandparents, uncles and aunts. It was common for an elder of the house to discipline any child in the family or even a child of the neighbour's family. I know this very well because I was usually at the receiving end.

The elders were strict, but in hindsight, their discipline paled in comparison to their overarching love for us all. The elders, especially the grandparents, had ample time and made the effort to pass on the morals. Through stories, poems and various anecdotes they taught us about honesty, devotion, reverence and faith. The elders would be the support system of not only the children, but of the young people in the village.

While the large families of the past had their advantages, there were some problems too. Everything from toothpaste to finances were shared amongst the family, which would sometimes cause friction. The decision-making was strictly top-down, and the elders made decisions, keeping in mind the greater good of the family. For example, marriage was a social arrangement where two families came together. The norm was that you loved the one you married. Women were respected, but they were not empowered. They sacrificed a lot for the family but had no say in property rights.

Do This

Talk to your parents or grandparents and ask them about their childhood. Ask them what it was like for them when they were growing up. Who were their caregivers? Who told them stories? How did they celebrate holidays? Ask them to go back as far as they can in their memory and share some incidents from their childhood. If possible, record these treasured memories. It will help keep the memories alive for future generations. It will also cultivate gratitude for the things that we have in our lives today.

Another big problem was healthcare, especially in dealing with infections. Hygiene was poor and infections would spread fast. Women often died during childbirth. Many children were also lost during birth. The past was not perfect, and this is true for most families.

In contrast, in today's families, younger people have much greater freedom in decision-making. Technology, healthcare and education have improved our quality of life. And while we still have a long way to go, the status of women in families and society has improved. But what happened to the village? What about the sense of community that we took for granted?

Research shows that good relationships keep us happier and healthier. The most comprehensive study on happiness, the Harvard Adult Study,[1] spanning over eighty-two years of research, shows that the village matters. The village is vital for the social and emotional well-being of our children.

The Nuclear Family Offers Freedom

The nuclear family is a recent phenomenon that started in the mid-twentieth century. As the world became more urbanized, people began moving to the cities. Some countries such as India, China and Brazil became talent suppliers. In India, during the early 1900s, it was taboo for someone to board a ship and cross the seas. Fast forward a century and one can see Indians migrating to every part of the globe; in the United States, every seventh doctor is an Indian.[2]

Our family also moved. From our humble beginnings in Kalla, by the early 1980s, most of my siblings settled down in the cities in Gujarat. My elder brother and his family take care of the village home and the farmland, but none of us live there full-time. As for me, after completing my studies in India, I went to the USA and started my entrepreneurial journey in New York City. My children, both boys, are married and have children of their own. They live in the USA and are busy building their businesses.

My story mirrors that of many from my generation. When I think about how families have changed over the years, one noticeable shift is the move from the *collective* to the *individual*. Within a family, individual priorities and preferences started becoming more pronounced. Over time, the community ethos shifted towards greater self-reliance. The result was the nuclear family.

A nuclear family is a self-reliant unit, and it offers personal privacy and freedom. The influence of the extended family does not figure much. For example, in most families today when the children start earning, their finances are separate from their parents. I am not suggesting that it's good or bad. It's simply different from the past. High disposable income, personal freedom and advent of technology have made it easier to spend money. Today, at the click of a button, one can buy anything from a cup to a condo on Amazon.com.

For most families in the past, life was simple but not easy. Today, for a nuclear family, life is easy but not *simple*.

Parents in a nuclear family are responsible to get everything done on their own. If a child falls sick, there is often no help. If the school has a snow day, who would watch the children while the parents go to work? Simple things like meal planning and play dates have become stressful because the *support system* is lacking. The cushion is gone. The DIY-lifestyle can feel like an assembly line of chores. Even a minor slip-up and chores begin piling up. I see many young families toiling away every day to keep it all together. Mothers doing the double shift of working professionals and homemakers. Fathers working multiple jobs. But what stresses out the parents is not the work, it's the lack of support.

And for a couple with a newborn it can get overwhelming. Welcoming the newborn home is a beautiful feeling, but it's also *expensive* and *stressful*. Not the typical words associated with the joy of welcoming a child into the family. According to the Max Planck Institute of Demographic Research in Germany, the decline in happiness experienced by parents in the first year after the birth of their first child is larger than when experiencing unemployment, divorce or the death of a partner.[3] Raising a family is an ennobling experience but doing it all alone can suck the joy out of it.

In the past, whether a family was rich or poor, everyone had a support system to lean on. Everyone had a cushion in case of a fall. Today, the rich can buy themselves a village. They can hire a nanny, a cook and a cleaner. But a middle-class family is stuck in the earning-to-afford-day care syndrome. For families with low-income, the situation is worse. To take care of the family, most parents are struggling with prolonged work-ism. And while they do that, the children who spend a lot of time on screens sometimes end up wandering alone into scary digital ghettos.

The isolation in today's nuclear families affects all of us. Isolation creates loneliness which becomes a public health issue. The health risks of prolonged loneliness are equivalent to those from smoking fifteen cigarettes a day. According to an AARP survey in 2018, one in three adults over the age of forty-five in the USA feels lonely.[4] For poorer families, this number is one in two. Other developed countries such as Japan and the UK also show alarming levels of loneliness. In the UK, the government created a special ministry and appointed a minister of loneliness.

Loneliness might evoke an image of a grandmother looking down from her apartment window with a blank expression on her face. But the picture is gloomier. A 2018 survey of 20,000 adults by health services company Cigna showed that the loneliest demographic is Gen Z.[5] It's our children who are suffering the most from loneliness.

In a world with less village, how do we raise happy and resilient children? To find a solution, we need to go back to what made human beings the most evolved species on earth.

Worried? Try This

Next time you catch yourself worrying about something, try this.

In your journal, write down what's worrying you. For example, say you are worried about losing your job. You could write something like this:

What: I am worried about losing my job.
Why: Because there may be downsizing in my company.
What can I do: Update my resume. Watch my budget. Start learning some new skills.

When we write down our worries, then we take the focus away from the negative emotions like fear and anxiety. Verbalizing chops the problem to its proper size. A journal will shift the focus away from repetitive thinking and orient you towards finding solutions.

Together We Thrive

We, human beings, are unique in what we call collective learning. It refers to the sharing, storing and accumulation of information over time and across generations. Information was initially passed down through gestures, then verbally, then with symbols and finally through other media.

When our ancestors learned how to make fire or hunt game, they taught it to their children. Through drawings in a cave and language both written and verbal, they passed on their learnings to future generations. But, in the animal kingdom, if a monkey learns to use a stick to pluck mangoes from a tree, that knowledge dies with that monkey. In general, animals don't have the ability to transfer knowledge from one generation to another. There are examples of some apes with limited ability to share one or two skills. But collective learning as a trait is unique to only human beings. It's the reason why we survived mass extinction events and continue to outlast other species.

And why is this anthropology lesson important for parents? Because a family is the *basic building block* of *collective learning* in our society. For a child, collective learning begins in the family. The first teacher is the mother. The right word is not teacher but 'initiator'. The mother gives birth to the child and initiates the child's journey into the world. The second initiator is the father, the third initiator are the elders. No doubt, school, friends and society play a role in the collective learning of a child. But, the family's role is foundational. The family lays the groundwork for the child's attitude, behaviour and character. Later in life as the child grows up, the teachers and mentors play an important role in the child's self-development.

The mother, father, elders and the teacher are the initiators whose presence we are aware of. The silent presence in all our lives is the fifth initiator, whom we may call God, Source or Nature. As a child grows up and begins to introspect the deeper meaning of life, the role of the teacher lies in imparting spiritual education.

Often, the words 'religion' and 'spirituality' are used interchangeably. But they are distinct words. Think of religion as knowledge and spirituality as putting the knowledge into practice. So the spiritual education of a child refers to nurturing the qualities of the heart. Kindness, honesty, humility, love, compassion, contentment and courage are all qualities of the heart that nurtures a child spiritually.

Think about Your Village

Growing up who were you closest to? How did their association help you? Where are they now? Do your children know them? What can you do to connect your children better to your village?

When I was growing up, collective learning was a part of life in the village. But children these days are growing up in increasingly smaller families. Without the village, especially the elders, children risk losing out on collective learning. The elders may not say much, they may not share much, but their presence creates an environment. The way they eat, the way they talk, the way they process emotions—everything is a learning moment for our children, and they are missing out.

How do we rebuild the villages? Perhaps the answer lies in technology. Maybe we need to make different life choices. Some might say the onus falls on the government. There's no simple answer. But it helps to remember that the village is the people. If families come together for each other, then things can change.

We are all connected intellectually, morally and spiritually, and woven together in a common destiny. When such is the connection we share, should minor differences set us apart? We need to remind ourselves that no matter how prosperous we become, how healthy we feel or how much progress we make, we still need one another. Our children and our elders still need the village. We all need the village. It's our duty to create one in which we all thrive.

It *still* takes a village.

Daily Dilemma:

My wife and I moved to the city five years ago for better living conditions. We recently had a baby, and we have no idea how to raise a child. We are constantly worried whether we are doing the right thing. Should we move back to our town and stay with our parents for a while? What should we do?

Daaji: Congratulations on your baby. Most couples nowadays don't have much prior experience in handling babies. So, your concern is understandable. Don't worry. You will learn as you go along. Trust your heart, and don't hesitate to ask for help. People are friendlier and more helpful than we imagine them to be.

If you can move closer to the family, it will be good. During the pandemic, the option for remote work has allowed many couples to relocate closer to home. The presence of elders at home helps in better bonding between parents and children, especially the mother. Many studies show, for example, how the presence of a grandmother helps the mother and child develop a better connection. You also have less stress and more freedom to move around and take turns caring for the baby.

2

Halo Parenting: Rebuilding the Village

During my college years, while studying for my master's degree in pharmacy, I happened to like a girl. Although we were friends, I never told her how much I liked her. This was India in the 1970s. Even if a boy's shadow touched the shadow of the girl he liked, for the next few days, he would be floating in the air. Somehow, on the last day of college, when we were about to graduate, I summoned all my courage and confessed my feelings to her. When I finished speaking there was an awkward pause. She broke the silence by saying it would not work out and then she walked away. I was hoping she would turn back, but she didn't. Then and there, in those few minutes, my maiden voyage of love sank like the Titanic. A long build-up of expectation that drowned overnight by an iceberg of rejection. Somehow, I sauntered back to my dorm room and just lay there in my bed staring at the ceiling.

It was also during college that I had started meditating. My trainer was an elderly woman, around sixty years old. She was like the loving aunt who welcomes you with a smile and feeds you till you can eat no more and doesn't let you leave without food to-go. I would meet her often and after meditation, I would read to her books on spirituality. The books were in English, so I would translate them for her. When I would read passages on spiritual experiences, she would often say, 'Kamlesh, I have experienced this,' and then she would tell me about it. Her descriptions would match verbatim with what was written in the book. Listening to her experiences, I felt blessed to be in the company of a luminous soul who was drenched in the manna of spirituality.

Now, on the evening of my love debacle, after sulking long enough in my room, I went over to meet my meditation trainer. She looked at me and knew something was wrong. But she didn't ask me anything. She gestured for me to sit and went inside. Soon she returned carrying a cup of tea and some snacks.

After a few minutes, I opened-up and told her everything. She listened to me quietly and after a brief pause said, 'Dear Kamlesh, it's okay. These things happen. Do not burden your heart.' There was such reassurance in her words that I felt anchored. Afterwards, she gave me a meditation session. We meditated for about thirty minutes and when we finished, all the sorrow had vanished from my heart. Everything that was weighing me down was cleaned away. There were no feelings of resentment and I was at peace with myself. I was healed in the silence.

My meditation trainer was a *halo parent*. Her protective gaze and loving support were there with me through my college years. She believed in me, and her presence was a pillar of strength for me. Growing up, I was blessed to be surrounded by elders who looked after my welfare without being overbearing. These noble souls were my parents when my parents could not be there for me. In situations where I would not have felt comfortable reaching out to my parents, my halo parents were there for me. They were guiding lights of wisdom whose halo illuminated my path.

The Idea and Its Origins

The term halo parenting is inspired by 'alloparenting' (which means care given by individuals other than parents). In some animal species, members outside the genetic parents take care of the young. They support the parents in nursing, rearing, caring for and protecting the young ones. Primates, jackals, macaques, whales and several other animals have been studied for their alloparenting behaviours. Research shows that the young ones benefit from alloparenting and it increases the probability of their survival.

For human beings, the village was an alloparenting community. Grandparents, siblings, uncles, aunts and caregivers looked after the child together. There were several attachment figures for the child besides the parents. Studies show that this was a healthy way to bring up the child and lessen the stress and emotional burden of the parents.[1] Stephanie Coontz, professor, anthropologist, author and researcher on contemporary families believes that 'children do best in societies where childbearing is considered too important to be left entirely to parents'.[2] I couldn't agree more.

As children grow up, it becomes difficult for parents to give direct advice. Children rebel against direct instructions. At the same time, they look up to leader figures and role models outside their home.

Studies show that the presence of a grandmother at home or frequent visits from a grandmother increases the infant's chances of forging a stronger bond with the young mother.[3] In low-income families, the presence of a grandmother helps develop better cognitive skills in children.

We know that as the children grow up, it becomes difficult for parents to give them direct advice. Strict instructions like 'Do this' and 'Don't do that', often lead to the children rebelling. At the same time, children look up to authority figures and role models outside their homes. They also look for peer validation from their friends. It's a natural process of growth, and it's healthy. Knowing all this in advance, parents can prepare for it by building the village for their child.

As I said earlier, the village is the *people*, not the *place*. In modern-day nuclear families, it's usually the mother who is alone in the task of raising the children; and for single mothers, everything becomes doubly hard. Then there's the added pressure of being an *ideal* mother where the bar for perfection is too high.

In halo parenting, parents consciously cultivate a network of friends and family members who can be present in the lives of their children as they grow into adolescence and teenagers. These are elders their children look up to and like to spend time with. Having a halo network goes a long way towards creating a village for the child.

Think about Your Halo Parents

As a child, did you have elders with whom you could share your problems? How did they help you? Looking ahead, who do you think could be good halo parents for your child, and why? Do you think you could be a halo parent someday, and why?

Halo Parenting Supports the Parents and the Children

Having a halo network is a reassuring feeling for the parents. For children, their halo parents support them in situations where they can't speak freely with their parents.

Community Support Has Long-Lasting Positive Effects: A Study

The community plays an important role in offering social support to mothers. In a study, the University of Colorado in Denver observed a group of nurses who visited pregnant mothers. After the women gave birth, the nurses made approximately twenty-one visits before the children turned two years old.

When the benefits to the children were studied, the researchers found that the children were emotionally less vulnerable to fear. The children learned languages sooner. They also had higher mental development scores than the control group without the nurses' support. The benefits to the children because of this simple intervention of the nurses' support were observed even fifteen years later.

—Sarah Blaffer Hrdy, PhD, *Mothers and Others* [4]

Social support is vital, and I do not think we give it importance or recognition in society or in the family. Halo parenting can help us rebuild the support structure we've lost.

There are times when parents struggle with getting their message across to their children. In such times halo parents act as an effective medium. Many of us have been halo parents ourselves and we have seen its positive effects. Like the time when your niece was chewing off her fingernails trying to decide between studying medicine or going to culinary school and you helped her make a list of pros and cons and guided her thought process. Or the time your nephew got into a spot at school and, after a few rounds of badminton with him, you nudged him back on track.

Think of how your support helped your niece or nephew and how having a halo parent can benefit your child. The halo parents aren't there to usurp your role. They are there to support you and your child.

One of the biggest worries for a child is disappointing their parents. So, at times children find it easier to confide in elders who may be better at listening and restrained from judging and constant worrying. Not that all parents are judgemental, but there's too much attachment in the parent-child relationship. Sometimes this results in a disproportionate emotional response. A child worried about disappointing parents, may think of father's shrug as a sign of disdain or an offhand remark from mother as a cause to declare war. Parents too can at times overreact or become too protective. Halo parents can help everyone chill and help put things in perspective.

Then there are times when there is distress. Let's say your teenager is feeling low because of some nasty comments on her social media account. You come to know about it, and you try to boost her confidence. You share some stories from your teenage years.

Even though she understands what you are saying, in her mind, the distress keeps growing. What works in such situations is external validation. Here halo parents can be the empathetic listeners who encourage and boost your teenager's confidence.

In most cases, they might say the same things you might have said, but coming from them, it registers better.

Halo Parent: What to Look for

Looking for a halo parent doesn't mean surrounding children with over achievers and go-getters who later influence them in career choices. I go back to the example of village elders, mainly grandparents. Has anyone ever wondered why children love their grandparents so much? Most of the time, the children have issues with their parents. But grandchildren adore their grandparents for one simple reason. Grandparents are their most enthusiastic cheerleaders. When the grandchildren sing a nursery rhyme, that's the best song ever. When the grandchildren graduate college, the grandparents beam with pride because they always knew they had a prodigy in the family. Grandparents love their grandchildren, and the grandchildren feel their love and support in the core of their being. That's the role of grandparents—showering the grandchildren with an abundance of love. Parents instil discipline, while grandparents get to spoil them with love.

> Halo parents are not perfect by any means, but they are people who are perfectly authentic in their interactions with your child.

When thinking of halo parents, think of elders who are wise, supportive and encouraging. Also, halo parents are not only from the elder generation. People in the community who are young and are good at heart can also play this role. These elder brothers and sisters can inspire children too.

When we think of halo parents, we think of people who understand the heart of a young child. As I mentioned, halo parents are not perfect, but they are perfectly authentic in their interactions with the child. They understand the potential of the child. They know how inquisitive and innovative the child can be. They know that love is the way to handle the child's defiance. They also understand how to channel the child's energy in a positive direction. They are not trying to teach and preach. Instead, they are eager to learn more about the child's world and what is happening in their universe. With all these qualities, halo parents are a pillar of support for the child.

Halo parents need not be the neighbours or restricted to one's town or community. They can be in another part of the world. The Heartfulness community is a good example of this. I have seen children of parents from Delhi develop a close relationship with their halo parents from Denmark and Dubai. The same goes for children from Denmark, Germany and the USA who have spent months with me in Chennai and Hyderabad. Over the years, the children and the families have become closer-knit, and everyone benefits.

These days, we are all digital-first in our interactions. Our children are spending more time in digital communities, and this opens-up new possibilities. Technology, that's being blamed for creating isolation can help us rebuild connections in the global village. Parents can embrace this shift and foster connections in the digital world too. The pandemic has taught us how to use technology to build deeper relationships, rather than the shallow interactions one has on social media. During the pandemic, I know of many families that used technology to set up regular chats with grandparents, aunts and uncles. Even as the pandemic restrictions eased, digital interactions in these families continue. In a flat, fast and frenetic world, halo parenting will offer the sense of community and togetherness that parents know is so important for children.

The generations before us knew the strength of the invisible thread of attachment that held families together. They knew how important it was to stay connected. That's why, across cultures, there's the tradition of uncles and aunts playing the roles of godfather and godmother. The idea behind these traditions was to have a safety net for the child. When families were closer and life was simpler, these relationships blossomed. Now we need to recast these ideas to fit them into today's mould. Halo parenting is a conscious step in the direction of rebuilding the village. It creates support structures for our children and brings together the family.

A few things to ensure halo parenting is not taken out of context. Halo parenting is a silent bond of trust. In your enthusiasm to create a halo network for your child, please do not go about throwing halo parent announcement parties. This is a quiet affair.

We find halo parents by becoming one for somebody. Not because there is reciprocity but because that is how a community works. A simple way to get started on the journey to becoming a halo parent is by finding common interests. For example, you may like to paint and a child in your circle is interested in art. That's a good place to start. Or you may like French and you may start a reading group with a couple of children interested in learning French. Shared interests are a great way to nurture a connection.

One may wonder, *how do we create time for other children when we don't have time for our own children?* This type of thinking is what created the problem in the first place. There's strength in numbers, and support comes from unity. When we come together as halo parents, we are recreating the best of what large families offered *while retaining* our privacy and personal freedom.

Recall the analogy I shared earlier in the book of a box of matches. When it is dark, it does not matter which match you pick; they all give light. In the same way, halo parents are a collection of people with whom we nurture a relationship. We do not know who will come in handy when there is a need.

It's possible we may never use the matchbox. Halo parents are not just for troubled times. They are a silent presence in your child's life. They make happy times happier and difficult times easier to get through.

Becoming a halo parent is creating a bond of trust and care. It is a benevolent act of taking responsibility for someone who is not yours. At its core, it is about going back to one's roots and rediscovering the universal brotherhood that makes us one large, thriving human family.

Daily Dilemma:

My son has a very close friend at school, who also happens to be our neighbour. The friend's parents are both working, so he often comes over to our place after school with my son. I almost feel as if I am his godmother but am scared about what his mother will think. What if my care and nurturing is seen as an interference?

Daaji: I have two boys. They spent much of their childhood with their elder aunt. They were fortunate to have two mothers who raised them so well. Not everyone is as lucky.

You are doing something similar. So don't second-guess your intentions, especially when they are coming from the right place. Check in with your neighbour occasionally to see how she feels and if anything is bothering her. Such small talk should make it easier for you both. Love, care and discipline go hand in hand.

Principle 2

Be Guided by Wisdom. Seek It. Cultivate It. Share It.

3

Wayfinders, Shamans and Grandparents: The Wisdom Bridge

Walking to the store with your grandfather and buying rock candy, licking the cake batter off grandmother's baking bowl, or in the case of my three-year-old granddaughter, cuddling up in my lap and watching the night sky: grandparents and grandchildren share a connection that makes even the mundane, memorable. In their togetherness, wisdom flows from one generation to another.

Sometimes I think about why the connection between grandparents and grandchildren feels so special. Is it familial love or is something else at play? There are many theories, and the one I find compelling is from the late American comedian and author Sam Levenson. I remember a joke which went like, 'Grandparents and grandchildren get along so well because they share a common enemy.' Ha!

Jokes aside, according to anthropologists, what makes the connection between grandparents and grandchildren special goes back thousands of years ago, to our days as hunter-gatherers. In those times, when children were old enough to stay apart from their parents, grandparents, mainly the grandmothers took care of the children. While parents hunted and foraged for food, the grandmothers taught the children how to spot water sources, how to make a fire and how to hunt; essentially, how to survive. Anthropologists believe that the care and nurturing by our grandparents is one of the reasons why the human race survived, while other species stronger and bigger than we are were wiped out.[1]

> What makes the bond between grandparents and grandchildren so special goes back thousands of years ago to our days as hunter-gatherers.

Fast forward to urban society, where forests and savannahs have made way for apartments and villas, parents forage in concrete jungles and server farms. And grandparents continue to do what they did. They teach the children life skills. No matter how little time the children may have spent with their grandparents, they would have learned something from them. It's as if grandparents and grandchildren are *hardwired* in a way that grandparents share knowledge, and grandchildren imbibe them.[2]

Thanks to this hardwiring, *generational wisdom* flows from one generation to another. From the basic skills like cooking, knitting, speaking and reading to virtues like humility, compassion and generosity, the term generational wisdom covers the gamut. In a family, the elders, mainly the grandparents, carry the mantle of transferring generational wisdom. For this reason, I refer to our elders as living *wisdom bridges*.

To understand a wisdom bridge, let's first understand what a bridge is. In simplest terms, a bridge is a connection where a gap once lay, a path where once none existed. The Norse gods built the Bifrost, a celestial bridge, to connect the nine realms. Lord Rama built a bridge that connected what we know today as India and Sri Lanka. With regard to us mere mortals, we are bridge builders too. To connect with another person, we build an attention bridge. To allow the flow of ideas, we build an awareness bridge. To transfer wisdom, we build a wisdom bridge.

The elders are the living wisdom bridges in society. Close association with the elders enables children to imbibe their wisdom in a natural way. For example, a child can be taught morals—be kind, speak with love, judge not and so on. But when a child is with the grandparents and sees their kindness in actions, feels the softness in their speech and witnesses the calmness in their demeanour, the wisdom flows straight into the child's heart. Parents too can teach all this, but they are busy. Grandparents have the time, and they love to share with the little ones.

If you are a parent, you know the smile the elders bring to your child's face. You know the special place your children have in their hearts for their grandparents. In societies where generations are close-knit, the transfer of wisdom happens naturally. And what happens when generations are disconnected? You live in your little islands, cut off not only from wisdom but also from each other. Over time, each generation feels more disconnected than the previous one. Centuries from now, when future humanity studies our society, what will they find? Will they discover that we preserved wisdom? Or will they study us to learn what not to do?

Centuries from now, when future humanity studies modern-day society, what will they find? Will they discover that we preserved wisdom?

Let me share with you stories from two ancient cultures that will help you understand the importance of generational wisdom. For centuries these cultures thrived, thanks to strong wisdom bridges, but today they are dying as the wisdom bridges collapse.

Two Ancient Cultures and Lessons in Generational Wisdom

History books tell us about the voyages of explorers such as Ferdinand Magellan and James Cook and their discovery of new islands in the Pacific Ocean. Lot has been written about their battles, conquests, mutinies and the sicknesses they brought with them. One aspect we don't read about as much is how surprised the explorers were when they landed on the Pacific islands.

The Pacific islands are thousands of miles apart,[3] and the explorers expected them to be uninhabited. Instead, they found a civilization of people with similar culture and values, thriving on island after island. What perplexed the explorers was that there was no navy or sophisticated sailing equipment on these islands.

'How shall we account for this Nation spreading itself so far over this vast ocean?' Captain Cook wrote in his journal during his third and final voyage in 1778.[4] To give you an idea of the vastness Captain Cook refers to, he was referring to the Polynesian Triangle. In the South Pacific Ocean, the Polynesian Triangle covers an area of 10 million square miles.[5] To put this in perspective, Europe and the United States together account for 8 million square miles. Captain Cook could not fathom how a nation without a navy was thriving across the islands that were thousands of miles apart.

Today, thanks to scientific evidence, we know that the Polynesians were masters of navigation. Centuries before the European explorers ventured out on expeditions, wayfinders from east Indonesia and the Philippines settled in Polynesia. The wayfinders travelled in simple canoes with sails. They had no special equipment, not even a compass. Yet, they conquered the seas centuries before the Europeans did.

The wayfinders' genius lay in their generational wisdom. The wisdom bridges spanning from one generation to another transferred the knowledge of navigation. Grandparents and grandchildren walked the wisdom bridges together. The elders, while catching fish with the children, taught them about ocean currents. While making sundials with seashells, they sang songs describing the movement of stars. Lying on the beach as they gazed at clouds, grandparents taught how to differentiate a storm cloud from three days earlier, which looked more like a flower, from those that had appeared recently. Wayfinders had an oral tradition, and the generational connection was crucial for their culture to thrive.

The responsibility of preserving the generational connection fell on the shoulders of the *palus*, the master navigators. The palus were among the respected village elders, and it was their duty to guide the people and mentor them. For the palus, the ocean was an extension of his being. While sailing, looking at the playful bounce of the water against the canoe, the palus could identify the islands that lay kilometres away. In the middle of a voyage, it wasn't uncommon for a palu to lie down in the hull of the canoe. It wasn't for a siesta, but to feel the vibrations of the waves against his body; that way the palus identified the ocean currents. With the slightest shift in the cloud patterns, a palu could predict a storm three days out. For most of us, it's difficult to remember a handful of phone numbers. But a palu, if you can find one today, can still name hundreds of stars and plot their movement across the sky.[6]

Like the wayfinders, one more culture also has an oral tradition. To meet them we will have to travel to the lungs of the earth, the tropical forests of the Amazon. There, the tree canopy is so thick that the forest floor is always covered in darkness. In these brooding forests live the enigmatic medicine men—the shamans of the Amazon. They have long been curing diseases ranging from simple fevers to even Bell's palsy. They are the walking encyclopedias of the Amazon jungles.

Ethnobotanist Mark Plotkin has dedicated his life to preserving the rainforests. In his popular TED talk from October 2014, Mark shares his encounter with a shaman:

Now four years ago, I injured my foot in a climbing accident and I went to the doctor. She gave me heat, she gave me cold, aspirin, narcotic painkillers, anti-inflammatories, cortisone shots. It didn't work. Several months later, I was in the northeast Amazon, walked into a village, and the shaman said, "You're limping." And I'll never forget this as long as I live. He looked me in the face, and he said, "Take off your shoe and give me your machete." He walked over to a palm tree and carved off a fern, threw it in the fire, applied it to my foot, threw it in a pot of water and had me drink the tea. The pain disappeared for seven months. When it came back, I went to see the shaman again. He gave me the same treatment, and I've been cured for three years now. Who would you rather be treated by?[7]

According to industry data, it takes $2.6 billion and, on average, fourteen years to develop a new drug.[8] The failure rate in finding a new drug is as high as 95 per cent.[9] So then why aren't TV studios streaming shaman specials or why aren't Silicon Valley entrepreneurs clamouring to decode the ancient wisdom? Because these once-thriving cultures are now reduced to an endangered tribe. The cultures that worshipped the seas and revered the trees lost out to cultures that exploited the seas and axed the trees.

Why does it matter if a tribe vanishes? What do we lose if there are no wayfinders or shamans left? When a wayfinder dies or a shaman passes on to the other realm, a library burns down to the ground. All the knowledge, all the wisdom passed down for ages vanishes in an instant. Across cultures, we are witnessing a mass extinction of wisdom, which affects all of us. When we lose wisdom, human progress halts. There is a cliched but useful adage, 'Don't reinvent the wheel.' When we lose wisdom, we keep reinventing the wheel. Problems that were already solved will have to be solved all over again.

Your elders need not be wayfinders and shamans to make the case for generational wisdom and how it impacts your family. Our detour into the Pacific islands and the Amazon shows that the generations before us faced problems like what we are facing today.

The elders in your family have life skills and learnings relevant to your family's flourishing. They may not have all the answers, but you can learn from their successes and failures. You can blend wisdom and technology to create a lifestyle that helps your family thrive. There are many stories in this book that show how science and wisdom come together to improve your quality of life.

Be curious to learn more about age-old customs and practices. Instead of discarding them as superstitions and rituals, distil the essence behind the customs and take what is valuable. It will help you re-imagine the village as a place that brings technology and wisdom together for your children and your family.

Also, you may not be a family elder or a grandparent yet, but one day you might become one. At that time, as an elder of the family, you will carry the mantle of passing on wisdom to the young ones. What kind of elder do you want to be? How do you want your grandchildren to remember you? Understanding the importance of generational wisdom today will prepare you for the future. What you share then will be the wisdom that your family's future generations will carry forward.

An Imperfect Past and a Work-in-Progress Present

I'm not a nostalgia merchant peddling wisdom ware to talk about the good old days and complain about how we have it all wrong today. Sometimes, we feel that we had it all figured out in the past, and as time went by, we lost our way. It's important to remember that the past wasn't perfect. When you read about the wayfinders and the Amazon tribes, you learn that prejudice, jealousy and greed affected their generations too. The fight for land, the rivalry between clans, the secrecy around knowledge and the hunger for power were present in those cultures too. But a lot of good was passed down from one generation to another, and a lot of evil also made its way down. Just as precious ore is found after sifting through tons of gangue, it's our responsibility to sift through what we receive and discern wisdom from waste. Your heart guides you in developing discernment.

The knowledge, experience and intuition of generations comes together to form wisdom. A life without wisdom is a life of ignorance. Wisdom helps you to avoid rookie mistakes and protects your families from unnecessary complications. The steadying hand that comes from generational wisdom is a positive influence in a child's life.

The living wisdom bridges—our grandmothers, our grandfathers and our elders—are the arteries through which life experiences have flown. There are 1 billion people in the world today who are grandparents.[10] It's a demographic dividend that is glossed over in urban society. In the modern lifestyle, a world steeped in pace, the living wisdom bridges around us have slipped away into the shadows. Through this book I am shining the spotlight back on them.

The governments have reduced them to line items in welfare and healthcare budgets. Families agonize over how best to care for them. The elderly themselves struggle to find a voice, a final hurrah. They deserve better. We have to do better. And most importantly, our children need their wisdom. As the world population becomes greyer and older, our efforts to rebuild generational connections will help us all. We need to make wisdom relevant again in our lives, through the wise who can pour it into those hearts that can receive it.

Daily Dilemma:

My children love reading and listening to stories. Their grandfather, who lives in a different city, instilled the habit of reading in them, and of listening to the exciting stories he'd tell. They miss their grandfather. I would love to tell them stories, but they just tell me I'm not doing it as well as he did. What should I do?

Daaji: Most families today live far away from each other. So, we should use technology to bridge the gap. Set up a regular time for your children and their grandfather to speak. Your role as a parent is to set up the conversation so that they meet regularly. Fix the timings, use a good device, ensure the internet bandwidth is good and so on. Try to remove the friction points that technology may cause. This will make it easier for the elders to use technology.

The elders are more comfortable in-person, and they find it easier to communicate this way. Initially, on a video call or e-meet, you may have to suggest some ideas, give some prompts to help them get into a flow. You only need to do this a few times here and there and then the conversation starts to flow. If you can, try and record some of these sessions. You will enjoy seeing them with the children when they grow up.

4

We All Pay the Price for Lost Wisdom

My grandmother was a quiet lady. She barely spoke, and when she did, she spoke in a soft, kind voice. Each morning, she placed one or two flowers at the deities' photographs in our living room and then stood there with folded hands. When her eyes closed, I could see how she melted away in the silence. After a few minutes, she would open her eyes and walk away still lost in thoughts of the Lord. I used to watch her from a corner in the room. Even though no words were exchanged between us, for me those moments were a masterclass in reverence towards the ultimate.

Six decades have passed since my time with my grandmother. A lot has changed since then. Our family moved from the village to the city. My wife and I raised two boys, both of whom are married and have children. Not long ago, I was in my room, getting ready to meditate. My door was open and as I got up from my chair to close the door, I could hear my three-year-old granddaughter run across the living room. When the little one runs her tiny feet make a soft pitter-patter sound, which I love. She ran to her mother, who was speaking with someone and tugged at her dress. Then she shushed her, saying 'Mama, Sssh . . . Sssh . . . Daada is meditating.' And then she ran back towards my room. Just as I had observed my grandmother, my little granddaughter was observing me. She saw that I was about to start my meditation and she wanted to make sure the house was silent. In her eyes, I saw the same feeling I used to have when my grandmother offered her prayers. Life came full circle for me that day.

Wisdom is not taught, it is caught. The intentions, thoughts and actions of the elders are caught by the hearts of the young ones.

Seeing the Wisdom beyond the Veils

When I talk about the wisdom of the elders, the image it evokes is one of saintly elders with serene auras. Gandalf the powerful type of towering personalities, who have a solution for any problem we may face. Simply breathing the same air in the room with them would make one wiser. Such imagination creates confusion because when you turn around and look at your own elders, they seem anything but Gandalf the powerful.

The elders most of us know are plain old people. They have auras of greying hair and wield creaking joints that need a massage (yet again). They are forgetful and repetitive. Conversations with them are short, interspersed with long pauses. So where are the all-knowing elders whose wisdom is supposed to guide us?

The idea that Gandalf and Yoda-esqe grand personalities would unleash life-altering wisdom is not how wisdom works. It's the opposite. Wisdom is shrouded in veils of simplicity. Wisdom is so simple that it escapes our attention. It's not a grand shiny object that one finds at the end of a quest. Instead, it's like the air we breathe. All pervasive, invisible and vital for one's life.

During my years with my Guru (we used to call him Babuji), people came to meet him in droves but most of them were turned-off by his utter simplicity. They expected to see a Homeric personality. Someone who delighted in arcane philosophical discourse and displayed miraculous powers. Instead, what people saw was a benign Indian elder managing a large family and raising nine children. When asked about philosophy, he would joke that philosophy was like catching a black cat in a dark room. When pushed further, he would simply say 'Meditate and experience. Do and feel.'

I remember an incident when Babuji went to receive a government official who was visiting him from a nearby town to learn meditation. Usually, he would send the help but since the gentleman was new to meditation and was visiting him for the first time, he decided to go and receive him. At the train station, the official saw Babuji and thought him to be a porter and had him carry his luggage. Babuji quietly obliged. When they reached home, the visitor realized what he'd done. It was an awkward moment for him, to say the least.

Most people who came to see Babuji looked at his outer appearance and never peeked into the magnificence of his heart. Like a child, when he used both his hands to break a roti, people were turned off by his awkward table manners. They didn't know that here was a Guru who could change their destiny in the blink of an eye. Appearances can cast a veil over one's eyes. My Guru's simplicity was his veil.

Elders do not go about touting their wisdom because they don't know they're wise. To them, they're just getting on with their lives.

In the case of your grandparents and your family elders, they may have their own veils that you need to look beyond. While you may have more money and better know-how than the elders, the elders have more experience. They have seen more sunsets. They know how life changes when we go from the vitality of the twenties to the midlife crisis of the fifties. They know how the ego taunts the mind as dependence on others grows in the sixties. They may not be eloquent in sharing their life lessons, but if you pay attention, you can pick up good habits to apply in your own lives.

Also, the elders don't go about touting their wisdom because they don't know they're wise. To them, they're getting on with their lives. They know they're walking towards the sunset, and they are happy to share what they know. It is for you to observe, ask questions and learn from their lives.

For example, notice the lifestyle of the elders. Most of them follow a disciplined routine with habits like waking up before dawn and having dinner before sunset. It shows you how they align with the circadian rhythm of their body (we will read more about circadian rhythm in the chapter on sleep). When grandmother or grandfather look at your face and know right away that something's wrong, it's for you to learn that empathy is their second nature. When you notice how little they consume, how their needs are reduced you can learn from their minimalist lifestyle. When through eye contact they convey more to each other than you do with words, then it's for you to appreciate how their relationship is now a communion of two souls.

I could keep giving examples, but the takeaway is that you need to peel the layers and discover the wisdom behind the actions of your elders. And when you do this, your children and grandchildren can also learn from it. But if you don't see beyond their infirmities and their other quirks, then you lose opportunities for self-improvement.

Grandchildren do particularly well in learning from the elders because children are innocent. They don't have rigid egos that say, 'Yes, I know everything there's to know.' They are eager to learn and don't resist learning. They don't see any veils because their hearts feel the love that grandparents have for them. Children are thirsty for love and grandparents dole it out in super-sized portions. In the short time that I have spent on this planet, I haven't heard anyone complain about getting too much love.

Generation Gap Has Become a Generational Chasm

I once met a gentleman who told me about a game he plays with his grandchildren. He picks some names of politicians, rockstars or even criminals from his generation. He then asks his teenage grandchildren if they know who those people are? He shares a tidbit or two and it starts off a conversation.

Next up, the grandchildren pick some names: social media influencers, rappers, scientists and so on. The *no-filter* view of the grandfather and the glass half-full perspective of the grandchildren make for a chippy conversation that spills over to listening to some music or watching movies together. The gentleman told me that the game creates common ground between him and his grandchildren. I think it's a brilliant idea.

In most families, there is a generational chasm where the distance between elders and the young keeps growing. The generational chasm is different from a generation gap. The generation gap is nothing new. Even our hunter-gatherer ancestors would have had a generation gap. The elder might have wanted to hunt antelope while the young one preferred geese, the low-fat option. In a generation gap, the young ones think about life differently from the elders. But in a generational chasm, the elders and the young ones share no common ground, even in the food they eat or the shows they watch.

Do This

Think about the elders in your family and see how they can teach your children. For example, an elder in your family may be an excellent cook. Set up a weekend cooking class so that you and your children can learn from an expert. Someone else in the family may be a history teacher. Why not set up story times with lessons from history?

Because we don't share common ground, other than looking after the children, most of us don't know where else to involve elders. Our fast-paced lives also make us feel that elders slow us down. But we forget that their *presence* is what makes the difference. For example, in a house, the presence of a roof is enough. It doesn't have to do more than being present. The same goes for our elders. Their presence creates an environment at home.

With families living apart, the distance makes the chasm wider. To make it easier for the elders to be present in our lives, we need to teach them how to use technology. Teach them the tools and create a simple set up for them to stay connected with the family. Technology is our friend in making generational connections stronger.

The elders don't need an invitation to jump in, but they hesitate. They are running low on confidence.

Technology Is an Enabler, Not a Replacement

Since its founding, Google's mission has been to organize all the information in the world. In 2005, a reporter asked Eric Schmidt, the CEO of Google at that time, 'How long do you think it would take to organize all the information in the world?'

'Three hundred years,'[1] said Eric Schmidt to the reporter. It wasn't a riff at the reporter asking the question. Eric Schmidt holds a BS degree in engineering from Princeton and a PhD. from Berkeley. He knew what he was talking about. The engineers at Google had already calculated the answer to this question.

What you need to think about is if it takes 300 years to digitize all the information in the world, can you imagine what it would take to capture the wisdom in the hearts of the people? Technology helps us in preserving information. Generational connection helps us in preserving wisdom. Both are necessary.

Technology helps us in preserving information. Generational connection helps us in preserving wisdom. Both are necessary.

Here's a situation most parents can relate to. It's late at night and your baby starts crying non-stop. You call your paediatrician but it's after hours and the on-call nurse takes a message. In the meantime, you try patting the baby. You carry her around, turn off the lights, play music and when nothing works, you try to drive her around in the car. But the moment you put her in the car seat she starts shrieking even louder. By now the parents are close to having a full-on panic attack.

You video-call the grandmother, your mother, and she hears the baby in the background. She tells you to take some lukewarm olive oil and massage the baby's stomach and back. Laying the baby on her back as you massage her, she calms down and, within a few minutes, she slips away into a deep sleep. With the crisis resolved, the parents start breathing again and grandmother also signs off.

In your bookshelf, you may have the books written by Spock and Farber, but what you need at such times is the wisdom that comes from experience. Grandmother knows what to do because she learned it from her mother, who learned it from hers. Maybe the warmth helped the baby. Maybe the oils had some effect. Maybe it's the years of experience that calmed the baby. Who knows what the reason is, but whatever grandmother advised, worked.

We have all had similar experiences where home remedies saved a trip to the pharmacy. When we bring together wisdom and technology, our families benefit from the best of the past and the present. And what happens when we don't care about wisdom? What happens when a society loses wisdom en masse? I'm not talking about losing grandmother's home remedies but about losing medical science itself. Can you imagine the havoc in a world with no doctors? It may seem like a doomsday scenario, but history shows us that such black swan events have occurred.

Caution from History: The Library of Alexandria and Lessons for Us

When Alexander the Great was crowned King of Macedon in 334 BCE, beginning his reign of ruthless conquest, he dreamt of creating a world library in Alexandria. From what historians could gather, at its prime, the library had botanical gardens, ten research laboratories and a vast collection of books and scrolls.

Eratosthenes, a Greek mathematician, held the prestigious job of director of the library for many years. It is said that while working at the library, he invented a tagging mechanism to connect the knowledge within the scrolls—what we would today call search engine technology. He also devised an algorithm to discover prime numbers. Using sticks and shadows, he inferred that the earth was a sphere and calculated the circumference of the earth with near accuracy.[2]

Heron—a mathematician and inventor, and one of the luminaries in philosophy, literature, science and arts who congregated at the library—is credited with inventing the world's first vending machine, a wind wheel, and here's the big one: a rudimentary steam engine.

Why then did we have to wait for centuries until 1775 for a Scottish engineer named James Watt to invent the steam engine? Because the library of Alexandria was burned to the ground. Almost all the scrolls by Heron and other great scholars were lost in the plundering and burning of the library that followed.

> History teaches us that fires and invasions damaged the library,
> but what destroyed the library was human apathy.

History teaches us that fires and invasions damaged the library, but what *destroyed* the library was human apathy. There are letters by Seneca the Younger, where he lamented that the new emperors of Alexandria were hoarding manuscripts as a trophy collection. He mused about how the emperors craved opportunities to show off their collection, but never took the time to read them.[3]

When the novelty of collecting scrolls faded, the wealthy moved on to collecting other treasures. Over time, the library lost patronage and the papyrus scrolls started decaying. But there was no impetus to copy them onto parchment or paper. Since the times when copies were made of books, came a time when no one cared if the scrolls were falling apart. Society was changing, and new beliefs were replacing old ones.

New generations thought the past was no longer relevant.

No doubt, the scrolls were a source of great knowledge. But the scrolls didn't hold the wisdom. It was the great minds of scholars such as Euclid, Eratosthenes and Heron who churned knowledge to generate wisdom. They were the living libraries who made the library what it was. Without the elders to teach and the young ones to learn, the scrolls were just mouldy souvenirs of the past. Like the library of Alexandria there are many stories in history that show burning libraries and loss of wisdom go hand in hand.

The present times are different. We have the unique opportunity to harness wisdom and technology. We still have the elders around us from whom we can learn. We also have the power of technology that has made access to information democratic. Inheriting the wisdom of the elders and using the power of technology is the opportunity of our lifetime. It can help our families thrive and society to advance.

Be thirsty for wisdom. Be guided by wisdom. Seek it. Cultivate it. Share it.

Daily Dilemma:

As a young child, I used to read moral stories. But I hesitate to give the same books to my child. Are the morals in the stories too old? Are they still relevant in the present times, relevant for my child?

Daaji: I understand your confusion. The times have changed, but the narrative in the stories hasn't kept up. Here's an example you can relate to. Cultures across the world recommend fasting. It was recommended for religious reasons. But today, we know through science the benefits of fasting and time-restricted eating. The practice of fasting remains the same, but the narrative has changed.

Morals and values are always relevant. What is needed is the right social context to explain the story. So, you, as the parent, need to play the translator so the children can enjoy the story and appreciate the wisdom. Some time ago, our team worked on a project to recast the stories from the Vedas and explain the wisdom behind them. The book was well received, particularly by parents.

Principle 3

Preparation Begins Long before the Children Arrive

5

Becoming a Parent: Approach and Attitude

My grandmother died before I turned ten. Life expectancy was shorter in the 1950s and 1960s, and one didn't get to share as many years with one's elders. Today things are different. Gen Z and the millennials share more years with their grandparents. Not long ago I met a girl whose family I have known for many years, and I have seen the little one grow-up. She is now in her mid-twenties. 'Who do you like the most in your family?' I asked her.

'My grandmother,' she said.

'Why so?'

'Because of the way she was. She taught me so many things, and she shared many stories.'

'When are you getting married?' I asked her.

'Oh, I have a lot of time. I'm only twenty-six, Uncle.'

'All right, so when do you think you'll get married? Let's put it that way.'

'Maybe thirty-two or thirty-three.'

'Do you want your children to also have wonderful memories of their grandmother? Like you did?' I asked.

'Sure,' she said. 'I would love that. My mother can tell them stories and teach them so many things.'

'But the way you are planning,' I said, 'it may not work out that way.'

She calculated her approximate age when she would have children and her mother's age as the children will grow up.

'If I do things my way, I don't think my mother will see much of her grandchildren,' she muttered while rechecking the math in her head.

'Why are you robbing your mother of her grandmother-hood and robbing your children of their grandmother's love?' I could see that she started thinking, but I wasn't sure where her thoughts took her.

Wage disparities, motherhood penalties, balancing the needs of career and family acutely affect women and the family they are helping to raise. For instance, during the pandemic, women faced an increase in their workload—had to work double shifts—and were compelled to quit work in droves. This mass exodus of women put gender parity at work back by at least thirty-six years by some measures.[1]

Men, even though in a better position, find it difficult to run a household on a single salary. Mainly for these reasons, I find young people delaying marriage and delaying having children. And among those who are married, many couples look for ways to deepen their relationship. So, whether you are newlywed or have a few miles under your belt, the topics covered here should be helpful.

Tik Tok: Both Men and Women Have Biological Clocks

In the American movie *My Cousin Vinny*, Vinny Gambini, played by the wise guy Joe Pesci, hasn't slept in five days. He's scheduled to appear in court to defend his nephew in a death trial. On that morning, his girlfriend Mona Lisa Vito, played by the effervescent Marisa Tomei, spews fire over Vinny's broken promises, their marriage and her ticking biological clock. As she stomps her stiletto heels on the pine floorboards, shouting out 'tik tok, tik tok,' Vinny breaks out into a rant of how *everything* is going wrong in his life, and on top of it the added pressure of a ticking biological clock.[2]

Although popular, the stereotype of portraying women as having limited shelf-life fertility is wrong. Both men *and* women have fertility clocks that are ticking away.

Let's start with the men first. In 2018, Dr Michael Eisenberg, Director of Male Reproductive Medicine at Stanford University, led a population study. He and his team analysed more than 40 million births in the United States between 2007 and 2016.[3] The study found that advanced paternal age (forty-five years and older) affects the children *and* the mother. They noticed that advanced paternal age was associated with an increased risk of premature birth, low birth weight and low Apgar score, the five-point assessment of a baby's health in the minutes after birth. The study also found that the odds of gestational diabetes in mothers were 34 per cent higher with the oldest partners (fifty-five years and older).[4]

The study also showed that advanced paternal age put the children at an increased risk of conditions such as dwarfism, psychiatric disorders and autism. So, it's no surprise that the American Society for Reproductive Medicine recommends the following for sperm donors: 'The donor should be of legal age but younger than forty years of age so that *potential hazards related to aging* are diminished.'[5] The data on advanced paternal age risk has been around for a while. Yet, awareness of the male biological clock and its impact on the mother and the child's health is minimal even in developed countries.

Switching gears, women hit peak fertility in their early twenties. Once women reach thirty-five years, they are considered a high-risk pregnancy in many countries, including the United States. Osteoporosis, gestational diabetes and reduced skin elasticity are some risks associated with pregnancy in advanced maternal age. There are many screenings prescribed for a high-risk pregnancy including tests like Amniocentesis. Most of these tests are inconvenient and some are even painful. Not to mention the stress that comes with getting the tests done. For women, giving birth in their twenties is in tune with the fertility rhythm of their bodies. Another benefit of giving birth to the first child in her twenties is that it makes planning for a second one easier.

Over the years, I have met some couples, who tried to conceive when they were younger in their peak fertility years. But things didn't work out for some reason, and they ended up having children later who are all in good health. I also know of couples who delayed having children. They had children later in life who are also doing well. So, planning a child is not about beating the statistical odds. It's about avoiding taking chances with something so important. There is merit in cooperating with the natural rhythms of the body. As a couple you should sit down and talk through your plans for raising a family. One key consideration in your discussion should be your biological clock and making sure that you use the window wisely. I pray that your circumstances support you and your partner in making these decisions.

Offering reproductive advice is a charged topic. It touches women's reproductive rights, social policy for childcare and religious beliefs, and no matter which line one treads someone will be unhappy. What I have written here, is what I told my children and loved ones. If my words caused you any hurt, I hope you can take it as advice from a well-wisher.

Energy, Fun and Finances

Besides biological rhythms, the other reason to have children sooner is the energy it takes to raise them. Children like to run around, play ball, ride bikes, paint pictures, have pillow fights and wage snowball wars. When parents are younger, their energy levels are higher. They can keep up with children's demands and manage their careers, social life and everything else that needs attention. When physical energy is waning the body struggles to keep up.

The energy advantage becomes clearer later in life when children become teenagers. For example, a mother who gives birth in the late thirties will have to deal with her own physiological and psychological changes related to menopause while supporting a teenager whose body is also changing. Both are on the edge, and it's a recipe for emotional showdowns. The same goes for the father who may be dealing with his midlife crisis and now has to support a young person dealing with uncertainties that come with youth. It can be challenging.

Having children while parents are younger has some auxiliary benefits too. When you are younger it's easier to find jobs. So, if you decide to move closer to family or take a break from work, it's easier to get back in.

When parents are younger it's likely that grandparents too are younger. That makes it easier for grandparents to offer both practical help and monetary help if needed. Most couples understand these benefits, but there are situations that throttle your plans. One such situation is balancing career and family, and it's most accentuated for mothers.

Career and Family: Supporting Mothers

Couples, in the present times, try to achieve some financial goals before having children. Women play a key role in achieving these goals. Considering how difficult it can be to raise a family on a single income, working women when faced with an option to choose between a career and starting a family, prefer to choose a career.[6] Also, if the partner dies or is unable to work, it's more difficult for a woman to re-enter the workforce after a break. Not to mention the disparity women face at the workplace. In the US, for example, women earn 49 per cent of what men do, mothers earn less than fathers, and mothers earn less than women with no children.[7]

Over the years, I have met many working mothers and not one of them has told me that they were happy to go back to work immediately after having a child. A mother feels tormented stepping away from her newborn. Her guilt for missing out on her time with the child and being unable to give full attention to them runs deep. Unfortunately, most women don't have a choice, and for single mothers, there's no other option.

Having a day care at work could be great. But in most places good quality day care is expensive. I once heard of a day care at a tech company that had a two-year waiting list. And the cost? Fifty thousand dollars a year! Most mothers take a break when they get tired of 'working-to-pay-for-day care'. But the transition from a career to a full-time homemaker is not easy. Imagine having worked hard towards a professional career and then setting what you've accomplished aside, even if temporarily, for childcare, which can be exhausting and less immediately rewarding.

In days when society was agrarian, women were married-off while they were very young, and as a result, they lost their childhood. From there we seem to have swung to the other end of the spectrum where we are delaying marriage and having babies for as long as we can. Somewhere in between is the place where a family's financial security and the desire to have children are not at odds with each other.

Having said that, there are no simple answers, and each family situation is different. If a couple can enlist the support of their parents or some close family members while planning a family, that would be helpful. It will give them an understanding of how others managed to raise a family. The family's support, be it advice, helping when the baby comes or having someone to speak with, takes away some pressure from parenting. Also, when couples involve the elders in their life plans, it brings the families closer.

So far in our discussion I shared my thoughts about the importance of having children in line with your biological clock and its benefits. I also touched upon the real challenges that make some of these decisions difficult. Now I shift gears to touch upon some relationship anchors that help a couple grow in their relationship.

Relationship Anchors: Acceptance, Friendship and Teamwork

All parents would like to be the best in raising children. So how do they do that? Research shows that one of the best predictors of *parenting quality* is *marital quality*.[8,9] In simple terms, happy couples make good parents. That said, couples can't be madly in love or blissfully happy in their relationship all the time. They're not going to agree on every single thing. That's why it's so important to manage expectations.

Relationships hit rough water because of mismatched expectations. Especially expecting the *other* person to change doesn't work. I am not saying people don't change. What I am saying is accepting the other person as they are his the first step towards change.

I tell my young friends, 'When you are in a relationship, focus on yourself. Everything you are expecting from the other person, ask yourself if you could offer that to your partner. The way you are today, do you love that version of yourself? My suggestion is you first build your own empire of moral qualities. Strengthen your moral muscles before you expect the same from the other.'

An attitude of self-improvement gives strength to a relationship. It shows that your ego is not rigid. Most of the time there's friction in relationships because of the clashing egos. When the couple focuses on self-improvement, they give each other the space they need to adjust. In the process, they start developing a friendship.

Discover Friendship in Your Marriage

Couples who have a strong base of friendship in their relationship, enjoy life transitions including welcoming a new member into the family. Think of your best friend and how you spent time together. With your best friend, life did not feel serious. Days just passed by, and any minor squabble ended with both of you trying to out-appease the other. When a couple becomes friendly, accepting the other becomes easy. When there is acceptance, love grows in the relationship.

Becoming friends also helps the couple appreciate the small joys of life. Science also backs this idea. John Gottman of the prestigious Gottman Institute found that the real difference between couples who stuck together and those who didn't wasn't their ability to tackle big problems well, handle conflicts and manage communication. Instead, it was the small things that made a big difference. Drinking coffee together, sharing a sandwich, going out for a walk, doing a crossword, sharing house chores and so on. The dull and mundane stuff turned out to be the glue in the relationship. Couples who stayed together cherished the small moments. They took interest in each other. They were friends first, husband and wife second. Rediscover friendship in your relationship. If you are already friends, continue to deepen the friendship. Raising a family is an ongoing adjustment of lifestyles. Early on in the relationship if the couple develops mutual respect and appreciation for what each one does, it keeps the relationship harmonious.

Do This

The partner's support is vital for the mother. Simple things like helping out with the dishes, making a cup of tea, helping with the laundry gives the mother meaningful support. For the men who are reading this, try to do everything your wife does at home for a week. Getting the children ready, the chores and everything else. It will give you an appreciation of how much effort it takes to run the house.

And for the wives, who may not be paying attention to financial planning, investments and other tasks often handled by men, start taking interest. Taking interest and supporting each other will help strengthen the relationship.

Relationships Are Teamwork

One evening, during my walk, I saw an elderly couple sitting on a bench near the river. They shared a sandwich and had some water while watching the river. Then they got up and started walking on the trail along the river. They didn't talk. They just held each other's hand and continued walking for a long way. The harmony in their evening ritual was heartfelt.

Often people think that they have to talk and impress the other with their intellect and smart conversation. In an authentic relationship, one doesn't need to impress the other person with words. Instead, the words are replaced with a reassuring silence. The desire to impress is overridden by the desire to care for the other. The care is expressed in one's actions. In a heartfelt relationship, silence is the best expression of love. Through mere eye contact, this elderly couple conveyed volumes to one another. Their picnic lunch ritual was a masterclass in togetherness.

Relationships are teamwork. Think of your family and close friends as one team running the relay race. Father, mother, children, grandparents, close friends—all are part of the team. Each member runs their race and passes the baton. We cheer for each other and boost each other. Sometimes, the baton slips. But because a teammate fumbled, we don't stop running. We don't walk away from the race. Instead, we run harder to make up for the lost time. Couples who are friends work as a team. They look beyond their individual identities. They see their strength in unity, and they complement each other.

As a couple's compatibility increases, they resonate with each other at a deeper level. Their relationship benefits not only them but those around them as well. We have all experienced this. Think of the awkward evening dinner with a couple that sparred over everything from parking to restaurant décor to which dessert to order. Spending time with such couples can drain one's energy. Contrast this with an evening spent with a friendly couple. Their banter, body language and ability to finish each other's sentences inspire couples' goals. The field of energy created in the two scenarios is of an opposing nature. One gives out an all-consuming and tiring vibration while the other gives a joyful and uplifting vibration.

Happy couples resonate better with each other, and their heart-mind fields create a welcoming space for a new soul to enter their lives.

Daily Dilemma:

My husband and I often have arguments. Sometimes things get loud. Should I be worried about the psychological impact this will have on my child?

Daaji: I suggest you and your husband try 'postponing anger'. In general, most of us are experts at postponing. We postpone exercise, meditation, financial planning and many other things in life. Try postponing anger. You will be delighted with the results.

In the Talmud, the holy book of the Jews, there is a line, 'The talk of the child is the talk of the elders at home.' So, it's wise to avoid arguments and fights in front of children.

6

All Parents Are Adopted

As soon as a child is born, everyone around is fixated on one thing: the child's cry. The doctor, the nurses, the midwife, the parents—all rejoice upon hearing the child announce her arrival into the world with a piercing wail. For a parent, the sound of the child's first cry is unforgettable. But sometimes, there is only quiet. And then efforts are made to make the child cry. The doctor pats the child and gently massages the child's back. If that doesn't work, the team rushes to use a suction tube to drain any residual liquid blocking the child's nose and mouth. If that doesn't work either, then the child is shifted to the NICU and put on a supply of oxygen. At the end of it all, if the lungs refuse to kick into action, then the family cries out in deafening grief.

Why didn't the child cry after birth? The interventions by the doctors are limited to the physical body. But they can't help it if something that was supposed to accompany the body at the time of birth did not come along. Something that triggers the baby to cry, an entity that jump-starts the baby's breathing, needs to accompany the child at the time of birth. The missing entity is the life-force. It is the bridge between the animate and the inanimate. Spiritual traditions address it by many names, including *soul, ruuh, atman* and *neshamah*.

Our soul resides inside us from the moment of birth and continues to be with us until the final moment, whenever that may be. The soul keeps the body going, and when it leaves us, we kick the bucket, as they say. The soul is not enshrined in a holy place or found on a sacred mountain top. We do not go on pilgrimages to visit it or summon it under a special tree. Animals, plants, birds and human beings—we are all carried by the life-force imparted by our soul.

And why is it important for parents to learn about the soul? It's because parents are not mere donors of genetic material. The mother and the father together create a field for the incoming soul. The soul chooses the parents. To understand this idea, I first explain a few important concepts about the soul and then explain how the soul enters the mother's womb.

Vibratory Field Created by the Soul

The soul is not like a battery that gets discharged over time. It is an eternal source. When it's time to go, the soul unplugs and moves on. When the soul unplugs, the body stops functioning and, over time, disintegrates into the elements. While the soul resides in a body, life-force keeps flowing through the body and it creates a vibratory field around the body. Take the example of a wire. When electricity is flowing through it, an electromagnetic field is created around it and when the wire is unplugged the electromagnetic field around the wire also drops to zero.

> Our thoughts, our actions and our lifestyle, all affect the nature
> of our vibratory field. Meditative practices and qualities such
> as compassion, love and empathy create a vibratory field with a
> welcoming quality to it.

In the same way, when life-force is flowing through our body, it creates a vibratory field around it. The vibratory field that you emit is your unique signature. Your attitudes create your vibratory field. Your inner qualities and thinking make your attitudes. And your attitudes are reflected in the vibratory field that you create. There's no faking it. So if you want to create a vibratory field with a welcoming and loving nature, you need to be a person with a warm and welcoming attitude. Meditative practices and qualities such as compassion, love and empathy create a vibratory field with a welcoming quality to it. Whereas arrogant and egoistic attitudes create a vibratory field of a domineering nature.

We do not have instruments to measure the vibratory field. But there is an indirect measure. The electromagnetic field generated by one's heart which can be measured up to 3 feet away from the body, is an indirect measure of one's vibratory field.[1]

You may be wondering what does the vibratory field have to do with a couple planning for a child. To understand this, we need to get a deeper understanding of how the soul enters the womb.

Entry of the Soul into the Body

Human life, as most of us know, starts with the sperm merging with an egg. It is a biological process that culminates in the birth of a child. You may think where is the soul during the biological process? Once conception occurs, a soul is drawn to the mother's womb. The soul hovers around the mother's womb and waits there. It waits for the right time in the biological process that has already begun in the womb. By remaining outside the body, in the vicinity of the womb, the soul starts applying its force. The soul's force gives momentum to the biological process within. It accelerates the division of the cells, and the first organ that forms in the foetus is the heart. From the heart, the other organs are nourished.

While the physical body of the foetus develops, its spiritual body develops alongside it. A network of energy channels is created in the foetus for the life-force to flow through. Think of how a house is built from the outside in. First, the foundation is laid, and then the walls and roof complete the outer shell. After this the electric wiring begins inside the house. In a similar way, for a foetus, the vital body parts start developing first. After that, the energy channels for life-force are created in the body. In the electrical layout of a house, there are junction boxes that manage the flow of electricity. In the human body also, there are junction points from where energy is channelled and distributed. These junction points are called chakras.

> Once the soul enters the foetus, it resides in the heart. The heart is the seat of the soul.

Most of us are familiar with the seven chakras along the spine. While these are the most known, there are several more chakras in the human body. One of the chakras, vital for fetal development, is the *Brahmarandhra*. When the foetus's brain is well formed, and the Brahmarandhra chakra is well developed in the brain (near the occipital area), the soul enters the body through this chakra.

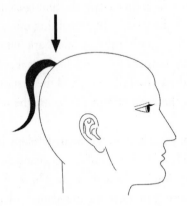

Location of the Brahmarandhra

The entry of the soul through the Brahmarandhra happens within the first three months of conception. Why does the soul not enter the foetus right away? The soul waits for the appropriate time. Think of it this way. If we take a gadget whose circuitry is not complete and plug it into a power supply, then things can go wrong. In the same way, the soul waits for the energy circuitry of the body to develop first. When the circuitry is complete, then the life-force can begin flowing in the foetus. Once the soul enters the foetus, it resides in the heart. The heart is the seat of the soul. Through the heart the soul's life-force reaches all the chakras in the body.

Attitude and the Vibratory Level of the Soul

These days, especially in India, it is common to see parents set up an appointment for a planned C-section to coincide with an auspicious date and time to ensure that a great soul will descend. I have seen families also consider the place, horoscope and so many other factors. Do such preparations help?

The soul, which is to come, has already incarnated. At the time of conception, the soul was drawn to the vibratory field created by the parents. The soul chooses the parents. We chose our parents, and our children chose us. Between lives, the soul contemplates and plans for the next life. In its wisdom, it designs a plan that carries the blueprint for its evolution. Then the soul awaits the womb from where it can begin the next cycle of its existence.

So, the preparation that helps welcome a soul lies in cultivating one's vibratory field. When the wife and husband love each other and support each other in leading a life of meaning and purpose, their attitude at the time of conception creates a vibratory field that will be different from the vibratory field created by someone with bad attitude and a misguided inner compass.

Mythological stories highlight how the attitude of parents plays a role in the soul they attract. For example, in the Christian tradition, the story of Samuel, the son of Elkanah, and his mother, Hannah, is an inspiring one. Hannah was a pious woman who prayed fervently to the Lord and she was blessed with a son, Samuel. Hannah offered her son to the Lord to be his servant. Samuel, who inherited his mother's pious nature, led a virtuous life of service. The pious attitude of Hannah and the loving relationship that Hannah and Elkanah shared helped them attract a soul with divine qualities. There are many such stories that highlight the importance of the parents' attitudes and the effects it has on their children.

One story I find revealing is from the Mahabharata, the great Indian epic. King Vichitravirya was the ruler of the kingdom of

Hastinapura. He had two wives, Ambika and Ambalika. At a young age, the king contracted tuberculosis and died, leaving behind a kingdom without an heir. The king's mother, Queen Satyavati, wanted to ensure the continuity of the royal lineage. In those days, under exceptional circumstances, it was socially permissible for a widow to temporarily cohabit with a man for the sake of bearing children. This social permission was called *Niyoga*. One way to understand Niyoga in today's context is to think of it as sperm donation. Such customs were prevalent across cultures. For example, in the Old Testament, Sarah had offered her slave Hagar to her husband Abraham to bear him children.

Satyavati decided to exercise Niyoga. She consulted the palace astrologer. 'This is the most auspicious time,' he said. 'If the queens can conceive during the next two hours, the children will be of a glorious nature, worthy of a king's succession.'

Satyavati had an eldest son, Vyasa, who at a young age, became an enlightened sage and lived as an ascetic. The queen sent an urgent summons to Vyasa, who was meditating in the jungle. He'd possibly been meditating for weeks, and upon hearing his mother's summon, he came as he was, unwashed and matted long hair.

Upon hearing the queen mother's request, Vyasa rebuffed the idea, but Satyavati insisted. After much pleading, out of obedience to his mother and for the greater good of the kingdom, Vyasa agreed. He went into the chambers of Queen Ambika, who was aghast when she saw him. Ambika had just lost her husband. She did not have an heir, which meant that anyone who attacked the kingdom would lay claim to the throne and the queens. In time of such despondency, she had to consummate with an ascetic who was her late husband's stepbrother. In the story, it is said that she shut her eyes in disdain and went ahead with the act. Likewise, when Vyasa went to the other queen, Ambalika, she saw him, froze and turned pale, as if her blood stopped circulating.

Two children were conceived of the union. The child born to Queen Ambika, who had closed her eyes in fear, was blind, and the child born to Queen Ambalika, who had turned pale with fear, had pale, leucodermic skin (the loss of pigment in blotches). These two queens also offered their loyal maid to the sage in case they had failed to conceive. For the maid, it was a great honour to be of service to the royal throne. She was grateful for being chosen to serve her master's house in such capacity. The child born to the maid was the wisest of the lot and he became the chief advisor to the king.

This story from the Mahabharata, the story of Hannah and similar stories from other cultures highlight the importance of attitude at the time of conception. Now the question arises, 'Can one manufacture a super fine vibratory level at that moment?' No. During conception, passions are running high and the last thing on your mind would be the vibratory field. More importantly, one cannot fabricate a vibratory level because one wants to invite a soul like Jesus Christ or a Vivekananda into one's family. Think about it this way. You can dress like a golfer, have the best set of clubs, and even fake a good swing. But when it's time to tee off, then one shot is all it takes to prove whether you are a pro or an amateur. Your vibratory field is the outcome of what you are inside. One must be authentic about inner transformation and approach it with all sincerity.

When a couple supports each in becoming better human beings and pursuing goals beyond the mundane, then their relationship also evolves. They connect at a deeper level. The union of such a couple creates a field that attracts souls with superior spiritual potential.

By the word 'spiritual potential', I mean souls with a higher level of consciousness. These incoming souls will have greater empathy, better resilience and a superior moral fabric. They carry the potential to positively influence their families and communities when they grow up. So, being authentic and becoming a better human being benefits not only oneself but also the future generations.

We don't have scientific evidence on the vibratory level of parents and the soul it attracts. But if we focus on one's attitude and its effects, science offers compelling evidence. Take for example, the attitude of happiness. There are studies that show that 50 per cent of our happiness is genetic. Meaning, we inherit the happy gene from our parents and the rest of the happiness depends on the environment we grow up in.[2] Similarly, studies also show that children born of extreme trauma are affected by it. For example, children born of traumatic incidents like rape are more likely to suffer from severe psychological disorders like PTSD and depression.[3] In such cases of extreme trauma, what helps is the loving care and support of family for both the mother and the child. Social support can go a long way towards healing from trauma.

Tackling Some Common Questions

Some of you may be thinking, 'I already have children, and I was not aware of the importance of attitude at the time of conception. Does this mean that my child's spiritual potential is fixed?' When a child is conceived by a couple, they attract a soul with certain spiritual potency. Think of it as the spiritual capital that the soul brings along with it.

The spiritual capital can be enriched all through one's life. The mother plays a pivotal role in this, especially during pregnancy and in the early childhood years. During pregnancy, the vibratory environment created within the womb nurtures the child spiritually. Later in this book, the principle 'happy mothers make happy families,' explains more about creating a nurturing vibratory environment within the womb.

After birth, the parents and the environment at home nurtures the child. So, if a child is nurtured well, the spiritual potential of the child continues to grow. On the other hand, parents may beget a child with immense potential, but if they are unable to nurture the child with the right thoughts and values, then the child is like the proverbial diamond in the rough waiting to be discovered. Parents play a foundational role in nourishing the child's physical, mental, emotional and spiritual development. The most opportune time for this is during the childhood years.

A second question that often comes up is around births that occur through IVF. It does not matter whether the egg is formed in the womb or in a test tube. The moment of conception will attract a soul of corresponding frequency.

Many have asked what happens in the case of twins or even triplets. Souls of similar frequency are drawn to the womb of a mother. Such souls share similar tendencies and temperaments.

The important takeaway from this chapter is that preparation begins long before the children arrive. Instead of worrying about timing the birth of your child, the place of birth and so on, focus on creating the right environment for the mother and the baby. And this takes us to the next principle, *Happy mothers make happy families.*

Daily Dilemma:

I have been married for seven years and I am currently at the peak of my professional life. I have held-off having a child till now because bringing a new life into this world is daunting. What if I am not a good mother? What if I end up hurting my child? How do I overcome this fear?

Daaji: Fear of the unknown is common to most of us. To be successful in anything in life, three things are needed: will, faith and confidence. Doubt poisons the will and affects faith and confidence. You have doubts about being a good mother.

To eliminate doubt, one must prepare. Most of the time, we are nervous because of our lack of preparation. As you plan for a baby, you and your husband can start meditating. If you already meditate, I suggest you both get your one-to-one sessions from a meditation trainer regularly.

Meditation prepares an environment of peace and harmony within you. This will help you overcome worries and doubts. Besides meditation, share your worries with your mother or grandmother. Listening to their stories will give you confidence.

I pray for you and your family.

Principle 4

Happy Mothers Make Happy Families

D-Day, Dutch Hunger
Winter and Epigenetics

In China, despite warp speed modernization, the age-old practice of *the sitting month* still flourishes. For one month after birth, the mother stays at home and follows a strict diet and lifestyle that keeps her and the child healthy.[1] In Columbia, something similar is practised for a period of forty days. In Nigeria, the first bath for the baby is given by the grandmother or an elderly aunt. The ceremonial bath is a much-celebrated milestone. In India, the expectant mother goes to her parents' home where many practices like the ones shared above are followed.

Are these practices mere cultural protocols or do they have a greater significance? To explore further, we start our conversation with a crucial moment during World War II, the D-Day invasion.

D-Day Invasion and the Dutch Hunger Winter

Following the D-Day invasion, the Allied troops took back most of France, Luxembourg and Belgium. Next, they were headed for the Netherlands. To make it easier for the Allied troops, the exiled government of the Netherlands called for a rail strike. Their plan was to hinder the movement of Nazi troops. The Nazis countered by blockading the parts of the Netherlands that they occupied. They cut off food supplies into those parts.

The winter was beginning, and the winter of 1945 turned out to be hellish. Mass food shortages hit the Netherlands. When relatives started sending food through the postal service the Nazis blocked the delivery of parcels. Men were forced to hide at home to prevent capture, so women and children became scavengers of food, often biking miles into the countryside. After hours of standing in lines, in the cold, most they managed was a bread loaf. Within a few months, it is estimated that 22,000 people died. The Dutch refer to this dark period as *Hongerwinter* or Hunger Winter.

When Tulips Became the New Chestnut

Many of us are familiar with the tulip mania of the 1600s when the tulip bulb prices reached record highs and caused one of the most famous market bubbles and crashes. But, few of us know that during Hunger Winter, tulip became the new chestnut. As food shortages continued, tulip bulb powder became a staple in recipes for cakes, cookies, stews and soups. The Amsterdam Local Committee for Domestic Education and Family Management also published a cookbook on the use of tulip bulbs. Sadly, thousands still died of starvation in a famine that was an act of man.

Despite the hardship they were facing, the Dutch doctors maintained detailed patient health records. There were about forty thousand women who were pregnant during Hunger Winter. Scientists and doctors worldwide still study the Hunger Winter health records to understand the effects of malnutrition on the mother and the child.

Dr Tessa Roseboom, a professor of Early Development and Health at the University of Amsterdam, led such a study. Her team found that the babies conceived earlier in the famine were affected with more severe health problems later in life as compared to babies who were conceived towards the end of the famine.

Dr Roseboom found that the mothers who starved for longer gave birth to children with low birth weight and smaller head circumference. She also found that these children developed problems that surfaced decades later in life. When the Hunger Winter children grew up and were in their fifties and sixties, they developed more medical complications. For example, the children born during the famine had twice the risk of heart disease in their sixties. These people also suffered from greater incidence of obesity than those who were born later. Throughout their lives, the Hunger Winter children had higher hospitalization rates. Scientists speculated that due to lower cognitive abilities their professional careers also suffered.[2] It is as if the body shut off some genes in the foetus and they never restarted again, even when times became normal.

We are talking about problems that show up *decades later* in life. Years later in their fifties and sixties, these adults developed many more medical complications

Not only this but some of the effects were transferred to the grandchildren of the women who suffered during Hunger Winter. So, the children who were born during a famine were affected and the next generation that was born after, when there was peace and prosperity, was also affected.

How do we explain such transference across generations? Do the genes carry some information that they pass along to the next generation? Can such genetic memory be reversed? These questions have been at the heart of a classical debate in modern science for the last few centuries.

It is called the nature versus nurture debate. Those in the nature camp believe that it's all about one's genes. The genes are what make you or break you. For example, you are intelligent because you inherited those genes. The nature camp promotes the idea that genes determine everything.

As opposed to this, those in the nurture camp counter by saying that genes don't matter. They propose that the human mind is a *Tabula Rasa,* a blank slate (an idea attributed to Aristotle). The nurture camp believes that it is the environment and the nurturing that makes all the difference. It doesn't matter who the parents are or what genes one is born with. When the child is given a healthy environment, then the child will thrive.

Its Nature and Nurture: Enter Epigenetics

While the debate between the nature and nurture camps raged, some scientists forged a new path in the field of biology called *epigenetics*. 'Epi' means something on the outside. Epigenetics studies the effect of the environment on one's genes. Epigenetics says it is nature *and* nurture, not nature versus nurture. You may be blessed with great genes, but if you were not nurtured well after birth, then the genetic advantage is lost. Nature and nurture work together.

> Epigenetics is showing us new ways of understanding the relationship between one's environment and one's genes.

Research in epigenetics shows that external factors can turn on or turn off genes. This process is called *methylation.* In the studies of the Dutch Hunger Winter, scientists found specific genes involved in metabolism showed evidence of methylation. So, the genes that were supposed to help the body grow and burn fat were *suppressed* from expressing as they normally would. As a result, later in life, while in their fifties and sixties, because of the suppressed genes, these adults suffered from obesity and heart disease.

Epigenetics is showing us new ways of understanding the relationship between one's environment and one's genes. One may be blessed with good genes but external factors like social status, income and access to healthcare can impact one's health at a genetic level. While reading these pages, some of you may start worrying about what your parents or grandparents did or didn't do and how it may have affected you. Please don't be alarmed. Firstly, research also shows that epigenetic changes are reversible. For example, in the case of smokers, it has been observed that smoking causes epigenetic changes in the body (specifically for the AHRR gene). However, when they quit smoking, these changes reversed over time.[3] Secondly, knowing what you know now, planning how you would do things differently is a better way to channel your energy. As a parent today and as a grandparent in the future, how would you play your role in creating the right environment that allows for the best expression of one's genes, that is a worthwhile effort.

Focusing on the Pregnant Mothers Care

While our elders may not have used the word 'Epigenetics', they must have understood its influence on a person's health. For example, in *Charaka Samhita*[4] an ancient Ayurvedic text, there is a section called *Garbhini Vyakarana* (meaning *Development of the Embryo*). It is the palm leaf version of *What to Expect When you're Expecting*. In it, there is a verse that reads, 'If a cup filled with oil right up to the brim is to be carried without spilling even a single drop, every step has to be taken with care.' This verse refers to the care and nurturing needed for an expectant mother during pregnancy.

What's special about this ancient text is it focuses on physiology as much as it does on the environment surrounding the expectant mother. The post-conception care as detailed in the texts offers prescriptions for diet (*aahara*), daily routine and activities (*vihara*) and medicines (*aushada*).[5] Everything from recommended foods for each month, types of massages and exercises, air quality, sunlight, moonlight, aromas and even music for the expectant mother are described. What we would today call epigenetic influences are well documented in the ancient text.

The wisdom behind sending the expectant mother to her parents' home was to ensure an environment free from any stress.

In Indian society, the tradition of sending the expectant mother to her parents' home reflects an understanding of epigenetic influence. The custom is still followed but many do not understand the significance behind it. For the longest time, Indian society was agrarian, where the men worked the fields, and the women took care of everything else. Raising the children, cooking, cleaning, helping during the harvest and anything else that needed to be done was handled by the women. It was a lot of work, and for a woman to not support her family by doing her share of the work made it difficult. But pregnancy brings on such an onslaught of physical and emotional changes that it is impossible to maintain the same energy levels as before.

The wisdom behind sending the expectant mother to her parents' home was to ensure an environment free from any stress. This way, the expectant mother could spend the time in the loving care of her family without having to worry about expectations from her in-laws, labour-intensive chores or her own guilt in not being able to help.

In her parents' home, her lifestyle was set up in such a way that both the foetus and the mother were nurtured physically, mentally and spiritually. The mother's daily routine was well planned in terms of the food she ate, the dietary supplements she would have, her resting hours and some light household activities to keep her busy. The devotional prayers of the elders created an atmosphere of piety and peace. Various rituals and ceremonies punctuated the pregnancy, the significance of which was to keep the mother to be in good spirits. Back then, families were large, and people had many children. A house filled with the laughter of little children uplifted the spirits of the mother-to-be. The social support at home acted as an immunity shield for the mother.

Even though I am referring to Indian households, across cultures of the world, customs that honour pregnancy and suggest special care for the expectant mother are pervasive. Earlier in the chapter I shared examples from China, Columbia and Nigeria. Anthropologists have also studied these customs. For example, in her seminal work *Coming of Age*, the anthropologist Margaret Mead writes about the customs of the Samoans. She says that for months before the birth of a child, the father's relatives bring gifts of food to the prospective mother, who lived with her parents. The mother's relatives busy themselves making baby clothes and tiny baby mats. The pregnant mother is advised against any solitary work, heavy work and avoiding extreme heat and cold. At the time of birth, the father's mother or sister is present to care for the newborn, while the midwife and the relatives cared for the mother.[6]

The physical, emotional and spiritual health of the parents affects their children. A 2018 study by Child Trends, a leading research organization in Washington DC,[7] reported that 'the parents' health is one of the strongest predictors of child's health'. Their research showed that parents' health was more strongly associated with the child's health than many other factors, including family income, family structure, parents' level of education, and the child's sex, age or race. Our elders intuited this knowledge and recognized that healthy mothers build healthy nations. Happy mothers make happy families.

Don't Start Packing Your Bags, Yet!

Before you start packing your bags and start asking your relatives to get busy with their knit kits for the baby, hold on. There are other factors, too, such as maternity leave, medical facilities near the parents' home, sibling care, financial constraints and so on, that need to be considered. The central idea is the *well-being* of the mother-to-be—a safe, stress-free environment where she feels comfortable and supported.

If packing bags and heading out to your parents' home is a good option, then by all means do it. But for any reason, it's not, then see what best can be done to create the right environment where you are. This may mean getting help from friends and family that's nearby. In some scenarios, the parents-to-be may need to evaluate their career choices. When making these decisions, prioritize the expectant mother's health and happiness. See what works best for her and then make plans.

In the coming chapter, we dive deeper into the epigenetic effects and explore the wisdom behind what the baby knows even before she lets out the first cry in the real world.

Daily Dilemma:

My wife is expecting. How can I support her and make sure she is happy and healthy?

Daaji: Congratulations to you both. Your support and presence play an important role in the well-being of the mother and the child. I suggest you start with getting your affairs in order. Make sure you have life insurance and a plan for financial savings. As the due date gets closer, arrange for domestic help. If you can be closer to elders who can support you, that would be wonderful.

This is a special time. Use it wisely to deepen your spiritual togetherness. Meditate together, read together and send positive suggestions to the child coming to your home.

8

Ashtavakra, Abhimanyu and the Scientific Theory of Foetal Origins

One of my fondest childhood memories is sitting in my father's lap and listening to stories. Countless times I heard the stories of Prahlada and Dhruva. Both were young boys and their fierce devotion for the Lord inspired me. Now, when I look back at those moments, those stories changed the environment at home. Their wisdom touched the hearts of all those who listened in—grown-ups and children alike. As a tribute to the storytellers in our lives, I share here two stories particularly important for couples expecting a child.

Ashtavakra: The Boy Sage and a Master of Masters

Sage Kahoda and his wife Sujata, lived in the ashram of Sujata's father, Sage Uddalaka. When Sujata gave birth to a boy they named him Asita Devala, but the world would come to know of him as Ashtavakra, meaning 'one with eight deformities'.

One day, Kahoda was chanting the scripture, and Sujata, pregnant at that time, was listening in. Kahoda while chanting one of the verses made a mistake and the baby in the womb immediately kicked hard. Sujata winced and Kahoda noticed it and continued chanting.

It so happened that Kahoda made another mistake and the baby kicked yet again. Kahoda made eight mistakes throughout the chanting, and the baby kicked all eight times without missing a beat. An unborn child pointing out mistakes did not sit well with the father. Kahoda's ego was hurt, and in a fit of rage, he cursed that the child be born with eight deformities.

When the child was born, there were eight deformities, thus receiving the moniker Ashtavakra. The deformities notwithstanding, Ashtavakra, was a prodigy. By the age of twelve, Ashtavakra completed his training and set out on a mission to impart knowledge to one and all. As a wandering monk, he encountered King Janaka, an emperor, who was also a seeker of divine wisdom. Their dialog resulted in the *Ashtavakra Gita*. It is an extraordinary treatise on consciousness consisting of nearly 300 verses spread across twenty chapters.

Ashtavakra's story has some key takeaways. First, the story showed that while he was in the womb he was learning. Not only did he learn scripture, but he became so adept that he corrected the mistakes made by his father. Second, while in the womb he was susceptible to intentions made by others. So much so that his father's curse affected him. Remember these two takeaways while we go to the next story. After that, we will see what science says about what a baby in the womb is learning.

Abhimanyu: The True North of Valour

The second story is of the teen warrior Abhimanyu, whose martyrdom was a turning point in the battle of the Mahabharata.

Abhimanyu was the son of the great warrior Arjuna and Princess Subhadra, the sister of Lord Krishna. One afternoon, in the privacy of their chambers, Arjuna was telling Subhadra, who was pregnant at that time, the secrets of a military formation called the *Chakravyuha*. When an army attacks in this formation, it acts like a tornado, destroying everything in its path.

Arjuna explained how a skilled warrior can break into a Chakravyuha using a secret manoeuvre. But if the warrior doesn't know how to break out of a Chakravyuha, death is certain. While listening to Arjuna, Subhadra fell asleep.

The story goes that Abhimanyu learned how to break into the Chakravyuha while still in the womb. But Subhadra fell asleep. So, Arjuna never finished telling her how to break out of the Chakravyuha. So, Abhimanyu only learned how to break-in.

Fast forward sixteen years, in the war of the Mahabharata, on the thirteenth day, the enemy lured Arjuna away into another battle. Using this tactical advantage, they attacked using the Chakravyuha. Arjuna was the only one who knew how to destroy this formation, and without him, it was a freefall.

Seeing the rout they were facing, young Abhimanyu led a powerful counterattack. The young lion tore through the formation and decimated the enemy lines. It's said that he used a weapon with a hallucinating agent that created a chimera of hundreds of Abhimanyu's. The enemy soldiers panicked and started killing each other. But since he didn't know how to break out of the formation, Abhimanyu was trapped. The enemy surrounded him like a pack of wild dogs and killed him off in an unfair fight.

As with the story of Ashtavakra, Abhimanyu's story also shows that while he was in the womb, he *imbibed* knowledge of warfare and recalled it later in life. Ashtavakra and Abhimanyu were prodigies in their own right. Both were groomed for a grand destiny. All the same, these stories raise many questions: 'What does a foetus learn about the world?', 'Are parents' mere genetic donors or something more?', 'Is there any scientific research into what the foetus already knows?'

What the Baby Knows before Her First Cry

Science reporter and author Annie Murphy Paul gave a TED Talk in which she quotes a research study showing how the foetus develops tastes and smells in utero. [1] 'In one experiment,' she said, 'a group of pregnant women was asked to drink a lot of carrot juice during their third trimester, while another group of pregnant women drank only water. Six months later, the women's infants were offered cereal mixed with carrot juice, and their facial expressions were observed while they ate it. The offspring of the carrot juice drinking women ate more carrot-flavored cereal, and from the looks of it, they seemed to enjoy it more.' [2]

Obstetrics and gynaecology focused on safe births, maternal health and child development for the longest time. Not much research was devoted to *how time inside the womb* might affect the child's health in the long term. But that began changing after a paper in the Lancet journal in 1989 by British physician and epidemiologist David Barker. While studying data on 5654 men from Hertfordshire, UK, he found that whoever in this group was born with the lowest birth weight *and* lowest weight by year one had the highest death rates from heart disease. [3]

To further understand what David Barker was saying, consider this. If a child in Hertfordshire, UK, born in 1923, had low birth weight and continued to be of low birth weight at the age of year one, then this child as a seventy-year-old man, had a high chance of dying of heart disease. In the 1980s, scientists were not looking at heart disease and correlating it to birth weight. The causes of heart disease were attributed to lifestyle, diet and hereditary factors.

But David Barker hypothesized that heart disease in the Hertfordshire study was because of genetic programming that occurred in the womb. He believed that the transmissions that cross the placental barrier acted as 'biological postcards' sent by the mother to the foetus. The postcards gave the foetus information about the world. If they carried messages of a peaceful and bountiful world, foetal development would be healthy. If the postcards carried trauma messages, then the epigenetic effects caused the child to have health problems later in life.

Initially, the findings of David Baker were not well received. But, over time, research collaborators from India, Finland, New Zealand, China and Canada started publishing research that proved David Barker was correct. Dr Tessa Roseboom, whose Dutch Winter study showed how mothers' health affected children, had worked with David Barker. In honour of David's work, Fetal Origins is also known as Barkers Hypothesis.

The foetus is not a tabula rasa, nor a pre-programmed robot. The stories of Abhimanyu and Ashtavakra and the scientific research point us in the direction that the foetus is in osmosis with the mother, and is learning about the world she is entering. Genetic donorship by the parents is the beginning. The mother and father's interactions, their joys and sorrows send messages to the baby inside.

Knowing this, how best can a family support the mother and her child? What to watch out for? Can we create positive epigenetic effects that benefit the foetus?

Addressing the Epigenetic Effects of Stress

The villain in maternal epigenetics is stress. It's a leading factor affecting pregnant women's health.[4] The form of stress that causes the biggest problems is *chronic stress,* which is the body's response to emotional pressure suffered for a prolonged period.

In today's world, the sabretooth tigers are all around us. Stress at work, stress at school, the stress of finances, the stress of relationships, and stress because of stress itself. We are always on the lookout for the sabretooth tiger lurking somewhere.

Psychologists give the example of the sabretooth tiger to explain how stress response mechanisms evolved in our bodies.[5] Here is how it goes. Imagine your caveman ancestor strolling in the jungle and a sabretooth tiger attacks. There are three options: fight, flight or freeze. If you freeze, well, that's the end of the story. If you fight the tiger or outrun the tiger (flight), there are chances of survival. It's a high-stress encounter where the body creates stress hormones such as adrenaline and cortisol. Blood is redirected from the digestive tract and other vital organs and moved towards the muscles and limbs to give the energy needed for fight or flight. If your caveman ancestor was lucky and survived the attack, then the stress levels in his body would have come down, and the body resumes its regular business. This, in short, is how the stress response mechanism evolved.

In today's world, sabretooth tigers are all around: stress at work, stress at school, the stress of finances, the stress of relationships and stress because of stress itself. We are stressed non-stop about the lurking sabretooth tiger. This type of stress where one is always on guard is called chronic stress. Chronic stress is known to cause issues related to high blood pressure, suppression of immunity, damage to muscle tissue and poor mental health.

Research shows the epigenetic effects created by a combination of finance, relationships, lack of community and racism induce chronic stress in pregnant mothers, resulting in premature deliveries. [6] Cortisol, a stress hormone, crosses the placental barrier and passes on to the foetus affecting its development.[7] The effects of chronic stress on the foetus also include lower weight at birth and longer-term effects, including personality disorders, cardiovascular issues and diabetes.

Building immunity against stress is crucial because stress, first and foremost, affects the mother. Proper nutrition, a healthy lifestyle and good social support help manage stress. While we know the harmful effects of chronic stress, avoiding stress altogether is not possible. We all have some level of stress in life. Studies show that moderate stress does not cause any damage to the foetus. What we need to avoid is chronic stress and burnout.

In medicine, burnout is defined as 'a state of emotional, mental, and often physical exhaustion brought on by prolonged or repeated stress. Though it's most often caused by problems at work, it can also appear in other areas of life, such as parenting, caretaking or romantic relationships.'[8]

In a research study on burnout, it was found that in a short period of time meditation lowered stress in a statistically significant way.[9] Not only did the stress levels reduce, but the length of the telomeres increased, especially in the younger population. Telomeres are cap-shaped sections of DNA found at the end of chromosomes. The length of telomeres indicates wellbeing. So longer telomeres are a good sign.[10]

Create Lightness Within

Stress can create such heaviness inside us, but we can ease that stress and feel so much lighter as a result. A simple way to beat stress is to laugh. Laugh often. Laugh at each other. Laugh at yourself. Laugh at the situation's life may throw at you. If you cannot laugh, try smiling. A simple, genuine smile will alleviate many triggers for stress. Get into the habit of smiling, practice smiling and see how problems become manageable. As you read these lines, it's likely you're smiling. A smile makes the heart feel lighter. Nine months for expecting mothers can feel like a long time and smiling can make it shorter and bearable.

During pregnancy, create a nurturing environment, wherever you are. Thoughts, actions and intentions create an environment. Meditation at home creates a wonderful environment. My request to expectant parents is to start meditation if you haven't already. Both the mother and the father benefit from meditation's calming and rejuvenating effects.

In Heartfulness meditation, the Transmission, which is the essence of love, nourishes the mother and the child. The mother's meditation creates a vibratory environment in the womb that benefits the child. These are matters of experience. I hope you experience the benefits and prove these words true for yourself. (In the appendix, you can find a link to locate a trainer near you.)

A significant cause for stress in expectant mothers is the amount of information and advice hitting them. Eat this, don't drink that. Get this test done. Get acupuncture. Do this exercise. Don't eat sushi and so on. So many dos and don'ts send the concerned mother-to-be into a Googling spree that ends with imagining the gloomiest scenarios. Making expectant mothers feel like ultra-fragile packages increases their burden and causes unnecessary stress. Meditation can not only help relieve stress, but it can help you navigate your way through this information by tapping into your inner wisdom.

My advice to the expecting mothers: you are gifted with an intuitive connection with your child. And I hope the knowledge shared here empowers you even more. I also hope that the book brings family members closer to each other.

In the not-so-distant past, when families were closer, mothers-to-be could have a chat with an aunt or a grandmother to better understand their bodies. Hands-on advice from an aunt, loving banter with other mothers and the reassuring presence of elders put the mother-to-be at ease. Such support helps decrease stress and increases self-confidence for the mother to be.

When Charaka wrote in *Garbhini Vyakarana*, 'If a cup filled with oil right up to the brim is to be carried without spilling even a single drop, every step has to be taken with care,' he was not pointing out the fragility of the pregnant mother. He was pointing out the role of loved ones in keeping the expectant mother happy and healthy. I hope that we, as a society, come together to support mothers and keep them smiling. And mothers, I hope you cherish yourself during this time and meditate even more during these days.

Daily Dilemma:

I am an expecting mother and I meditate daily. I follow a healthy diet and observe all the instructions by my doctor. But it does not seem enough. I want my child to be healthy and born without any complication. Please let me know what else I can do.

Daaji: Stay positive, cultivate positive thoughts and talk to your child often. Don't worry about complications or other problems that *might* occur. You are doing all the right things. Whenever you catch yourself worrying about imaginary situations, just shift the mind from negative thoughts to something uplifting. Listen to some music, call a friend or read a book. You can also let your trainer know that such thoughts are worrying you.

9

Japanese Fishing Village, Oxytocin and Mother–Child Bonding

In Japan, it's customary for expectant mothers to return to their mothers' homes sometime during the third trimester. Then, after childbirth, they spend at least a month there. This custom, called *satogaeri shussan,* ensures that the mother and the child receive all the care they need. For the mother, actually, the right word is 'pampering'. The new mother is treated with care and warmth, like a baby. Everything is taken care of. Someone is ready to feed her; someone is around to help her to the restroom, and so on. The mother's only task is to feed the baby and stay snuggled up together. For some reason, if the mother is unable to travel, others from the family (usually mother or sister) come over to help. How does such support help the mother? Do we have any research that shows the benefits of such care? In the early 1980s, Dr Terry Brazelton learned something which he then shared with the rest of the world.

Baby Whisperer in Japan: Poise and Calm

For those who don't know, Dr Terry Brazelton was a towering personality in Developmental Paediatrics and a patron saint for panicked parents. To give you an idea of how he practiced, he insisted that parents bring in the child four times without charge. Each visit was to build trust with the child. Here is how it went:[1]

First visit: The parents and child would sit in the waiting room. Dr Brazelton would offer a lollipop to the child. That's all.

Second visit: Dr Brazelton would offer a toy to the child from across the waiting room. To get the toy, the child needed to climb off his or her parents' lap, cross the room and take it.

Third visit: The child would again take a toy from across the room, and this time around, Dr Brazelton would wear his stethoscope.

Fourth visit: By now the child would be at ease. The parents would sit in the office with their child. Taking his stethoscope, Dr Brazelton would first examine the parents, then, while the child sat on his or her parents' lap, he'd examine the child. For his innate ability to understand babies, he was nicknamed the 'baby whisperer'.

During his travels to Japan in 1983 for a lecture series, one of the Japanese doctors recommended he visit the Goto Islands. It is an archipelago of 140 islands in the East China Sea. There are five main islands, and the rest are smaller. When Dr Brazelton visited the Goto Islands, they were dotted with fishing villages. Men fished the seas and women made fishing nets and cleaned the fish. Dr Brazelton observed that new mothers were treated like newborns. 'They were wrapped up with the baby, and they were put on a futon with nothing to do but nurse the baby. They also were picked up and taken to the john and fed like a baby. There was absolutely no postpartum depression.'[2]

Dr Brazelton studied the parents and the babies on the Goto Islands for several years. He observed that the mothers were poised and calm. There was no rush about anything. The newborns were quiet and gentle. In an interview, he says, 'A baby in the Goto Islands could hold attention for twenty-four minutes without a break.'[3] When he studied children in Tokyo, which was much busier, the twenty-four minutes dropped to eighteen. When he conducted the same study in Los Angeles, the time dropped to eight.

Over the years, the lifestyle of the island community created children with high attention spans. The mothers were cared for with a lot of love, and they were happy after childbirth. The child and the mother had ample time to bond. For families and parents-to-be, the message here is not about moving to a fishing island. The message is about the importance of poise and calm in one's lifestyle. Earlier in the book, we discussed that one cannot manufacture a special vibratory state at conception. The preparation takes much longer. The same goes for cultivating poise and calm.

One cannot transform overnight and become poised at the time of pregnancy. The couple should start the preparation long before. Meditation is a proven method to achieve poise and calm. Think of it this way, to build immunity, we take vitamin and mineral supplements. In the same way, to build resilience, we meditate.

Romanian Orphans: The Tragedy of Deprived Early Attachment

In 1966, believing that a larger population would beef up Romania's economy, Communist leader Nicolae Ceauşescu curtailed contraception and abortion. He wanted more workers in the country, and to achieve this, he imposed tax penalties on people who were childless. At the same time, the state celebrated mothers who gave birth to ten or more children as 'heroine mothers'. When parents could not afford to raise so many children, they'd say of a new baby, 'It's Ceauşescu's child. Let him raise it.' Orphanages were flooded with such children. Unfortunately, the orphanages were soulless institutions. No one held the children, played with them or soothed them.

After the Romanian revolution in 1989, little children kept in worse hygiene than a sewer were discovered in the orphanages. The media crews were scarred by what they saw. In 2000, the Bucharest Early Intervention Project launched a twelve-year study following 136 infants and children who had been abandoned in Romanian institutions.[4]

The findings suggest that early institutionalization leads to profound deficits in cognitive ability, socio-emotional behaviours, brain activity and structure, reward sensitivity and processing alterations and a heightened incidence of psychiatric disorders.

Uninterrupted time for infants with their mothers creates a strong bond of attachment. This bond between the mother and the child helps the child's transition into this world. The newborn knows the mother by the heartbeat. By the eighth day, newborns know the smell of their mother's milk.[5] In a matter of days, they seek out human voices and can identify their mother's voice from the rest.[6] As the children grow up, their father and elders play an important role as attachment figures.

Special Souls and Your Simple Gestures

A few years ago, I travelled in the US, conducting meditation workshops and conferences. During my visit to Austin, Texas, I took an afternoon to spend time with some family friends. They have a child who is autistic. The child is around fifteen years old but needs help with all activities. The mother and father have reoriented their life to care for the child. The mother stopped working, and the father took up a job with predictable work hours.

During our conversation, the parents expressed their keen desire to meditate more and even spend time doing volunteer work. But most of their time went into taking care of their child. I told them that special souls choose parents who have a special ability to love. They choose parents whose hearts are oceans of love and serve with a selfless spirit. The soul chooses such parents to help it go through what it needs to in this life. I told the parents that their child is their meditation, and the pain they go through while raising their child will create such tenderness, empathy, acceptance and love in their hearts that their lives will become the most beautiful offering to the maker. The child's soul completes its karmic cycle because of the parents' support, and the parents, too, evolve, thanks to their immense sacrifice and labour. One may not see it this way during one's incarnation, but I can assure you that such parents are chosen for their unique gift to give boundless love.

When you know someone in your friend's circle who has a child with special needs, make sure you are available for them. Even simple tasks like helping with a grocery run, arranging to pick up the dry cleaning, cooking meals during the weekend and anything else you can do will give these parents the thing they badly miss: a little time for themselves.

Nurturing the Bond of Love

The mother's care makes the newborn feel secure and embrace their new environment. In the field of psychology, the connection between a mother and the infant falls under the study of attachment theory.[7]

> Studying the attachment bond between the mother and the child and, by extension, the attachment with the father and the elders helps researchers gain insights into how a family can best care for their children.

Intuitively, we understand the importance of the mother–child connection. But is there a need to research this further? Think about it this way: We live in the twenty-first century, an era of technology and innovation. What seems intuitive today may not have been in the past. Take the example of a child born in the early twentieth century in a Victorian royal household. Just based on birth, the child hit the lottery. But is that enough?

Here is a quick snapshot of how the children might have been raised. For the most part, a nanny would raise the children. If the newborn children were crying, picking them up was a bad idea because that would reinforce the habit and the children may demand to be picked again and again. Let them cry. For select times of the day, the children would be *presented* before their parents. Family life was formal, with no hugging and kissing. Children could speak only when spoken to. Until the age of twelve, children would eat at a separate table. After they reach the age of thirteen, they could be *invited* to the table with their parents for dessert.

Nothing about raising a child in this way sounds intuitive. It may feel inhumane and harsh. But in the uppermost echelon of society back then, children were raised in this way. And what about a child born into a poor family? Life was a waiting game to grow up and start pitching in.

Thanks to attachment research, we've seen a sea change in how we care for children. Studying attachment between the mother and the child and, by extension, the attachment with the father and the elders gives researchers insights into how to best nurture children.

Dr Ruth Feldman is the most cited researcher about mother and child attachment. During the last fifteen years, she and her team have published more than 300 papers on the neurobiological system for Oxytocin, also known as the love hormone.

In one of the research projects, her team compared fMRI scans of two categories of people: lovers and new mothers. The scans showed that the brain regions that lit up for lovers and the brain regions that lit up for new mothers overlapped.[8] And it explains the euphoric feeling new mothers and fathers experience. Having a child is like falling in love. Oxytocin, the hormone responsible for the feeling of love and euphoria, is released generously in lovers and new parents. Not only that, the regions of the brain that are associated with negative emotions like social judgement and mentalizing were deactivated.[9]

During pregnancy and postpartum, Oxytocin plays a crucial role in developing *synchrony* between mother and child. Synchrony is defined as the spontaneous rhythmic coordination of actions, emotions, thoughts and physiological processes across time between two individuals. [10] Simply put, when your eyes meet your child's and you both smile, nodding together in agreement during a chat with a friend, cracking up at the same time on hearing your partner joke are all examples of synchrony. It plays an important role in interpersonal and social skills. Dr Feldman says, 'Our ability to engage in other relationships with partners, with friends, with strangers, and eventually parent the next generation, are all set by the experience of synchrony we experienced during the first few months of life.'[11] Please pause and read the previous sentence again.

What Dr Feldman is saying is that our ability to *effectively function* as a social being depends on the bonding experience we receive in the first few months after birth. An extreme example of what happens when children are deprived of such a bond is the orphans of Romania. Oxytocin triggers the feeling of love and care between the mother and the child, and, as a result, synchrony develops. When the mother looks at her child, hears him, smells him, sings to him or snuggles up with him, Oxytocin is released. Touch between mother and child also releases Oxytocin.

The mother and child are hardwired for love. For example, when the mother breastfeeds the child, Oxytocin is released. The flow of Oxytocin makes the mother feel calm and deepens the bond of love between them. The baby also produces Oxytocin during feeding and snuggling up with the mother. Oxytocin makes the child calm and sleepy.

There are times when a mother is unable to breastfeed despite help from a lactation nurse. For whatever reason, if breastfeeding doesn't work, then mother and child will figure out ways to compensate. Working mothers also store their milk for caregivers to feed the child. If the caregivers can think lovingly of the mother while feeding the child, such an attitude will benefit the child, the mother and the caregiver.

Sometimes parents of adopted children go through immense struggle in developing the parental bond. Despite a lot of efforts from the parents, the child doesn't seem to integrate. This is because, during the critical period when the body is attuned for bonding, loved ones weren't around for the child. After adoption, parents and family members have to recreate an environment where the green shoots of attachment can grow between the parents and the child. It can take months and sometimes even years for this to happen. So, a lot of patience is needed.

In a family when there is love and attention, unknowingly there is a transference of burden between the family members. Think of it like surrogate support for carrying the burden. When you have more on your plate than you can handle, some of that emotional load and burden shifts to a loved one who can carry it for you. It doesn't happen consciously where someone says, 'Okay, give me your load and let me carry it.' It happens naturally. The young child who is adopted may be carrying a big burden within. At a tender age, the baby felt orphaned, and all the traumas got cooped up. In a loving environment, the child can work through the baggage and emerge stronger.

The lessons from the Hunger Winter, the theory of foetal origins, research by Dr Brazelton and Dr Feldman helps us understand the profound ways in which the bond between the mother and child and the rest of the family is strengthened. Science helps us discern what to do and what to avoid. Wisdom shows us how to implement it in our life. The well-being of humanity lies in the well-being of mothers. Happy mothers do make happy families.

Daily Dilemma:

I love showering all my love on and spending my time with my newborn daughter. I hold, bathe and cuddle her. I also sing to her. But is it enough? Should I be doing something more?

Daaji: Yes. Do more of the same. Early childhood, especially the months immediately after birth are a unique window where the child and the mother are still in osmosis. They were one and now they are separate. But the connection is still strong. The time spent in bonding helps the child and the mother. Also, no one complains about getting too much love, especially the little ones. So, enjoy and have a blissful time.

Principle 5

Early Childhood Is the Foundation

10

Early Childhood: The Neural Goldrush and the Art of Relaxed Efforts

Here's a snap quiz on the early childhood years:

1. What percentage of the child's brain develops by age three?
2. What are some catalysts for brain development?
3. How many connections are there in a cubic centimetre of the brain?

If you know all the answers, well done! If not, that's fine too. Most parents are experts on all things to do with their child. They know how to trick their child into eating broccoli. They know their child's favourite bedtime stories. By simply looking at their child's face, they know if a cold is on the way. Becoming a parent opens-up a new level of sensitivity where parents can pick up on the slight hints and micro-expressions of their child.

To enhance your sensitivity further actively cultivate presence. Your presence helps in sifting between the child's signals: ones that need attention and ones that can be ignored. Signals, or cues, indicate what the baby wants or needs, and can include fist clenching, yawning, reaching out to be held, the type of cry and so on. As I mentioned earlier, presence is more than being around physically. It means nurturing the connection that the parent and the child share.

A simple way to nurture presence is to pay attention when interacting with children. When speaking to them, make eye contact. When they are talking, let them finish their thoughts and only then respond. Make yourself accessible so they know they can reach out at any time.

During my school days, I remember my father once made a surprise visit. I was studying at the Arya Samaj school a few hours away from home, and I used to live in the hostel. My father spent the day with me, and I was so happy to see him. He did not say much, but he returned to see me again after a week or so. This time, he had a small wooden box with tiny glass vials of aromatic oils. He told me that I should smell the oils if I felt low or sad.

I was feeling low at that time, but I did not share that with my parents. My school fees were already a strain on the family. But my father's intuitive gaze picked up that something was amiss. The aromatic oils helped me, and in a few days, I was back in the game.

Most parents intuitively understand their children. But only few have the knowledge of how much cognitive development happens in a child during early childhood. These years are a golden period for a child's development. When the parents' intuition is complemented with knowledge, it will help them take better care of their child.

There are two key concepts I want to discuss in this chapter. The first is a Neuroscience101 lesson about the child's brain and your role as a parent. This bit is going to be technical and at times it can feel dry. But please read it (even if you aced the snap quiz).

The second concept, equally important, is about your eagerness to get everything right about child-raising. I will talk about why it's essential to slow down and cultivate an attitude of relaxed efforts. But before any of that, here are the answers to the snap quiz:

What percentage of the child's brain develops by age three?

Ninety per cent of the child's brain develops by age three. This doesn't mean the brain is wired and integrated like an adult. The integration of the brain continues well into the teenage years. But in terms of the physical growth of the brain, most of the work is completed by age three. Healthy nutrition, quality family time and sensory development are crucial in the early years.

What are some catalysts for brain development?

The catalysts for brain development are our five senses. Touch, smell, hearing, taste and vision send inputs to the brain. When inputs are received, neurons wire and fire. The inputs from the senses are the growth catalysts for the brain.

How many connections are there in a cubic centimetre of the brain?

There are as many connections in a cubic centimetre of the brain as the number of stars in the entire milky way.[1] Last I checked, the number was 100 billion.[2] Imagine how much activity is happening stealthily during early childhood brain development.

Childhood Brain Development: A Primer

Brain development can be categorized into four main stages. The first stage is in the mother's womb, as the foetus grows.

The second stage is early childhood, from birth to three years. The third stage is between four to twelve years, and the fourth is during teenage and adolescence. This chapter will focus on the second stage, which is the early childhood years.

The human brain is walnut-shaped, jelly-like in texture, made up of 90 per cent water. It functions somewhat like a complex logic circuit that is powered by electric impulses. Special brain cells called neurons carry the electric impulses.

If you burst a water balloon on the ground, the water forms a splash pattern. A neuron looks something like that. It has an *oval* centre from which tentacles, or dendrites, protrude outward. The dendrites act as the messengers for the brain. They receive and send information. When dendrites from one neuron meet dendrites from another neuron, their connection is called a synaptic connection. Electric impulses in a synaptic connection carry the information.

Babies have nearly 86 billion neurons at birth and 50 trillion synapses.[3,4] These synapses connect the neurons and form the brain's architecture. During the first few years of life, more than 1 million synaptic connections form in the brain every second.[5] By age three, the child has 1000 trillion synaptic connections in the brain.[6] While different parts of the brain develop and reach adult levels at different times, by mid-adolescence, these connections drop to 500 trillion and stay in that range through most of the adult's life.[7]

But the number of brain connections we form is far more than we end up using. Those we use most, strengthen and multiply. Those we don't, are eliminated or pruned. Because of all the activity, the brain needs a lot of energy. In general, the human brain consumes 25 per cent of the net energy intake of the body.[8] That's why parents should pay close attention to their child's nutrition at a young age. A healthy balanced diet of carbohydrates, proteins, fats, minerals and vitamins is important for the healthy brain development of a child.

The brain is a constant *work-in-progress* project—wiring and rewiring itself. Neuroscientists call this 'neuroplasticity' or simply 'plasticity'. The inputs from the senses sculpt the connections in the brain. When similar inputs are received, existing synaptic connections are wired stronger. When new inputs are received, new synaptic connections are formed.

In early childhood, connection-forming or the plasticity of the brain is at its peak. The brain is like a super magnet attracting information. Each input to the brain breaks down further into thousands of synaptic connections. The richer the inputs, the more connections the brain forms. During early childhood, moments of intimacy and connection are rich inputs for the brain. When you hug your babies, rock them, sing to them, make eye contact, laugh with them, play with them, hold them, you're laying down the architecture for the child's brain.

In the case of adopted children, who weren't held enough and just lay in their cribs, the adoptive parents would end up spending years in sensory integration therapy to help the child to catch-up. So don't lose any opportunity to hug the little one. Cuddles do a world of good for the brain. The wiring of the brain is most prominent up to mid-adolescence. Later in life, the wiring and rewiring continue, but forming new connections is nowhere close to early childhood.

In the first three years, the brain lays the foundation for language, aptitude, vision, thinking, analysing skills and several other key traits. It is an energy-hogging, gold rush of connections. Children, especially infants, sleep so much because the neural connections consolidate during sleep. The consolidation helps in firming up the neural connections.[9]

In the first three years, the brain lays the foundation for language, aptitude, vision, thinking, analysing and several other key traits. It's a gold rush of connections in the brain.

When the child is overstimulated or tired, then its information overload for the child. The tantrums and the howling matches kick in because a lot is being taken in and not enough sleep to process it all.

The environment you create also plays an important role. In early childhood (the ages of zero to three), the mind of the child and the parents are in osmosis. Like the air in a room carries the sound vibrations from one corner to another, the child's extraordinarily sensitive mind registers even the slightest suggestions made by the parents. How parents talk to one another, how they talk to their child, their actions, intentions and emotional states subtly influence the child's mind.

A good atmosphere and thoughts of purity are essential in supporting the wellbeing of a newborn. Across cultures rituals like Baptism (in Christianity), *Naamkaran* (naming ceremony in Hinduism and Sikhism) and similar rituals highlight the importance of a pure and nurturing environment for the child.

Knowing what we have learned so far about the child's development, what do you think you could do better to nurture your child? More bedtime stories, lullabies, making eye contact, playing peekaboo, having siblings and family around and walks in the park all help with the child's growth.

As you read this book, sometimes the urge to memorize everything may kick in. Just take a breath and slow down. You already do most of these things. Revisit the book once in a while, and it will help with what you are already doing.

Relaxed Efforts Go a Long Way

Saint Kabir, wrote a couplet that goes like this:

Dheere dheere re mana, dheere sub kucch hoye
Mali seenche so ghara, ritu aaye phal hoye

'Slow down, dear mind, slow down. Everything happens
in its own time. The gardener may pour a hundred buckets
of water, but only when the season is right will the trees
yield fruit.'

In a few words, Saint Kabir shares the wisdom behind doing things at the right time and waiting patiently for the results. Parents know about doing things at the right time. And even if they don't, they can read about it and learn. But waiting for the results is an attitude one needs to develop. Especially in today's world of FOMO (Fear Of Missing Out) and instant gratification, waiting can be a tough exercise.

What do we mean by waiting? In its real sense, waiting means allowing a process that has begun to complete without interfering. Just as we sow a seed and then wait. We put the potatoes on to boil, and then we wait. We teach children good habits, and then we wait. We offer a prayer, and then we wait. If you analyse it, life is nothing but waiting interspersed with moments or bursts of activity. Waiting takes up a large part of our life and not activity. Waiting comes from the faith that actions done well will yield the right results. It is waiting that is the art.

As parents, there is hardly anything more important to you than the well-being of your children. So, you do everything you can to help your children succeed. All the sleepless nights and ferrying your children from one activity to another, is to prepare them for their life ahead.

I commend the efforts parents put in these days in raising their children. I do have a suggestion. Once in a while, *relax. Do less.* You are already starved for time, don't try to squeeze more into your day. Less is more. One advice new parents often get from parents with grown-up children is, 'Spend as much time as you can with your little ones. It goes by too fast.' They are right.

If you need to drop something to get more time with your child, then do it. If you both enjoy cuddling and poring over a book together more than the piano class or the taekwondo training, go ahead and do that. If you feel like taking the day off and going for a picnic with the children, then do that. Our fondest memories are usually of childhood. There is no need to rush children through their childhood. Don't force your children to grow up fast. Your son is being clingy and wants to spend more time with you? Great, spend time with him. Your daughter doesn't feel like reading the story book on her own? No problem, read it to her. Let them take their time.

Each child is unique. Some learn math fast while others create wonderful art. Some love helping in the kitchen while others like to spend time running around the park. Children's minds are like flower buds. Do not force them to bloom. Be patient, be present and be loving.

Patiently wait for your child to bloom, in the same way a flower blooms on its own. Children's minds are like flower buds. They should not be forced open. Do not push them too much.

In the next three chapters covering Principle 5 'Early childhood is the foundation', I will share some ideas on how to nurture the sensory development of children. After that, in Principle 6 (Nurturing character blossoms the personality), I discuss the foundation of character, importance of teaching virtues, developing observation and other qualities. These chapters covered in these two principles give insight into the skills parents need to develop. The chapters are not a blueprint to produce a perfect child in an imperfect world. Instead, think of them as a travel guide for a fulfilling parenting journey.

Knowing what to do and what not to do equips you better on the parenting journey. Gaining knowledge is an important step. Most of us know a lot more about the global economy or the statistics of the last ball game than we know about the development cycles of a child. Educating ourselves on the best practices of parenting is helpful. This happens organically in a family with elders around. If that's not the case, reading and learning about parenting is helpful. A group of parents getting together once every few months, *specifically* to share notes and ideas on parenting, will also help.

What helps the most is *listening* to your child. Listening will teach many things that are otherwise lost in the noise of life. The tantrums of your child, the meltdowns, the loving hugs, the shyness, the mischief are all opportunities to listen to the unsaid feelings of your child's heart. Keep listening with your eyes and ears, and your heart will speak its guidance more clearly.

While our life circumstances can be unique, a common factor that unites all parents is a perennial dearth of time. So, be kind to yourself. Your reading this book shows your keen interest in becoming a good parent. Learn to wait and understand that everything happens in its own sweet time. Enjoy the journey because the destination is a moving goal post.

Daily Dilemma:

My child seems to lack confidence. She hesitates in asking the teacher about her doubts and even when I remind her, she doesn't. What to do?

Daaji: Some children are shy. It's part of their make-up. Parents often remember their own so-called shortcomings and are over cautious about such tendencies in their children. Please introspect and see if that's what is happening in your case. Also, positive suggestions and indirect advice work well over time. Be patient and keep me posted on how things come along.

11

I Once Asked a Three-Year-Old Her Favourite Colour. Her Answer Still Makes Me Smile

I've never been much of a television person but when I did tune in, I watched *Mister Rogers' Neighborhood* with my children. This was during the 1980s when our family lived in Staten Island, New York. I admired the poise of Fred Rogers. His words were uplifting, his message was clear, and he epitomized the values the show stood for—respect, compassion, kindness, integrity and humility. One of the most striking aspects of the show, besides the man himself, was the language (simple, focused and precise) and the tone (even, warm and gentle). His pacing was even—not too slow, not too fast, just the right speed for the message to sink in.

> Words matter. Words are the connecting bridge for a child crossing over from the womb into our world.

In his book *The Good Neighbor: The life and work of Fred Rogers* Maxwell King, a former director of the Fred Rogers Center, reveals the methodical process by which Fred Rogers ensured that everything the children heard on the show nurtured them. In fact, the scriptwriters had a term called *Freddish.* It was a nine-step checklist to make sure that each sentence on the show gave the children the right message. [1]

Words matter. They form a bridge for a child crossing over from the womb into our world. The words of the mother and the father are reassuring sounds for the baby in the womb. After birth, their voices give the newborn a sense of continuity and assurance. The rhythm of the mother's heartbeat, the comfort of her lullaby, the gentle words of the father—all create a cocoon of protection for the baby.

Words also help in instilling values. There is a story about the Founding Master of Heartfulness, Ram Chandraji of Fatehgarh, in this regard. His mother was a saintly woman and treated everyone with love. When she sang her prayers, the devotion in her voice would pull young Ram Chandra to sit by her side. Many times he would see his mother, absorbed in prayer while tears rolled down her cheeks.

Poor Ram Chandra lost his mother when he was seven years old. Even though their time together was short, his mother's spiritual life had a profound effect on him. Later in life, referring to his mother, he would reminisce about how her words laid the foundation for his spiritual destiny.

Cultures across the world have rituals for newborns. The togetherness of families during such rituals has its own grace, and we all enjoy such events. Priests recite religious texts and often read a sacred word or a hymn to the child. But what do we know about the importance of words for a newborn? Do our words matter? Are we talking to our children in the right way? And how often should we be talking to them?

The Story of Thirty Million Words and Your Three-Year-Old

How much parents talk to their child during early childhood (till three years old) has a lifelong impact on the child. In 1995, United States researchers Betty Hart and Todd Risley wrote a paper titled 'The Early Catastrophe'.[2] For two years, the researchers studied families from different socio-economic levels. When they analysed the results, they found that the children whose families were on welfare heard 1500 fewer words per hour than families that were better off financially, which meant, the families on welfare spoke less to their children.

Over a three-year period, this gap translates to nearly 30 million fewer words heard by the child in a welfare supported family than a financially well-off family. During these three years, a child's brain develops at hyper-speed. Words are like nutrition for the brain. They enable the development of the brain and sustain long-term benefits. For example, when the researchers revisited the same children in the Early Catastrophe study after eight years, they found that the children whose families had been on welfare performed remarkably poorer on language tests and assessments than their higher-income peers.

This United States' study's bleak findings had a seismic impact on social policy and funding for child development. New programmes to help families and communities were put together. Investments were made in reading programmes. New public awareness programmes like 'Sing, Talk, and Read

(STAR)' and 'Talk with Me Baby' were launched across the US to educate parents and caregivers.

The Early Catastrophe study helped in driving positive change. Several new studies followed the Early Catastrophe study, in which the measurement methods were improved. The newer studies used automated recorders to capture data. They used MRI machines for brain analysis. They also designed better study groups to correct some of the assumptions made in the original study. For example, they dove deeper into aspects like economic disparities and social divide.

Thanks to all the new studies, today we have a better understanding of the relationship between poverty and the development of a child's language. Research shows that besides economic status, ethnicity and education, the knowledge of parenting is also a crucial factor.[3] It means knowing how to raise a child and how to care for their wellbeing plays a big role in how we bring up children.

Serve and Volley Conversations and Avoid Interruptions

Does this mean parents just talk to their baby about anything that comes to mind, just so they keep the words flowing? Are all conversations the same? No and no. Studies in neuroscience show that the most beneficial conversations are those with open ended questions and back and forth dialog. Such conversations have a positive impact on parts of the brain responsible for language skills and comprehension.[4]

When mommy laughs out loud and the baby giggles in response, it is an example of back-and-forth dialogue called a 'serve and volley' conversation. In the initial months, there is a lot of serving going on from the parents. The child returns with volleys of goo-goo-gaa-gaa's—a string of sounds but a response, nonetheless.

When the child can respond in words, it's important to have conversations with more volleys, more back-and-forth dialog with the child. Asking open ended questions like: 'Why do you like playing in the muddy puddles?', 'What do you think the moon is made of?', 'Why be kind to others?' 'Do you have an idea for a recipe?' and so on, spark interesting conversations. Such conversations also give parents a glimpse into the vibrant creativity of their child.

Do This

Here are some open-ended questions to jump start conversations:

- What are the clouds made of?
- Does it hurt the grass when we cut it?
- Do potatoes think?
- What smell do you like the most?
- Who is your best friend?

Record the answers on your phone, in your journal or wherever is convenient for you. Make some memories.

Once I asked a three-year-old what her favourite colour was, and she promptly replied 'rainbow'. No pink, yellow or orange, but rainbow. This little girl wasn't going to limit her answer to one colour. She loved them all. Such a delightful answer. Children's hearts are flowing with a stream of consciousness that's soaked in innocence. Unlike adults who become somewhat cynical and narrow minded with the passage of time, children see the world with a sense of awe. When we ask open-ended questions, we stoke their imagination and tap into their unhinged creativity.

Exchanging funny ideas, telling each other stories and recalling fun memories are some ways to create back and forth conversations. Any activity that you are doing, use it as an excuse to have a conversation with your child. For example, show them a painting and ask them what they feel. Listen to a piece of music together and ask them what they liked in it and what they did not.

Don't push children for answers or force the dialog. Allow children to take pauses. Let them flutter from one topic to another. Meet them at their level and allow the conversation to develop on its own. In natural flowing conversation, the minds merge, as though parent and child have one mind, and there is transference of ideas and emotions. A conversation, a joke, play and banter, are all learning moments for the child.

Parents should try to avoid interruptions during such learning moments. Repeated interruptions create wrinkles in learning. The common culprit is the cell phone. Say you are reading aloud a Dr. Seuss book and your child points out a new word and just then the phone rings. The call interrupts a learning moment, and the child may miss registering the new word fully.[5] Before reading, try to put the phone on silent mode and avoid interruptions. If someone knocks at the door, then don't race to answer it. First let your child know that you will pick up the story shortly, then you might both answer the door together. The idea is to avoid abruptness and create gradual transitions.

Importance of Teaching Your Child Your Mother Tongue

There is one more aspect all parents are concerned about and that's teaching the child the parents' native language. Especially if you are an immigrant in a country where only a few speak your native language or in countries like India where languages can change from state to state. From what I have seen, parents teach the child one language. While this may be a pragmatic choice, the best time to teach children multiple languages is during childhood. Children can learn two or even three languages growing up. At birth, an infant can tell the difference between each of the 800 sounds of all the world's languages combined. 'They become attuned to whatever language is spoken by their caregiver . . . By the time the baby is eleven months old, the brain activity reflects the language or languages the baby brain has been exposed to.'[6] So if you know more than one language, it's ideal to teach them to your child from birth. Children will learn fast, but it is a bit of work for the parents.

In the US, I have seen school districts that offer dual language instruction. Early results indicate that such an approach helps the children develop better cognitively.[7] It also helps them appreciate cultural nuances better. In the recently unveiled education policy in India, the policy makers have incorporated a stronger focus on regional language skills, which is a step in the right direction.

If you have caregivers at home, especially grandparents, then I suggest that you ensure that they speak with the child in the native language. Parents worry what might happen if the child goes to school and doesn't know English. You will be surprised to see how fast the child will pick up English or whatever language is spoken outside. The main effort involved is from parents and elders to keep at it and continue speaking in a tongue that may not be in common use at home daily.

> Early childhood is the time for seeding the garden of the child's mind. It is the time to invest. Read, share and communicate as much as you can.

A healthy sense of self develops from a good understanding of one's cultural identity and tradition.[8] So if you are from China or Korea living in, say, Germany, it's important to teach your child about your culture and guide the child in assimilating the local customs. St Martin's Day, Christmas, Chinese New Year and Spring Festival can all be celebrated by the family together. Teaching the child about one's culture and appreciating diversity removes the seeds of cultural bias.

When I was ten years old, my father sent me to the village mosque. For a few months, I received lessons in Islam in the Urdu language. I became so good at reciting the Quran that I even offered azan at the mosque. It was my father's decision to make sure that I learned the basics of Islam. I am grateful that he did this for me at such a young age. There were some days where in the morning I offered the azan, in the afternoon I read books on yoga with my father and in the evenings, I read aloud the stories from the Mahabharata. When I reflect on this experience, I feel that it helped me understand the essence of unity across religions.

What Comes before Language? Gestures.

A child points to an object and the mother answers with its name. Gestures enable learning for the child. They increase retention and facilitate faster learning. Across generations, grandparents' stories and songs were also accompanied by gestures. Research shows that children, whose parents gesture to them, acquire an expansive vocabulary over time than those with parents who don't gesture.[9]

Early childhood is the time to invest in your child. Read, share and communicate as much as you can. As your child grows up, you will be delighted to see how the essence of all that you shared blossoms.

Conversation that Touches One's Heart

The previous sections show the importance of talking to our children. Now I want to share some ideas about *how* to talk to our children. And for that matter, how to talk to each other.

Sometimes we encounter situations where the speaker unleashes a torrent of words, yet not a single word registers with the listener. The words just bounce off like oil droplets in a Teflon pan. And then there are times when just a few words are enough to convey a message which stays with the listener for a lifetime. What causes this difference in the impact of the words?

When we resonate with someone's words, we are resonating with the sincerity of the speaker. It is as though the speaker's words are imbued with life that enlivens the listener's heart.

The deeper the level from which the words surface, the greater their impact. The authenticity behind such words cannot be fabricated. This is the reason why the words of sages and prophets such as Saint Augustine, Hazrat Bibi Rabia, Lord Jesus, Sahajo Bai, Saint Therese, Prophet Mohammed and others are still thriving even though centuries have passed.

Talk to Children Respectfully

I learned something profound from Babuji about how to speak with children. In the Hindi language, when speaking with an elder, man or woman, we address them using the pronoun *'aap'* meaning 'sir or madam'. It's a respectful way to converse with elders. Usually, when we address children, we address them using the pronoun *'tum,'*, meaning 'you'. 'Tum' is more informal.

Babuji, though, addressed children as 'aap'. He never addressed them as 'tum.' Even when children were making a ruckus, he would chide them, but he never used language or a tone that showed any form of disrespect. Even his scolding's were respectful.

By speaking to children with respect, they learn what it means to communicate in a respectful way. They understand that respect is not something you extend to someone depending on who they are, what they do, their age or which race they belong to. Children learn that respecting one and all is the way to be.

Now, what about common folk like us? How do our conversations take shape? We have all been in situations where a conversation feels like peaches and cream, and one flippant comment later it feels stoic and sandpapery. Spoken words cannot be taken back. They cannot be unheard. Biting words inflict deep cuts. People may forgive what we say, but the scars remain. When parents remove sharpness in their tone and develop inner softness then their words transmit love and kindness into the children's hearts.

Is there a way to develop softness in our voice? Is there a way by which even simple words become imbued with the deepest feeling? Is it possible for us to develop such depth that our words melt hearts?

Many years ago, I discovered a letter that was written in the late 1800s. It contained what I refer to as the *Principles of Conversation*. It was written by the great yogi Ram Chandra of Fatehgarh, whose story we read earlier in the chapter. He shared these tips about communication in a letter to his associates in a small town in Northern India. If there is only one practice you implement from this book, let it be the Principles of Conversation. In my life, discovering this letter was like hitting a million-dollar jackpot. It is the treasure that keeps on giving.

Here is an excerpt from the Principles of Conversation:[10]

The style of speech should be devoid of rise and fall in pitch. On the contrary, it should be like the divine current, flowing evenly since the beginning of creation. I had copied just that and innumerable are its benefits, beyond the possibility of narration.

This is a philosophy, that when the flow of conversation proceeds in conformity with Reality, there develops a state of harmony between the two. Through that harmony, the divine way starts developing automatically. This results in effectiveness as whatever is spoken goes on touching the hearts of others. In other words, a sort of relationship with the current of Reality gets established. When a relationship is created, effectiveness has to be there. If someone copies it, only those words will be flowing out during conversations which are intended and are right.

To achieve this, we first of all try to remove the rise and fall in the voice while speaking, which is also called sharpness. This flow of speech will go on acquiring harmony with the current of Reality, to the extent that such a reduction is achieved progressively. By 'sharpness' I do not imply only anger, which is very heavy and should not be allowed at all in this context. What I mean is that the flow of speech should not carry any kind of weight in it. An illustration of this is a current of still air. It is very difficult to achieve, but everything is possible through sustained effort and courage, if the grace of God is there.

The balanced condition of mind is an expression of the right attitude in all our activities, under varied circumstances. In a broad sense, it is the reflection of our character. It has a deep impact and a favourable influence on those people who are associated with us. It reveals itself in conversation, which can be either serious and long or light and short. Such conversation is devoid of excitement or any high-pitched emotional outburst, and devoid of any rapid, short-tempered and moody reaction. It is a prompt, methodical and civil expression of one's own self and it is soft, cultured and smooth like the harmonious descent of divine grace.

A person whose tongue is polite, civilized and cultured, has a large, pure and noble heart, and thus has a wide sway over the minds of others. The pure heart, in communion with the Source, pours itself forth naturally with nobility, magnanimity and love. It leaves an impression immediately and it progressively makes deep inroads and establishes itself in the minds of all. But ambiguity and indecision are not to be encouraged.

A civil tongue is a prerequisite to achieve the goal of human life. A cultured tongue rules the kingdom of the heart. A polished tongue in discourse or conversation influences humanity and reigns supreme.

Anger is a poison to spirituality. Unless we are free from the plague of anger, moderation can never be obtained. The effect of anger is that the system becomes heavy, and tension is produced. There will be continuous pressure on thought. This human frailty leads to loss of self-respect and individuality and results in unhappiness. Anger does not allow the free and subtle current to enter; in other words, it restrains the flow of divine grace.

If anger is overcome, and a nasty and short temper is avoided, there is scope for the attainment of a balanced condition of the mind. The greater the control over anger, the freer and more bounteous is the celestial gift.

It is a pity that this important and essential principle of the use of the tongue in the inevitable and constant activity of people is often overlooked and neglected. It is no doubt very difficult to control the mind.

To free oneself from anger, we should think of ourselves to be polite and humble. A cool and calm disposition alone is required for spirituality. The heart is so tender that it begins to droop even by the slightest circulation of the wind.

The technique of developing softness is to create extreme humility in temperament, so that it is filled up with such a sentiment of love, as to have no inclination to cause any hurt

to anyone's heart, and the words are also such as not to hurt
anyone's heart in the least.

When I first discovered this letter, I read it again and again. I highlighted parts of it and meditated on them. I would put the principles into practice and observe how it would change my temperament and how the listener responded. This letter taught me the importance of listening over speaking. I understood how important it is to allow the other person to complete whatever they are saying. I also realized that when I listen to others, it reflects humility. When I want others to listen to me only, it highlights my ego. There are many other hidden gems in these lines that I hope you also discover.

If parents can start following these principles, children will benefit immensely. When parents speak while staying connected with the deepest access within their heart, children will also resonate with that depth. By following these principles, the mundane act of talking will become a vehicle for deeper connection.

When children see elders speaking with poise and equanimity, such behaviour becomes natural to them as well. As parents, we can guide our children by making these principles a part of our life. In this world filled with loud voices and belligerent rhetoric, our children will naturally lead the way to heartful communication.

Daily Dilemma:

My child does not listen to me even when I try explaining errors to her in a calm voice. How do I get my child to listen to me?

Daaji: Children or grown-ups, no one likes to be corrected. Our ego rebels against authority. So, what you are facing is difficult. If your child is a teenager, it's trickier because they will push back on indirect hints also. Try to focus on building good habits instead of fixing bad habits. It's easier to wire new behaviour than trying to eliminate the older patterns. Let's say you want your child to brush daily before going to bed. Then start with a habit that comes before this activity like turning off the lights and making sure the doors are closed. Once you start doing this together for a few weeks together, then stack on the brushing at night as a next step. It takes time, patience and repetition, but it's worth it.

12

East Meets West, Massage Meets Research: The Story of Touch

Hippocrates of Kos (460 B.C.E–375 B.C.E.), the Greek physician and the man considered to be the father of modern medicine, was credited for introducing elm bark to treat fevers. Centuries later, European scientists synthesized the molecule salicylic acid from sources like elm, willow and myrtle to create the wonder drug aspirin, which we take to treat everything from aches and pains to inflammation and fevers. It's even prescribed as a blood thinner for heart patients. The discovery of aspirin shows how we benefit when scientific research meets generational wisdom. Through science, we understand *why* something works the way it does. It helps us build a bridge between cultural norms and their relevance in daily life.

In the 1980s, a scientific discovery as profound as that of aspirin occurred, revolutionizing the way we care for premature babies. This discovery, explained in the next section, is the poster child for the coming together of generational wisdom and scientific research. Because of this discovery, we've saved the lives of countless premature babies.

Massaging Rat Pups and Neonatal Intensive Care

In the womb, the foetus is covered in fine hair known as lanugo. The lanugo appears at around sixteen weeks. When the amniotic fluid gently swirls around the baby, it rubs along the lanugo creating a gentle and soothing feeling for the baby. Touch is the first sense that the babies develop. This chapter covers the story of touch, and it begins in 1979, with a team of scientists in the Department of Pharmacology at Duke University in North Carolina.

The team, led by neuroscientist and physician, Dr Saul Schanberg, worked on a research project funded by the National Institutes of Health. Their task was to measure the factors affecting growth in rat pups. The pups were kept in a controlled environment but separation from the mother did not go well, and their growth markers declined. Dr Schanberg's team observed that the separation from the mother shocked the pups, which increased their stress hormones. The rat pups went into survival mode and stopped growing. Uniting the pups back with their mother reduced the stress and they resumed growth.

When the pups were with the mother, she groomed them by licking them vigorously. The team wondered if this act of motherly care was making all the difference in the growth markers. Was the physical touch and licking by the mother helping the rat pups grow faster?

The team decided to do the same thing, minus the tongue.[1] They replaced the licking by swabbing the pups with a fine camera lens brush repeatedly. The team performed this laborious task for weeks. And this time around, with all the stroking, the growth markers rose. The rat pups were growing again. The stroking worked like a charm, every time. Dr Schanberg and his team discovered one of the principal triggers for communicating with a newborn: *touch*. [2]

The story gets more exciting.

Around the same time Dr Schanberg's team conducted their research, Dr Tiffany Field, a psychologist at the University of Miami, was researching premature human babies and whether massaging premature babies helps promote growth.

Premature infants who were massaged for fifteen minutes, three times a day, gained weight almost 50 per cent faster than those who were left in the incubators and received no massage.[3]

When Dr Field heard about the rat pups' experiment and the beneficial effects of massage on them, she decided to experiment by applying moderate pressure when massaging the premature babies. Eureka! The results were nothing short of miraculous. The moderate pressure acted like a growth supplement and the stress hormones dropped immediately. The heart rates, which were erratic, also slowed down. Prior to applying the moderate pressure, the premature babies' growth rates were abysmal —twelve to seventeen grams a day, which is less than half the growth rate inside the womb. After the touch therapy, the growth rate shot up to thirty grams a day.

In her research papers, Dr Field has noted that premature infants who were massaged for fifteen minutes, three times a day gained weight almost 50 per cent faster than those who were left in the incubators and received no massage. The massaged infants were more active and alert, and were discharged from the hospital six days earlier than those infants who were kept in incubators and were not massaged.

Besides the immediate benefits observed right after birth, the benefits of massage kept on giving. The studies by Dr Field's teams showed that even eight months later, the massaged premature infants tested better on mental and motor abilities than the premature infants who were not massaged. Not only this, but they also held on to their advantage in weight.

Premature birth is a serious health concern globally, the leading cause of death in children under the age of five years.[4] In the United States, one in ten babies is born premature. Premature birth is a significant cost in healthcare spending. According to data from 2005, Neonatal Intensive Care Unit (NICU) spending was estimated to be at least $26.2 billion in the US, nearly $52,000 per infant. Dr Field and her team published a cost benefit analysis that showed annual savings of $4.8 billion per year by simply massaging all the premature babies.[5]

The research findings and the associated savings in medical costs spread like wildfire. People took notice, not in an academic way but more in a manner of 'We need this now!!' Massage became a must-have skill in the neonatal care unit. But in the 1980s and 1990s there were hardly any massage therapists in US hospitals. Today most of the natal care units have touch therapies. Many hospitals have programmes involving grandmothers and trained nurses who regularly touch and massage extremely low-weight infants.

In a conversation with Dr Field, where she reminisced about her travels to India for medical conferences, she said, 'They massage babies in India, actually, and that's where massage originated. When they did studies on rats and provided a moderate amount of pressure on the skin of rat pups, they found that the hippocampal region (the region for memory) was more developed. When these rats became adults, they performed mazes just as if they were infant rats. They never became senile, and they interpreted this to say there are statistics showing that people who were born and raised in India are able to recite numbers. If you put a whole page of numbers in front of an Indian child and then take it away, they'd read those numbers back to you. They say that's the reason why there are a disproportionate number of Indians who are computer geniuses because they have more developed hippocampal cells.'

'That means that in an fMRI of the hippocampal region, the dendrites that carry the information from the axon are more elaborate – they have more arborization as a result of this early infant massage. That means they have more branches that can collect messages. That's why you can put a page of numbers in front of an Indian child, and they can read it back to you.'[6]

When we look back at the sequence of events starting in 1979, when both the teams started their research, we can only marvel at how everything came together. What started as research for growth markers in rat pups led to a lifesaving procedure for premature babies. Imagine how many precious little lives were saved and how many mothers were saved from deep anguish and hurt.

Kangaroo Care: Benefits of Skin-to-Skin

In South America in the 1970s, two physicians in Bogotá, Colombia, didn't have enough incubators to care for all the premature babies in their hospital. [7]So, they placed these tiny naked babies on their mothers' bodies with both mother and baby covered by an exterior wrap, which allowed the mom's body heat to warm the baby. The babies thrived. The doctors named their technique the kangaroo mother method. This method shows the importance of skin-to-skin contact between the baby and mother after birth.

Skin-to-Skin Contact Benefits

The skin-to-skin contact benefits both the mother and the baby.

For Baby

- Babies cry less often when they receive skin to skin.
- They can better absorb and digest nutrients
- Increased weight gain
- Higher blood oxygen levels
- Long-term benefits, such as improved brain development, stronger immune systems and stronger parental attachment

For Mother

- Experience more positive breastfeeding
- Improved breast milk production
- Likely to have reduced postpartum bleeding and lower risk of postpartum depression

Do This

After birth, if there are no medical emergencies, take these three steps:

1. Have the nurse place your naked baby on your bare chest so the two of you are chest-to-chest.
2. Keep the baby's face sideways so she can breathe well.
3. Remain this way for at least an hour and only then let the baby step out for weighing.

Science Backs Massage

Some of you, mainly those from India and other Asian countries, must be wondering, 'Why is this information such a big deal? Massaging babies is what you do. Massage makes babies stronger and healthier. Everyone knows this. Right?' Not exactly. In the West, massage is a recent addition to people's lifestyles. Now, it is common for one to see a Massage Envy or Hand and Stone store in a strip mall, even in a remote town in the US Midwest. And the shiatsu massage chairs are a common fixture in most shopping malls.

But remember, our story takes place way back in the 1980s and 1990s. Back then, massage was not mainstream in the West. Massage as a profession was just picking up. More importantly, for the medical community, the benefits of massage for a premature baby were unknown. For doctors, these findings were the equivalent of discovering a miracle drug.

Our elders understood the importance of *touch*. They understood that skin is the largest organ of the body and caring for it has positive effects for the body. Across cultures, there are many examples of using massage. In India, special massage oils made from herbs are used for different types of massage. Grandmothers in India use such oils to massage the baby. It is believed that this helps to improve bone density and build stronger muscles.

In Bali, massage is thought to be useful for preventing infant colic. Maoris in New Zealand massage babies' knees and ankles to keep the joints supple and make the overall frame graceful. Traditional medicine, be it Ayurveda, Chinese or Greek, all have documented the benefits of massage. This knowledge, though, stayed in its own cultural sandbox for a long time.

Benefits of Touch

Touch reduces stress: Touch starvation is a real thing. Cortisol and the other stress hormones that build up in the body are reduced by touch. Holding hands, hugging and massaging counters the fight or flight response. Companies around the world offer professional cuddle services to the touch deprived. The existence of such companies shows the need for touch in our societies.

Touch sharpens cognitive ability: One of Dr Field's studies showed that medical school students who received short chair massages had an increase in Theta waves, meaning a relaxation of the brain.[8] The relaxed students did better in their cognitive performance. The same students performed a mathematical computation in half the time and with higher accuracy, on average, after receiving the massage.[9]

Touch conveys support and enhances one's confidence: For older people, touch is a tactile rejuvenation. I have seen grandparents feel delighted when their grandchild offers them Heartfulness relaxation instructions while holding their hands or touching their feet. Try this and see how it helps.[10]

The work done by Dr Schanberg, Dr Field and their teams made the crossover to mainstream possible in the West. Science was instrumental in establishing the wisdom behind massage. When we see the science behind a ritual or a custom, then it becomes easier to appreciate why something is done the way it is.

In many instances, science refines wisdom to make it even more applicable to today's lifestyle. For example, in the case of child massage, Dr Field observed that some of the herb-infused oils were causing allergies in children. She worked with the research teams of large pharma companies and shared these concerns. Today we have hypoallergenic oils that no longer cause allergic reactions.

Massage, fasting, oil pulling, lighting camphor at home, adding turmeric to food and following sleep cycles are all practices with wisdom behind them. Research is catching up fast to measure and quantify the benefits of such practices. The challenge we face is that we're losing wisdom much faster than science can catch up. Since we don't know the wisdom behind the practices, we tend to dismiss the practice as superstition or mere ritual. So, the question we face is: Do we wait for the scientific proof, or is the proof of our own experience enough? Either way, could we trust our elders that maybe over the years they figured out the benefits behind the practices being followed? While which source to trust is a personal decision, what applies to all is our duty to at least listen to what the elders have to share with us.

I say this because I can vouch for the scientific benefits of massage and touch therapy. When I was about a year and a half old, I had started walking. Around that time, I was hit by a massive attack of polio that affected my left leg. In those days polio crippled millions of children in India. For months on end, my parents would give me massages with medicinal oils. Twice or thrice a day, I would get a massage along with many other treatments, but the massage was the main thing. After months of touch and massage therapy, I was cured of the polio. Now I do not even have a remnant limp or a bend in the leg. I attribute it to the loving care of my parents and the rigorous touch therapy.

But, if you ask my mother, she will tell you that every week, she carried me to the temple of Lord Hanuman and sat by the steps of the temple and prayed for my health. She is convinced in her heart that it is the blessings of the lord that healed me. Whether it was her faith, her love or pure science, this incident from my life like many other examples of your lives shows that all three can not only co-exist but thrive.

Next time you meet your grandparents or some other family elder, ask them about their lifestyle. Ask them about how they were cared for while growing up. Ask them what homemade remedies they use and what habits they follow. Some of the tips may save you a run or two to the pharmacy. Our elders are like living libraries. Our efforts will save their wisdom for future generations. Our efforts will also give science the time it needs to show us that the more things change, the more they stay the same.

Daily Dilemma:

I am struggling with making time for all the things I want to do for my family, especially my children. How do I become a better parent?

Daaji: Time poverty is a reality. Whether you are rich or poor, live in the city or the suburbs, parents everywhere are overscheduled. There isn't enough time to do everything you would like to do. Focus on consistency. Children like consistency in their routines. So, if you can aim low but be consistent, it will benefit the child and also boost your morale. For example, you want to read many books to your child. Start with a page each day and keep that going. Similarly, you may want to give your child a massage every week. But what can you do if you work on the weekends? Maybe start with once a month. Try to adjust and adapt to your circumstances. And remember, your thinking about becoming better is already a big step in the right direction.

13

Explore the World Together, See More

Harvard scientists Tosten Wiesel and David Hubel won the Nobel Prize for Medicine in 1981. In a breakthrough discovery,[1] they found that if an infant's eyes don't send inputs to the brain, then the brain does not see. In one of their experiments, they covered one eye of a newborn kitten. The cover acted as a cataract and the eye wasn't sending any inputs to the brain. After three months, the scientists removed the cover and studied the kitten's brain under MRI. They found that the kitten's brain had *rewired* itself.

The brain re-allocated the neurons reserved for the closed eye to the other open eye. No matter how much visual stimulus was given later, the eyesight in the covered eye never returned because a critical period of development was lost. The scientists also did another experiment where they covered one eye of an adult cat with good vision for a few months. When they opened the covered eye of the adult cat the scientists found that the cover did not affect the cat's vision.

Hubel and Wiesel helped us understand how the brain allocates resources. They showed us how inputs from the eyes train the brain. Thanks to this research, doctors began removing cataracts from newborns within weeks of birth, thereby helping the children develop good vision[2].

In the hierarchy of our senses, sight is our alpha sense. Visual stimulation is vital for the brain development of a child. But what are the best practices to help with the child's visual development? And what should we avoid?

Digital Diet for Early Childhood

A digital economy runs on attention currency. Social media apps, news feeds, blogs and other products are designed to grab our attention. Screens are a magnet for our attention and a source of worry for parents. Articles with titles like: 'Have smartphones destroyed a generation?', 'Digital multitasking detrimental to a child's health' and 'Are smartphones destroying your relationship with the children?' amplify the worry of parents.

According to industry estimates, almost 50 billion connected devices are out there. This means the number of network-connected devices per person in 2020 was close to 7. In 2003, it was 0.08 connected devices per person.[3] You can guess what the number would have been in the 1950s when I was growing up. The first time I saw a television was when I was seventeen years old.

Buying groceries, calling a cab, paying bills, trading stocks, tracking health data—everything is digital. We can't push this toothpaste back into the tube. 'When you invent the plane, you also invent the plane crash. Every technology carries its own negativity,'[4] said French philosopher Paul Virilio. Knowing what we know of the benefits and pitfalls of digital life, what we need is the discipline to use technology to our advantage.

Let's start with infants and toddlers. The American Academy of Pediatrics (AAP) has long recommended keeping away *all* screens from children under the age of two, including smartphones, TVs, tablets and computers.[5] The World Health Organization (WHO) guidelines are more stringent than AAP in this area. The WHO states that screen exposure creates a deficit in the child's learning ability by the time they enter school.[6]

> Studies have shown that just having a television run in the background in the living room, even if *no one is watching* it, interferes with the child's problem-solving and communication skills.

It takes about eighteen months for the child's brain to develop to the point where they connect what they see on a screen with something in the real world. For healthy brain development, the child needs a colourful medley of all the senses. Changing sounds, varying textures, interactive gestures, different smells—all play a role in sensory development. But if a child is glued to a screen, then such interaction of the senses is curtailed. Screens hijack the sensory apparatus. Studies show that a television running in the background, even if *no one is watching,* interferes with the child's problem-solving and communication skills.[7]

Studies also show that a toddler sitting alone and watching educational videos doesn't help with learning. Educational content through screens at such a young age can only help if the parent is with the child and is actively engaged.[8]

In 2016, the American Academy of Paediatrics (AAP) made one noticeable exception to limiting screen time for children under the age of two. Video chat does not count as screen time with adverse effects.

When parents are mindful about the aesthetic they curate around their children, it helps the children. By aesthetic, I mean that which pleases the heart and not just the senses. A sense of orderliness, flow and harmony contribute to the aesthetic we create around children. For example, art, music, fashion, décor and writing all have a sense of aesthetic.

Now, we all have days when a child won't eat food without the TV rhymes or the purple dinosaur swaying on the screen. Exceptions are fine, but as far as possible, keep screens and devices away from children under three. In our household, we have figured out a routine. Daily after lunch, my grandchildren come to spend some time with me. This is our time. My grandson sits in my lap and my granddaughter shares the couch with me. We all watch Tom and Jerry together. Off late a few Coco Melon videos also snuck into the playlist. Outside of this safe window in the afternoon, the children don't interact with phones or tablets.

After early childhood (that is, after three years), the child's brain consumes information differently. Some of these changes make screen time in moderation permissible. But even there, my recommendation is less is more. Then again, there is one exception you could make.

In 2016, AAP said that video chat for children under two does not count as screen time with adverse effects.[9] AAP recognized that the benefits of video calls with grandparents and other relatives far outweigh the potential harm. A child giggling away while playing Facetime peekaboo with Nana or listening to Dada tell the story of the Big bad wolf and Piggy is not only fun but also healthy.

WMDs and FOMO

In the lines below, what does '*this*' stand for?

'If men learn this, it will implant forgetfulness in their souls; they will cease to exercise memory because they rely on that which is written, calling things to remembrance no longer from within themselves, but by means of external marks.'[10]

The word '*this*' in the above paragraph is a reference to writing. These are the words of Plato complaining about a new technology that was in vogue in those days: *books.* He believed that books would make people dull and forgetful. I wonder what Plato would say about WhatsApp.

Be it books, seat belts, typewriters, ATMs or the mRNA vaccines, any new technology brings progress and debate. In this backdrop, WMDs or wireless mobile devices have made our life convenient, but they have also hacked our attention.

Studies show that a cell phone with notifications turned off can still hack the attention of a grown-up.[11] According to the study, even when a device is turned off, the user is still thinking of the missed messages and notifications, thereby reducing working memory and problem-solving skills.

Our daily life is an interplay of two currents: energy and attention. When our attention is only in the world outside, then our focus keeps wavering from one thing to another like a kitten chasing a laser dot on the carpet. Wavering focus causes attention entropy.

A more common name for attention entropy is FOMO. It's the uneasy, all-consuming feeling that sets in when we're worried about missing out on that news update, the email alert or the WhatsApp notifications. Alerts, pings and updates that hit us non-stop create FOMO within, which in turn creates a feeling of helplessness and even a lack of self-worth.

Advertisers use slick designs and catchy messages to clickbait our collective FOMO. Newer technologies like AR (augmented reality) and VR (virtual reality) offer new tools for attention hacking. Many of us have grown-up in an era where screens came much later in our lives. But our children are digital natives. They've never known a world without digital devices and connectivity. Understanding how to navigate our digital world seems to be in their DNA.

What our children need help with is digital discipline. They need to learn to use technology as a tool: use it when needed and then put it away. As children grow up, they will use computers for schoolwork. Today, even middle school children turn in assignments electronically. Some parents also give children a phone so they can stay in touch.

Try This: The Focus Pouch

One of the engineers in the Heartfulness Community came up with a novel idea of a focus pouch. Otherwise, an ordinary-looking plastic pouch for the phone, the focus pouch has a unique feature: a signal shield that blocks all signals. Once you put the phone in the pouch and seal it, all notifications, alerts and sounds are silenced. Whenever you need to do focused work, put the phone in a focus pouch and get uninterrupted working time. Once the work is done, take a break and check your phone.

I have two requests for parents.

First, teach your children the basics of attention management. Make relaxation and meditation a part of their routine just like sports, music lessons and other activities. When they're about fifteen years old, introduce them to regular meditation practice. Contemplative practices will help children to manage their attention. Also allow your children to get bored. You don't have to keep them occupied non-stop. Boredom will inspire ideas and creativity in your child.

Second, lead by example and teach children digital self-regulation. Some ideas include turning off alerts and notifications from social media on your phones. At night, leave the phone in the study. While driving, do not text and use hands-free. For the weekends, plan your digital sabbath as a family. Give the devices, especially phones in their rightful place as tools and not make them, as the author Gopi Kallayil says, 'the 79th organ of the body'.[12]

The Sensory Spa of Mother Nature

Take nature walks with your child. While walking, have a conversation or enjoy the silence, whatever the setting calls for. Interactions with Mother Nature will benefit your child. You will also enjoy the ecotherapy.

A team of neuroscientists at the University of Bristol studied the effects of soil-based bacteria. They found that contact with soil activates serotonin in the body.[13] Serotonin is a neurotransmitter that helps with regulating our moods, feelings of well-being and happiness. The feeling of satisfaction after working in the garden or potting plants at home is because of the chemistry Mother Nature triggers in us. If you have a backyard, then plant a vegetable patch with the children. If you are close to the beach, then build sandcastles with them. And if you are a city dweller, then some pots with soil will do just fine.

Whatever you can do to increase the offline experiences for your child will be beneficial. Today, children are increasingly spending their time indoors. Because of COVID-19, the outdoor time has been further reduced. So, any opportunity for outdoor playtime is welcome. In my childhood, when it rained, we would make paper boats from old newsprint and calendars. Watching those boats glide away in the rainwater was such a joy. Try it sometime with your children. Children and adults both benefit greatly by decompressing in a natural environment. Later in this book, (in the chapter 'Interest and Observation are Twins'), I share more ideas and activities for families.

Although sight is our alpha sense, if your child is not blessed with sight, don't be disheartened. Mother Nature is generous, and she jump-starts other senses to create novel connections. These connections may not compensate for the lack of sight, but your efforts to nurture other senses through touch, hearing and smell go a long way.

Before we end this chapter, here is a story for you.

Once an old man was walking down the road in the dark with a lantern in his hand. As he walked, a young man, also walking on the street, stumbled into him and apologized. The young man realized that the older man was blind. Now he felt worse and apologized again. They walked together for a little while and then the young man asked, 'Sir, why do you carry a lantern when you can't see?' The old man replied, 'Dear boy, so that others can see me.'

Much like the young man crossing the road, we have eyes, but do we *really* see? While we may be blessed with sight, do we have the vision? How to elevate our senses so they become instruments for self-development?

Character and values transform a sensory life into sentient life. A good character and a stable personality make us a humane being. While early childhood is the foundation for a child's development, character is the foundation of life itself. In the next three chapters devoted to Principle 6, we dive into the key aspects of character formation and understand the important role parents play in laying the foundation of character.

Daily Dilemma:

My friend has a six-year-old son. He keeps hitting and pinching my daughter who is four years old whenever they play. His mother, my friend, never intervenes. What should I do?

Daaji: Reinforcing positive behaviour through positive suggestions and actions is the duty of a parent. I think you should have a conversation with your friend about the need to guide children in their behaviour. Request her permission to intervene and counsel the children while they are playing. If the behaviour still continues, you should try and find new friends for your daughter.

Principle 6

Character Builds Personality

14

Character Is the Foundation of Life: The Role of Parents in Laying the Foundation

In 1998, Warren Buffett, the acclaimed investor, gave a lecture to MBA students in the University of Florida. 'Think for a moment that I granted you the right to buy 10 per cent of one of your classmates for the rest of his or her lifetime,' he said. 'You cannot pick one with a rich father, that does not count. You have to pick somebody who is going to do it on their own merit. I give you an hour to think about it. Which one are you going to pick?'

Buffett raised the stakes by adding another condition, 'To buy the 10 per cent, you would have to *short* 10 per cent of another classmate.'

'If you think about it the correct way,' he said. 'The person selected would be someone who is generous and honest. Someone who gave credit to other people even for one's own ideas. Also, the person picked to short, would not be one with the lowest IQ. It would be someone who turned you off for some reason. The person who is egotistic, the person who is greedy, who is dishonest and cuts corners and all such qualities.'

> Character matters above everything else. Ambition and IQ are no doubt important but to *get* to the top and *stay* there takes character.

Through his thought experiment, Warren Buffett helped future corporate leaders in the room to understand that character matters above everything else. Ambition, creativity and intellect are all important, but to *get* to the top and *stay* there, takes character.

You may wonder why I began our conversation about character development with an anecdote from Buffett, an investor, and not with the examples of the Buddha, mother Sita or Jesus Christ. Here's the thing, when we think of the holy ones, the sceptic in us tends to box their teachings and label them '*good but not practical*'. The popular idea is that real-world Gordon Geckos (*Wall Street*) and Ricky Romas (*Glengarry Glen Ross*) need smarts and aggression. To succeed in life and business, one needs killer instinct and not kindness. Charismatic personality matters more than character integrity.

And that's where Warren Buffett comes in. He is at the pinnacle of wealth creation. After cutting his teeth on Wall Street, overcoming one financial crisis after another, he and his firm have only grown in stature and net worth. When Warren Buffett looks to buy 10 per cent, he looks for character over IQ, energy or initiative. The other traits are important but without character, as Buffett would say, it's not a value investment.

Whether it's worldly affairs or one's spiritual development, character is the bedrock of life. Parents' efforts in instilling a good character are vital for the child's future. The moral habits, etiquette and life lessons all help in strengthening the child's character. Sometimes parents get confused between personality and character. Here is a simple way to understand the two.

Character and Personality: The Tree and Its Fruit

A gardener knows that to enjoy the fruit, one must take care of the tree. Nourishing the soil, watering the roots, preventing pestilence and doing this year after year will ensure that the tree is healthy, one with deep roots and strong branches. And then, on a fateful spring, the blossoms turn into fruits, and we enjoy a bountiful harvest.

Character and personality share a similar relationship. Character is the tree and personality is the fruit. Character is the inner core and personality is the outer shell. Character is the cause and personality is the effect. Someone with a good character will have an authentic personality. Someone with a flawed character will let you down. If the character is not attended to, then life becomes a struggle to establish one's true personality. One may end up donning many avatars as they go through life without ever realizing who they are and what their true potential is.

The word 'personality' has its origins in the Latin word *persona*, which means 'mask'. During theatrical performances in the Roman period, performers wore masks that personified either the type (mother, noble, old man) or nature or psychological trait (angry, happy, worried) of the character. If the character was a warrior, the mask represented the features of a warrior archetype.

If the character was jealous, the mask depicted jealousy.[1] In the same manner, our personality, or persona, blossoms from and depicts our character. It makes sense then for parents to focus on building the character of their child. The personality will develop on its own. In other words, it will take care of itself.

> For parents, the important thing to remember is that character formation is a conscious effort. It takes as much deliberate effort and attention as developing other life skills like STEAM (science, technology, engineering arts and math) and communication.

Personality traits such as public speaking skills, networking ease, general aptitude and so on are important, but in the long term, authenticity, integrity and good moral values play a more important role.

Character will help children make wise choices. Choosing the right company, setting the right priorities, pursuing the right goals and making correct decisions—all are guided by one's character. The important takeaway here is that character formation takes a conscious effort on the part of the parents. It takes as much deliberate effort and attention from parents as developing other life skills such as STEAM, leadership and communication. Character formation also has immense significance in shaping the spiritual destiny of your child.

The Spiritual Significance of Character

A house is supported by the ground. The ground is supported by layers of Earth. The Earth is supported by the planetary forces of our solar system. Our solar system, in turn, is supported by other galactic forces in the Milky Way. Tracing this thread of who supports whom, we reach a point where we realize that there must be a common foundation that supports everything. A common substratum that acts as the absolute base for all existence. Science refers to this absolute base as singularity.

In the Heartfulness tradition, the elders have referred to the absolute base as *Bhuma* or the Centre. Before creation, existence was in a seed form within the Centre and there was perfect balance. When the time came, a stir in the Centre triggered an impulse of creation (science calls it the Big Bang). That impulse continues on and on, and as we speak the universe continues to expand.

In yoga, the goal of meditative practices is to create within oneself the perfect balance that existed before creation came into being. In a human being, the condition of perfect balance is reached when one's character attains perfection.

> A perfect character is when everything in a person is in a state of balance. The senses, the tendencies, the thoughts, the actions are all in a state of harmony with the inner guidance.

A perfect character is when everything in a person is in a state of balance. The senses, the tendencies, the thoughts and the actions are all in harmony with the soul. In such a person, the personality is one with character. There is no duality. Think of it this way. There is space outside a room and there is space inside a room. How would you describe the space if the walls were removed? The outside and inside are no longer separate. With the walls removed, oneness is pervading all around. When the character is perfect, there is oneness of being.

Such a person's behaviour and etiquette are exemplary. There is total naturalness in their way of being. Wherever they go, they radiate love and spread their light. They exude lightness and all those around them benefit from it.

As duty bound trustees of the soul that chose us, nurturing the child's character is our primary duty as parents. When we work to ennoble the character of our children, we are guiding them on the path of achieving oneness and balance.

Giving Children the Right Perspective

When we interact with our children, our biases, our attitudes and our habits, all play a role in shaping them. For example, we often ask our children: 'How much did you score on the test? Who scored the highest?', 'Does your teacher appreciate your work?' or, the question all children are asked, 'What do you want to be when you grow up?'

> How often do we ask our children questions like: 'Whom did you help in school today?', 'What kind act did you do?', 'Did you give others the chance to speak before you?'

Now consider this. How often do we ask our children questions like: 'Whom did you help in school today?', 'What act of kindness did you do?', 'Did you give others the chance to speak before you?' I don't think we discuss such questions as *often* as we should. We tend to focus more on the muscles of intellect and ambition. The same rigour is not applied to building the muscles of kindness, empathy and humility. Perhaps we assume that these qualities will develop naturally. But it helps to emphasize the importance of character. And there is a reason for this.

Children, deep inside their hearts, understand what their parents *truly* care about. When parents celebrate good grades, winning awards in school and similar achievements more than their child's acts of compassion and kindness, then the child gets a subliminal message of what parents truly care about. This is how a child becomes conditioned.

I want to share an incident from the 1990s when I was running my pharmacy business in New York City. My business was bootstrapped, and whatever I earned, I reinvested into the business. In a short span of time, the business grew in terms of size and reputation. Our employees stayed with us for years. The few who left us did so to start their own businesses.

On the days when there was bumper-to-bumper traffic on the Verrazano Bridge which I took to get to work, my customers waited for me. Large chain pharmacies were around the corner, and yet they chose to give us their business. I no longer play an operational role in the business, and it's been around fifteen years since I last filled a prescription. And to this day, some of the customers still ask about my welfare.

Back then, when I was busy growing the business, I was working on a deal to open a new pharmacy in the city. My business associate had negotiated favourable terms with a prospective seller. Both parties were ready to ink the deal, and I invited the sellers to my home for brunch on the weekend.

That morning, my associate told me that the contract had a clause that stretched the truth from our side. He told me that it wouldn't be an issue because the clause would be inconsequential in a few weeks after the deal closed. My associate was convinced that there would be no damage to the seller or to us. But as it stood, the clause was a stretch. There were other buyers competing with us for this deal, and I was coached that if a question about the clause came up, I should say, 'It's all good.'

Soon the sellers arrived. We were having a great conversation and a feeling of camaraderie was in the air giving one the feeling that the paperwork was a mere formality. As we headed to eat, the seller asked if we were compliant with the contract. From his tone, I knew it was a routine checklist question. And I politely answered no, and also mentioned the clause where we had a problem.

No one was expecting this turn of events and what followed was a stoic brunch. No papers were signed that day. After the sellers left, my associate, who was upset, asked for an explanation. He was like my younger brother and his anger was understandable. Here's what happened that afternoon.

As we were having our conversation, I saw my son playing in the living room. He was a young boy, six years old at that time. For a moment our eyes met, he smiled at me and continued playing. But my heart became heavy. I asked myself, 'Why are you doing this?', 'What are you teaching him?', 'Is this what I want to break bread over?' I was already hesitant, and when I saw my boy's face, it gave me the nudge needed to act on my heart's guidance.

After a few months, I met the sellers at a social event. After some small talk, the seller told me that they made a deal with someone else. He also confided in me that the new buyer had stretched the truth and did *not* disclose it at the time of the deal. Even though we didn't have a deal, our mutual respect increased.

I shared this story to point out that even if parents don't tell their children what is *truly* important to them, the children pick it up. Your moral dilemmas today can become theirs in the future. Children subliminally absorb our thinking patterns even when we are not in the same room with them. Children are like sponges, soaking up everything. And children want to achieve whatever their parents value. Parents and close family members sometimes play the role of potters, shaping the children's character. At other times, they are the gardeners, grooming and nourishing the child. At all times they are the guardians of the child's moral compass.

> Children are like sponges, soaking up everything. A child's character is a result of the environment and the suggestions their elders make.

It's up to the parents to truly value compassion, kindness, love, courage, empathy and other qualities. Only then do we pass on the right message to our children.

The Role of Parents and Teachers Has Increased and Not Diminished

At home, it's the family that guides the child, and outside of the home the teachers play an outsize role. In my school days, my mornings began with *Shanti-Paath*, a group prayer for universal love and peace. During the prayer, we applied a few drops of water on the chest and on the forehead and this was followed by recitation of hymns. This daily ritual was a good way to centre myself and begin my day. The teachers taught us the curriculum subjects and also focused on our moral development.

The relationship between the student and the teacher was one of respect and reverence. Historically, especially in India, a reverential attitude was a cornerstone value in life. There is a reason for this. When there is reverence, there is care and love. In the yogic times in India, an elder after waking up, would not set foot on Mother Earth without offering a prayer that thanked Mother Earth for allowing us to walk on it. Since those times, reverential attitudes towards Mother Earth, towards parents, elders and teachers has been praised and nurtured. For the longest time, teachers through their behaviour, direct instruction and stories taught children the importance of reverence.

Today, most of you will agree that parents are struggling to instil such values because they are alone in this effort. The elders are missing in action, schools and colleges focus mostly on skill development and the prevalent political correctness creates barriers to openly discuss the entropy in values.

As a result, the surroundings are filled with noises of callousness, superficiality, pride and self-indulgence while sincerity, authenticity, depth and humility are left for families to figure out. For example, in the US, data from 37,000 college students shows narcissistic traits grew just as fast as obesity between 1980 and 2004.[2] In a survey of children in the UK, 6 per cent wanted to be a lawyer, 8 per cent a writer and 34 per cent wanted to be a YouTuber.[3] One of the main reasons is fame. And in India, crass displays of wealth and a flippant attitude towards the elderly are becoming more common. And the hypocrisy of shouting from the rooftops about how great our culture is but not applying those standards to oneself is appalling.

Even a few generations ago, the elders in society, especially India, could provoke a meaningful conversation about character. Teachers whose position was next only to God-inspired students to seek true knowledge. The past was not perfect, but when it comes to character development, diligent attention was given by the elders. In the present, this is an area with a lot of scope for improvement.

As parents, you are the role models for your children. Don't underestimate your role in shaping your child. Sometimes you may feel that whatever you are doing isn't working but stay the course and nurture your child with values. The way you talk, the way you interact, the way you deal with others and the way you express your concern, all are opportunities to inspire the child. Use these opportunities to shift the conversation at home from acquiring to becoming, from ambition to aspiration, from superficiality to authenticity. If you nurture the roots; the fruits will take care of themselves. Most parents and teachers who I interact with are looking for simple and practical ways by which their children can learn character development.

In the coming chapters, I share some ideas on how to build character. The age group for these chapters is broad spanning from toddlers to seniors because it doesn't matter how old one is, we are all work in progress.

Daily Dilemma:

My child is eight years old and has stranger anxiety and doesn't socialize as much. Should I be worried?

Daaji: Nowadays, most children grow up in small families in urban settings. In a city environment, children are taught from a young age to not be friendly with strangers. Children are taught to curtail some of their natural openness. It's necessary to observe some of these precautions.

On top of this, most children are not exposed to large gatherings or people showing up unannounced at home. So if someone shows up unannounced and you want the child to be social and interact with confidence, it's a little much to ask.

When you are expecting guests at home, let your child know in advance that someone is coming over. Include your child in supporting you with hosting the guests. For example, you can request the child to help you with a glass of water for the guest. Don't push the child too hard, otherwise, they might develop deeper resentment. Involve the child more and things should improve. If this tendency continues after a few months, seek the help of a therapist.

15

As You Do, So They Learn: The Story of Mirror Neurons

Picture this: It's a golden spring afternoon in the park. Children are running around, families are having a picnic and as you enjoy your walk among the trees, a sudden movement catches the side of your eye. You notice a bike rider lose balance and skid across the gravel. Seeing the rider fall, you also recoil as if the gravel is scraping against your skin.

One more scenario: You see someone using a hammer, and they miss the nail and end up banging their finger instead. You also wince from the imaginary pain.

Okay, final scenario: On television, a black woolly spider slowly crawls up a woman's leg, and as it crawls up, you also feel the critter crawl on your skin.

Why does this happen? Why do we feel in our bodies what's happening to others? For years, this topic has been a subject of intense research for neuroscientists, psychologists and philosophers.

The breakthrough research in this area came in the 1990s from a team headed by Professor Giacomo Rizzolatti of the

Department of Neuroscience at the University of Parma, Italy. The team at Parma was researching the motor region in the brain and their test subject was a macaque monkey.

One day in the lab, Professor Rizzolatti picked up a peanut to eat, which triggered the neurons in the macaque's brain. But the macaque hadn't moved.[1] It *observed* what the professor was doing, and in its brain, the same neurons were triggered as if the macaque itself had picked up the peanut. The macaque understood the professor's *intention,* which triggered the same neurons as if it were picking up a peanut to eat. This was a serious breakthrough.[2]

Professor Rizzolatti's team also conducted experiments with actions that did not any intention associated with them. For example, waving hands in the air or swaying around in random movements. The team observed that for actions with no specific intention, the neurons in the macaque's brain did not register any activity.

After years of research on this subject, Professor Rizzolatti and his team published their first paper in which they identified a special class of cells called 'mirror neurons'. These neurons are special in the sense that they fire in response to the observed action. When the team first submitted their paper, they sent it to a top scientific journal. The journal rejected the paper for a lack of broad interest in the topic. Shortly after, the team submitted their paper to another leading research journal that accepted it. After publication, the paper ended up creating waves in the neuroscience community.[3]

Further research by other leading scientists showed that humans have a system of mirror neurons that are far superior to those found in monkeys. The mirror neurons in humans appear to be present in several regions of the brain, including the inferior frontal cortex (responsible for processing speech and language and impulse control) and the superior parietal lobes (functions include processing sensory information, understanding spatial orientation and body awareness). The research indicates that the human mirror neurons not only respond to the actions of others, but to their emotions and intentions as well.

Today, mirror neurons are a hot research topic. Scientists around the globe, including luminaries such as neuroscientist Vilayanur Ramachandran, Distinguished Professor of UC San Diego are looking at the implications of mirror neurons into areas such as language, empathy, autism, therapy and more. In his 2009 TEDIndia talk, Prof. Ramachandran said, 'For the longest time people have regarded science and humanities as being distinct. C.P. Snow spoke of the two cultures: science on the one hand, humanities on the other; never the twain shall meet. So, I'm saying the mirror neuron system underlies the interface allowing you to rethink about issues like consciousness, representation of self, what separates you from other human beings, what allows you to empathize with other human beings, and also even things like the emergence of culture and civilization, which is unique to human beings.'[4]

Mirror neurons explain the reason why we feel what we feel when we see the biker fall to the ground, the hammer hitting the man's finger or the spider crawling up the woman's leg. When we see someone perform an action, our mirror neurons automatically simulate that action in our brain. When I clench my fist and pull it backward, the mirror neurons in the observer's mind will read the intention of what I may do next. When I see someone who's grieving, my heart will also feel that grief. When I see the joy in someone's eyes, I too feel the joy. Mirror neurons support the transference of feelings.

> Mirror neurons move us from *thinking* to *feeling*. At some level, they show how we share a common consciousness and how the fabric of oneness ties us all together.

Mirror neurons move us from *thinking* to *feeling*. At some level, they show how we share a common consciousness and how the fabric of oneness ties us all together. The more aware we become, the more we can appreciate the beauty of the mirror neuron system within us. Once a neuroscientist from a leading university visited me at a meditation gathering in Pune, India. Close to a thousand people were meditating there in rapt silence, and a bubble of peace had enveloped the space. The scientist observed the environment and commented on the importance of measuring mirror neuron activity in such a setting. He was of the belief that such studies will help advance the adoption of meditation in families for reasons beyond religious beliefs.

Children are wired to mimic their parents and elders. They learn by observation and inspiration. Our actions and intentions shape the child's sense of self and their mental model of the world. In this regard, childhood is the right time to start laying the foundation for moral values. Think for a moment about the qualities you want to see in your children when they grow up. Would you want them to be loving, caring, empathetic and confident individuals? And in that case, how would they develop such qualities?

The teacher in preschool, the caregiver at the day care, the grandmother and grandfather—all have a part in shaping the child's mind. So, if we want the next generation of humanity to be loving, caring, empathetic and strong, then it is our duty to practice and reflect these qualities in us.

Exercise: Key Character Traits We Will Discuss

In the next few chapters, I share some foundational character traits. To help you with a deeper understanding of these traits, why don't we do a pre-quiz. Here are four questions for you.

Take a pen and write a few lines to answer these questions. After you complete reading the next two principles, you can revisit your answers and compare your understanding of these topics.

'What is the importance of humility?'
'Does courage mean no fear?'
'Does generosity mean giving money to the needy?'
'What do we mean by living in tune with nature?'

Mirror Neurons: An Evolving Area in Neuroscience

While on the topic of mirror neurons, it's important to level-set our understanding in this area. Mirror neurons are a developing area of research. There are some in the scientific community who think the claims of mirror neurons are overhyped. They feel that science is still catching up, but pop culture conversation may have taken over the topic.[5] This is a fair assessment because it's common to see articles with tall claims regarding mirror neurons. Helping children learn music, improved therapy experiences, and even addressing causes of autism in children, mirror neurons have been cited as the panacea. But the science isn't there to establish many of these claims.

I am in the camp of the mirror neuron advocates, but I also understand the counterargument being made. It's part of the scientific method and through the experiments and findings, science continues to make progress. My advice about mirror neurons and their implications on how we raise our children is to stay updated on the emerging science. I am hoping in the coming years, we will see some interesting updates in this space.

The important takeaway for parents is *that mirror neurons or not, our children mirror us.* Through our behaviour may our children mirror the best angels of human nature.

Daily Dilemma:

How to manage children lovingly when they completely refuse to do something that is necessary for their well-being and they have tantrums? What is a good way to communicate with them? E.g., go to bed, get dressed for school and eat healthy food?

Daaji: 'Tell me and I will forget, show me and I may remember; involve me and I will understand,' said Confucius. This is true for children and grown-ups. So, the key to instilling good habits in children is by becoming role models. Parents are the role models for children, especially little ones (pre-teen years).

Instead of telling, *do* with your children. You want them to go to bed early, then change the routine at home to allow early bedtimes. You want them to read, then read with them. You want them to stay away from screens, you lead the way. Also, make it playful and light-hearted. As we grow up, we somehow begin to take ourselves too seriously. Children come into our lives to re-instil our playful nature. Play with them and guide them during play.

A tantrum is a pre-emptive declaration of war. If you confront a toddler having a tantrum, they will win the howling contest. Distract them, humour them and de-escalate the situation.

16

Interest and Observation Are Twins

When someone says, 'Hi! How are you?', what's your response? Usually, we respond by saying 'I'm good' or 'I'm doing great!' Civil, pre-programmed responses. The person who is asking is extending a social courtesy and proportionate to the question, your short, automatic response is enough.

For a moment, reconsider the question 'How are you?' with greater interest. Before you answer, can you take a minute to observe yourself? How does your body feel—fresh, stiff, relaxed or sluggish? Think of a word that describes the feeling. Now observe your mind. How does it feel—busy, calm, agitated, overwhelmed or alert? Try to describe the state of your mind in a sentence or two. Next, move your attention to your feelings. Are you feeling anxious, happy, serene or meh? In a sentence or two describe your feelings. With this simple exercise, you can have a good understanding of your body, mind and feelings. When we take an interest and observe, we establish a deeper connection with the observed.

Interest and observation are twins. When we take interest, we observe what might otherwise escape our attention. Interest and observation make the mind contemplative; and a contemplative mind reveals the true nature of the observed. Many years ago, I learned a valuable lesson about the contemplative capacity of the mind.

> Interest and observation are twins. They come in pairs. The keener one's interest, the better the observations.

In 1980, deep into the winter, I spent a few days with Babuji in India. One morning, he was sitting in his recliner in the courtyard. It was a crisp morning, the kind where you let the sun gently thaw you. I was sitting on the ground, a few feet away from him. It was just the two of us. He was lost in himself, and I was admiring the silence that enveloped us. Suddenly he looked at me and said, 'Come here.'

I moved closer to him and sat near his feet. He turned towards me, extended his hand, and scratched at the top of his wrist to draw a line. In winters, in India, skin can get dry and cracked. His nail formed a pale white line on his wrist.

'Look here,' he said, 'this is a water canal.'

'Yes, Babuji,' I said.

Then he drew one more line from the centre of this line, going outward, like a 'Y' shape.

'Now, the power of the water has reduced by 50 per cent,' he said.

Then he drew one more tributary.

'Now it's reduced even further. Do you understand?'

'Yes, Babuji. I understand very well now.'

After this brief exchange, he turned away from me and slipped back into his thoughts. I sat there in silence as his teaching took root in my mind and heart. What he meant to say was that we form many channels in our minds. The mind's power dissipates across these channels. The more the channels, the less we observe. Through meditation, we develop the discerning capacity to regulate the flow of the mind and focus its capacities. When the mind is focused the contemplative capacity is enhanced.

When children are young, up to six years old, they are keen on doing what their parents are doing. So whatever the parents do, the children also want to do. These years offer a rare window of time when interests can be *inherited*.

Parenting Tip

Rather than worrying about what enrichment activities to take your children to, make the daily activities at home enriching for them. Involve them in chores and other tasks at home. It will teach them to take on responsibility as they grow up.

For example, if you start reading to your children, they will develop an interest in reading. The same goes for chores at home. No matter how small your children are, share chores with them. Ask for their help while making the bed or cleaning the kitchen. Get them involved. They might make a mess or they may get distracted midway, and that's okay. But get them into a habit of being involved with the activities at home. Such involvement will instil the idea of taking responsibility later in life.

Exercise the Child's Senses by Asking Questions

From the age of two, encourage children to listen. Sit with your little ones, and ask them to observe what is happening around them: 'Do you hear birds?', 'How many birds do you hear?', 'Close your eyes and listen again. What else do you hear?' You can also ask, 'What do you see around you?', 'What do you smell?' and so on.

Do this in different settings—at home, in the park, in the car while running errands. Make it a game that you play with your children. They love playing games like, 'I spy with my little eye.' Create your own versions of this game that includes seeing, smelling, tasting, hearing and feeling.

Another area to focus on is helping them develop a sense of direction. I do a particular exercise with my granddaughter. As I write this, she is three years old and when we go out on a walk, I ask her, 'Should I go this way or that way?' She chooses the correct direction every time. We also stop at the intersections and spell out the street signs. She enjoys our evening activity, and as we walk, she is developing her sense of direction.

When going to the grocery store, ask your child to memorize the names of the roads. Ask them to keep track of the directions. As they get better, you can also ask them, 'How many right turns did we take?', 'How much did we pay for the tomatoes?', 'What song was playing in the store?' and so on. The idea is to develop alert observation.

Interactions with Mother Nature are a wonderful masterclass where the family can learn together. Starting with how a flower blooms, how the stars shine, how the clouds move, how the raindrops fall, these are all simple ways to sharpen the observational capacity of children.

Sometimes I take my granddaughter to the terrace, and I ask her, 'Is it morning or evening?' I have drawn two lines on our terrace, to mark the position of the sun. When the sun is on one side of the line, it's morning, and when the sun is on the other side, it's evening. Initially, she would look at the lines and tell me if it was morning or evening. Now, she doesn't use the lines and can say, 'The sun will rise on this side,' and 'The sun will set on this side.' Her sense of direction has developed from an early age, and yes, I am beaming with grandpa-pride as I write this.

On a starry night, step outside and let the children gaze at the stars. It's a beautiful moment to see a child lost in the beauty of the night sky. Maria Montessori, Italian physician and educator, said, 'The things children see are not just remembered; they form part of his soul.'[1] To help them understand the beauty and concept of the cycle of life, as the seasons transition, let the child observe the leaves changing colours, falling to the ground, and the new leaves sprouting in the Spring. Each day, take the child to the same tree or plant and say, 'Look at this tree. We'll come back tomorrow, and we will see what has changed.'

The sense of smell is important to the development of memory, emotions, behaviours and other senses, such as taste. When you take nature walks, invite the little ones to develop their sense of smell by breathing in the different fragrances of the leaves and flowers (without plucking them). Then, because smell is intertwined with emotion, ask them how the smell makes them feel. Encourage them to feel, so they develop their sense of touch. Let them experience the textures of the leaves in the garden, the roughness of bark and the feel of the soil—moist or dry, sandy or claylike, pebbly or free of stones.

Exercise the Senses

Here are some sensory exercises you can do with your children:

- Listen to the bird chorus in the mornings and evenings.
- Watch the rising and setting sun.
- Observe wave patterns and moon phases.
- Pot plants together.
- Observe the surroundings.
- Recall dreams the child may have had and chat about them.

If you live near the sea, take your child for a morning walk or an evening walk at a fixed time. Let them observe the water level in the sea and have them place markers in the sand for the water level daily. Let them also observe the phase of the moon for each day. In a few weeks, the child can correlate between the phase of the moon and the level of the water in the sea. Let them form a conclusion about their observation on their own.

After visiting friends when you get back home, ask your children, 'What did you see?' 'How many sofas did you see? What colours were they?' 'What were the family members wearing?' The idea is to ask a few questions to trigger their observation mechanism and strengthen their memory.

When children wake up in the morning and are still sitting in bed, ask them what they saw in their sleep. A child might say 'I saw this red flower in my sleep and I was sitting in it' or like my granddaughter who went through days of saying 'I saw snakes. A black one, a brown one'. For weeks all she saw were snakes and she enjoyed meeting them in her dreams. It doesn't matter if children repeat themselves. What you are doing here is allowing the children to express themselves. You are allowing them to share a part of their subconscious workings with you. When a child knows that you are interested in hearing what they have to share, then they also become more observant and perceptive to their inner workings. With this exercise without much effort, children will develop skills in observing the subconscious.

In Kanha Shanti Vanam in India, where I live, many families come to visit the meditation centre and spend a few days in the serene environment there. They come with their children, and this gives me an opportunity to meet with so many children daily. Sometimes I ask a young one to go into my room and look at a portrait on the wall. Most of them go in, quickly glance at it and come out. Then I ask them what they saw. After listening to their answers, I ask them to look at the portrait again. This time they notice that the portrait is a collage of thousands of smaller photographs. In the first attempt, most children miss observing that detail. But when asked to look keenly, they get it. This shows that a nudge is enough.

Children learn through play. So, create simple games at home. For example, ask them to observe one of your bookshelves. Tell them the next day it is going to be different. Add a few new books, place some trinkets and move some things around. The next day, ask them to spot the differences. Your children, too, can set up such puzzles for you. One-way traffic makes parenting monotonous. Involve your children and implement their ideas for setting up activities.

The important behaviour from parents is that whenever children share what they saw or what they felt, listen to them and encourage them. Every child is different. Some like to draw, paint or create new things. Others like to run around and explore. Say your child likes art, then show them a painting and ask how they feel when they look at the painting. If your child loves sports, show them a clip of a game (any game), and ask them how the winner and loser may have felt.

After the age of ten, parents can raise the level a few notches and guide children to observe subtler aspects of their feelings.

Observing Feelings

When children are around ten years old, encourage them to observe their feelings. Help them focus on their inner state: 'Are you feeling peaceful, calm, still, happy, joyful or blissful?' This is a spectrum of feelings. Even most adults cannot differentiate between happiness, joy and bliss. But being able to do so helps in a better understanding of oneself. And it is not difficult to develop these skills. Once children start observing, for example, happiness, joy and bliss, they will learn that bliss is lighter, happiness is heavier and joy is somewhere in between. Similarly, when they are sad, help them to interpret the spectrum of sadness.

> Help children focus on their inner state: 'Are you feeling peaceful, calm, still, happy, joyful or blissful?' This is a spectrum of feelings.

We want to guide children in the direction of mastering their feelings. When they are tired and you ask, 'Are you tired?' they will answer 'Yes.' They will know the feeling of tiredness and they can express it. When they are fresh from the shower or bath and you ask, 'How does it feel to be fresh?' they describe what freshness feels like. In this way, through simple questions, we can help children develop a vocabulary for expressing their emotional states.

Verbalizing feelings also helps children regain their composure faster. Let's say a child is upset and about to cry. At such time, comfort the child and take a few deep breaths along with the child. Then ask how they are feeling. Ask them to find the words that describe how they feel. Such an exercise takes away the focus from the emotion. It helps the child move past the feeling without repressing it. The key to such interventions is asking the right questions at the right time.

The Science behind Asking Questions

At the beginning of the chapter, when I talked about that simple question, 'How are you?', it was enough to focus the mind on how you were feeling so you can answer the question. Questions are the catalysts for observation. When a question is suddenly directed at us, we are hard-wired to think and respond. Behavioural scientists have shown how asking questions drives our behaviour.

For example, in a research study, participants were asked if they would buy a new car in the next six months. Asking this question, increased the purchase rates by 35 per cent.[2] In another study, people were asked if they would donate blood, and that question increased the number of donors by nearly 9 per cent.[3] Asking the right question drives the right thinking and behaviour.

Positive, encouraging questions from parents enhance a child's observation skills. Serve-and-volley conversations make children more aware. Warm empathetic conversations elicit a child's deeper thoughts and forge stronger bonds between parents and children.

Questions you ask children can vary from age to age. In general, keep it light-hearted. Pepper in some funny questions here and there to keep the children engaged and motivated. Share jokes and anecdotes from sports and politics to religion and spirituality to affairs of this world and the other world. Questions will make children thinkers.

Start simple. Say you have a four-year-old. Hold up two fingers in each hand and ask how much? Fold in one finger and again ask how much. This is a simple way to teach concepts of addition and subtraction. Focus on the concept and don't rush and teach new concepts. Take your time and keep creating new ideas for the same concept. This will strengthen the fundamentals of understanding.

Similarly, ask them questions like 'Who are your friends?', 'What is your teachers name?', 'Was your friend happy today? What made your friend happy?', 'Whose birthdays are there in this month?', 'What made you happy today?', 'What made you sad?' Whether you have a four-year-old or a fourteen-year-old, such questions will show you what your children are thinking, and such conversations deepen the relationship.

Observe Breathing and Energy Patterns

With teenagers, parents can ask them to observe their breathing patterns: 'Are you breathing fast or slow?', 'What is the pattern of your breathing when you are happy?', 'And when you are angry, how does your breathing change?', 'Which nostril is dominant at various times of the day?' Don't give answers. Let them observe and note it in their journal or notebook. They can then study these patterns on their own.

Next, they can observe whether they are radiating or absorbing energy at any given moment. This is a subtler aspect of observation and can take a more nuanced approach. There are times of the day when we are radiating energy and those times are more suitable for high energy tasks like sports and games. Likewise, there are times of the day when we are absorbing energy and those are suitable for contemplative activities like studying, art and meditation.

Observing the exchange of energies with the environment will help the children learn more about managing their energies. Co-relationships between absorbing and radiating energy level and how they affect one's working or not is an important aspect of their understanding of self. It helps them appreciate the concept of the ease of swimming with the current versus the difficulty of swimming against it.

When children start observing their energy patterns to understand whether they are radiating, then ask them to observe which nostril is dominant when they radiate energy and which nostril is dominant. Doing so, they may discover that they perform better on analytical tasks like a school assignment when the right nostril is dominant, and they are absorbing energy. If they are attentive, they may also catch the moment when the breathing switches from one dominant nostril to another.

I suggest that parents do these activities with their children. You both can keep notes on observing the exchange of energies. After doing this for a couple of days, sit down and exchange notes. It will be a wonderful exercise for parents to connect with their children.

When children have learned to meditate, ask them, 'As you go deeper into your meditation, observe the lightness within you. How light do you feel after meditation? What goes away that makes you feel lighter inside? How does the feeling of lightness change during the day?' With such questions, we are transcending feelings. We are helping them go beyond observing the body and the feelings. What we are doing is inspiring them to take interest in the subtler aspects of life. When they take interest, they will observe and through observation, they will introspect. Wisdom develops with self-introspection, but it takes time. Those who take interest will find the time.

Do This: Left Nostril Breathing to Calm Down

There are times when your child (or even you) feel angry or anxious. In such times, try this. Close your right nostril with your thumb and take a slow, deep breath through your left nostril, breathing deeply into your abdomen and releasing the breath fully each time. Then continue to breathe like this eight to ten times through your left nostril. This simple exercise helps with calming down and regaining composure.

Do this: Right Nostril Breathing to Get Energized

There are times when you feel low on energy or sluggish. All you need is a boost of energy to get you going. In such times, close your left nostril with your thumb and take a slow, deep breath through your left nostril. Breathe deeply into your abdomen and release the breath fully each time. Continue to do this eight to ten times and you will feel a difference in your energy levels right away.

Even if It's a Few Minutes, Be Present

So far in this chapter, we covered a variety of exercises in developing observation and interest. From observing Mother Nature to being attentive in car rides to observing one's surroundings to being mindful of your feelings, we have covered a lot of ground here. Again, to remind you, be patient, be consistent. These skills take time.

Observation and interest are not analytical skills like learning a language or math. They are more nuanced skills and need greater attention and encouragement. Once developed, these skills enhance sensitivity and centeredness. The *presence* of parents and elders helps children with developing interest and observation. As I mentioned earlier by presence, I mean your attention at that moment. Presence in a conversation, presence in the park, presence during play—all create active participation. Active participation creates engagement. And engagement furthers interest. One doesn't have to spend hours in such activities. Even if it's a few minutes, be present.

Daily Dilemma:

How to talk to children about death? Someone in the family dies or is very sick. How to discuss these situations with children?

Daaji: Our home in Staten Island, New York was close to a graveyard. So, it was only a matter of time before my children asked me about death. I told them about how the body ages, and we eventually die. I don't think we talk as much about death as we should in our homes. Death is natural and it comes to all living things. While we talk about death, we should also teach children ways to process the grief that comes with the passing on of loved ones.

When my father died, my children were there with me in the village. There were a lot of rituals and communal grieving that they witnessed. But, what they still remember is that during that time, I was silent. I would meditate often, and the children got the idea of how to process grief through prayer and meaningful silence. I share this with you because years later when I was having a conversation with my children, they told me how they remembered my conduct during that difficult time.

In your family, when you suffer the loss of a loved one, pray together for a few days. Include children in these prayers. I hope this helps you.

17

Confidence, Courage and Self-Awareness: The Gifts of Humility

If I asked you if it's important for your child to learn public speaking or to describe how sports help with a child's development, you could answer my questions easily. But if I asked you, 'What are the benefits of humility?' that might be trickier.

Most of us know that humility prevents one from becoming egoistic. Other than that, what are its benefits? How does humility ennoble one's life? How do we teach children humility? Most parents don't have clear answers to these questions. In general, humility is not a mainstream discussion in parenting for many reasons.

First, when we think about humility we think of saints and reformers like Jesus, Gandhi, Mandela and Mother Teresa. Their lifestyles exemplified humility. But Mom and Dad are not aiming that high. Parents are focused on raising happy, healthy children. If the children grow up to be luminaries, that's like winning the jackpot.

Second, humility suffers from an image problem. Think about this. What picture comes to mind when you think of a humble person? It's someone who is soft, naïve and easily pushed over. The words *loss* and *humility* are often clubbed together. For instance, when your favourite cricket team loses, the commentator talks about their *humiliating* loss. Thereby making the point that losers are humbled. Or even worse, the humble are losers.

But then there is a flip side too. I'm referring to the glib variant of humility that appears with victory. Think of acceptance speeches at award ceremonies that begin with the clichéd 'I am truly humbled.' So, there's humility that comes with losing and there's humility that comes with winning.

So, there are so many facets of humility, and it's no surprise that you might be confused. Parents have asked me questions like: 'Does humility show a lack of conviction?' 'Will humility side-line my child?' 'Will humility affect my child's confidence?' This chapter is written with the idea of demystifying humility and helping parents with how they can teach humility to their children.

A Quick Primer on Ego: Enemy, Friend or Frenemy?

We cannot understand humility unless we understand ego. Ego is what gives a person the feeling of 'I'. It creates the identity.

Think of the ego as a spectrum, starting from zero and ending at, say, one hundred. For an activity like brushing your teeth, your ego might need to be at 3 per cent. To give a speech in front of ten thousand people, say your ego needs to be at 80 per cent. But if your ego stays at 80 per cent after the speech while having coffee with some of the attendees, then it's a problem. Now your ego no longer matches your activity level. When interacting with people, your ego needs to be at say 30 per cent to make you more approachable and courteous. A constant 80 per cent ego means having an inflated ego. And if your ego stays at 3 per cent when you need to inspire a room full of people, then you might fail in your task.

What's necessary is a flexible ego, one that matches your activity. For example, if you are pitching a product, addressing your team or giving an interview, your ego needs to be at a level where it portrays clarity and confidence. Once the job is done, your ego should return to a humble state.

> Humble people do not think less of themselves, but more of others.

Humility, like love, is a natural state of the heart. Impurities like prejudice, jealousy and competitiveness impede the flow of love. In the same way, a dominant ego suppresses humility. Humility emerges as one's ego becomes refined.

Going back to the analogy of ego as a spectrum between zero to hundred, let's take the example of a musician. If the musician thinks, 'I am the best performer ever, and no one is better than I am,' it's a case of an inflated ego. If the musician thinks, 'I performed well today, and it was my best so far,' it is confident pride. If the musician thinks, 'I performed well, thanks to my training and the best wishes of everyone,' such thinking shows humility.

Humility is the mother tincture from which many other qualities like truthfulness, reverence and courage are distilled. Many of the problems we face in life, such as prejudice, inequality, intolerance and apathy, all stem from hearts lacking in humility. Self-promoting ideas that put me, mine, I, myself first at all costs take root because humility is lacking. Humble people don't think less of themselves, but they think more of others. Especially as a person grows in power, it is one's humility that ensures that power does not block the flow of empathy.

Humility: What It Isn't and What It Is

Let me tell you a short story.

Once, there lived a mighty emperor. His subjects loved him, and his enemies feared him. One day, he was resting in his pavilion at the palace gardens. It was a hot, humid afternoon and the emperor slipped into a reverie. After a brief snooze, he woke up. He was thirsty, and he looked around. But there was no water. For whatever reason, none of his guards were around either. From the pavilion, the emperor could see the well from which the palace gardener drew water for the plants.

He walked over to the well and cast the bucket into the water. His palms were sweaty, and as he raised the bucket, he lost his grip. He tried to hold on with one hand, but his fingers were squeezed between the rope and the pulley. Wincing from pain, he somehow managed to free his hand, and the bucket along with the rope fell into the well.

The emperor was dizzy from pain and thirst, cradling his bruised and swollen hand, he limped towards a tree and sat down to rest. The cool shade helped him regain his composure. He steadied himself, looked up at the sky, and said, 'Lord, you are so generous. I am not even capable of pulling out a bucket of water to quench my thirst. For something even as simple as this, I need help, and yet, you made me an emperor.'

The story of the emperor signifies a moment in his life when he embraced what he was in that moment. He understood what he was capable of and acknowledged what he was not. Humility is a sign of great self-awareness.

> Humility is a sign of great self-awareness.

Humility is not debasing yourself. Fawning over someone or falling at a person's feet is not humility. We see too much of that today—people falling at an influential person's feet or a rich person's feet just to get something in return. That's plain flattery to serve a personal agenda, and it has no role to play in humility.

> Humility is not debasing yourself. Humility is not servility either.

When one is aware of what they know and that there is a lot they might not know, that level of awareness shows humility. Most of the great scientists, maestros and experts have an innate quality of humility, making them lifelong learners in their area of expertise. Their perfection comes from the humility they carry within their hearts.

Humility gives the person a feeling of insignificance that helps him grow. The feeling of insignificance comes because the person looks up to something much superior to them that inspires them to keep growing. Let me explain.

From the discoveries of Copernicus to Carl Sagan, our relative size in the universe has diminished, but our knowledge of what surrounds us has grown exponentially. We have discovered new galaxies, new planets, new black holes and so on. At each stage, when we understood how small we were in the grandness of the cosmos, we also grew our knowledge by light-years. The more we become aware of our insignificance, the greater our growth. Humility gives new knowledge.

Does this mean that humble people live in perennial doubt? No. Those who are humble are truthful: there is truth in what they say and truth in what they do. And when they don't know something, they are comfortable in sharing that they don't know. They are comfortable with their ignorance, and their ego does not put-up false pretences of their superiority. Humility makes one authentic. It endows one with the feeling that 'I respect myself so much that I cannot be untrue to myself. The purity within me cannot be honoured if I allow hypocrisy and falsehood to breed within me.' And it leads us to the next aspect of humility, and that is courage.

Humility breeds courage. The courage of humble people helps break through barriers. Have you seen the tiny, tender, hairy roots of a tree break through the toughest rock? These insignificant, almost invisible and powerless roots forge the way for the mother root to drive deeper into the soil and make the tree stronger. In the same way, the most impenetrable ego barriers are broken down by a heart filled with humility.

A humble person is respectful by nature. Humility cultivates reverence in one's heart. When we bow down with respect and not fear, when we adore with sincerity and not falsehood, when our eyes meet those of an elder and we automatically look down in politeness, it's all humility. Reverence and humility go together.

And how does a humble person thrive? Humility blesses the person with moral treasures. In nature, a tree laden with fruit bends. In the same way, humans bearing spiritual fruits become increasingly humble. Humility manifests in their actions. When you are in the company of a humble soul, you will find unexplainable peace and serenity.

As we have seen so far, self-awareness, clarity, truthfulness, courage, reverence and authenticity are all the virtues that descend into a humble heart. Who wouldn't want their loved ones, especially their children, to be blessed with such inner wealth? Parents are busy and what they need are practices that they can take and apply in daily life. In the rest of the chapter, I offer some practices on developing humility.

How to Develop Humility

While the suggestions I share here are for parents to teach their children, they are applicable for parents too. Dive into these ideas and put them to good use.

Prayer Creates Space for Humility to Develop

Teach children prayer early on. Prayer creates the emotional space within for humility to grow. When parents teach children to pray, or even better when they pray with their children, it will help them all develop humility.

Prayer is not a religious ritual, nor is it just the words that we chant or sing. Instead, prayer is a feeling created in the heart, and the words we use are a bridge to arrive at that feeling. Whether you believe in God or not, whether you are religious or an atheist, it doesn't matter. Prayer opens the heart to the possibility of deeper levels of communication within oneself. When your heart is moved with awe at the beauty of a majestic mountain, when it melts in pain because of the misery of a fellow human, when you feel yourself drown in gratitude, the state created inside one's heart is akin to prayer.

Prayer is the universal song of a humble heart.

Prayer is the universal song of a humble heart.

Here is one way to teach your child how to offer prayer. At bedtime, while seated, gently close your eyes and let a feeling of love and compassion fill your heart. Think about the acts of the day and seek forgiveness if your actions even unknowingly caused hurt to someone. Suggest to yourself that all through the night, the beauty of the heart will grow and grow. Sit in silence for a few minutes and allow the love to envelop you. Praying with children is a beautiful experience. Through prayer, children will develop humility.

In the resources section, at the end of the book, I have shared the prayer that we offer in Heartfulness. You may try this one or any other prayer you prefer. Please write to me about your experience of offering prayer with your children at bedtime. I have shared my email address in the appendix.

Sense of Sacredness towards Efforts

In 1789, Ben Franklin, one of the founding fathers of America, in a letter to French philosopher Jean-Baptiste Leroy, wrote, 'In this world, nothing can be said to be certain, except death and taxes.' We all die, and while we live, we pay taxes. But there is one more thing that's certain in life: failure.

We all fail.

Only by repeatedly failing does the baby learn to walk. By falling and tipping over a few times, does the child learn to ride a bike. By making enough mistakes in math is how one learns to calculate. Failing in love is how we learn about true love.

Failure is a natural part of learning. A perfect SAT score, a flawless piano recital or making the cut for the soccer team are all great, but children need to know that if they don't win, it's not the end of the world. Children dread disappointing their parents. As parents, we need to give our children the reassurance that we don't mind them failing.

Parents can support their children by shifting the spotlight from *results* to *efforts*. Creating a sense of sacredness towards efforts is important. For example, if your children are preparing to take the SATs, encourage them to put in good efforts. Teach them the importance of planning well and having a routine. As your children put in the effort, encourage them, test them, and when they are frustrated, allow them to vent. Appreciate your children's success, acknowledge their failures. The key is to instil a sense of sacredness towards efforts.

Make Humility a Conversation Topic at Home

Saying 'I don't know' is the beginning of knowing. Saying 'I was surprised' is the beginning of rethinking. So here are some questions for you to think about:

- When were you last wrong?
- What surprised you the most recently?
- What were you absolutely sure of, only to discover you were incorrect?
- What did you learn recently?

All these questions tie into the definition of humility, which I shared earlier: humility is an attitude where I know what I am, understand what I ought to be, and acknowledge the gap between the two.

Share stories with your children about when you were wrong and how you realized it. For example, an incident from your work where you thought a colleague was hasty with an assignment, only to realize later that he had to rush home to take care of a sick child.

Conversations about rethinking and re-evaluating help children understand the importance of humility. Also, at a certain point in their lives, children go through a phase of 'I know . . . I know'. Anything you want to teach them, the answer is 'I know'. For a time, it's okay to have this attitude.

But at around eight years old, if this continues, children need guidance. In such instances, sit down with them and discuss a time about when you thought you knew, but it turned out that you didn't. Share it as a story and those lessons will stay with the children. During adolescence if this habit makes a comeback, try giving some indirect advice and hints. Halo parents can also help in nudging the child.

Humility: The Highest Virtue

Saints and spiritual teachers have extolled the importance of humility in one's life. For example, in the Gita, Lord Krishna shares a list of twenty qualities that enrich one's life. The first quality is humility.[1] Saint Augustine is credited as having written these words: 'Do you wish to rise? Begin by descending. You plan a tower that will pierce the clouds? Lay first the foundation of humility.' Lao Tzu captured the importance of humility when he wrote, 'All streams flow to the sea because it is lower than they are. Humility gives it its power. If you want to govern the people, you must place yourself below them. If you want to lead the people, you must learn how to follow them.'[2]

Across cultures of the world, the drop and the ocean have been used as metaphors to signify the individual self (drop) and the higher self (ocean). When the drop and ocean merge, it marks a new beginning. The merger of the individual self with the higher self is the triumph of human life. Saints and spiritual teachers have inspired us to undertake the journey towards merging with the higher self (God, Nature or the Ultimate).

The journey, though, is fraught with temptations and mired in labyrinths of ego. A humble heart offers a safe passage through these obstacles.

Without humility, there is no merger of the individual self and the higher self. Humility attracts grace. When a low-pressure area is created in the atmosphere, the wind rushes in to fill the void. In the same way, when we empty ourselves of arrogance and pride, we create a low-pressure area in the heart, which gets filled with grace. When there is humility within, grace descends, automatically.

There is a naturalness that pervades a person filled with humility. Others may think you are humble, but to you, you are free from any such description. You are your natural self. You will find that, slowly, the world recognizes your innate worth, and not only follows you but *wants* to follow you. I hope these few pages inspire you all to instil the virtue of humility in your children. I pray that your efforts bear the most bountiful fruit.

Daily Dilemma:

Daaji, my child asked me about heaven and hell? How do I explain?

Daaji: Hell and heaven are both here on this earth. If we are loving, kind and compassionate, then we find heaven inside. If we are cruel, wicked and selfish then we create a not-so-good place inside ourselves.

Principle 7

Youth Are the Future. Guide Them, Don't Break Them.

18

Youth: A Time of Promise and Potential

If we plant a seed, it cannot jump thirty years and become a fruit-yielding tree. It must go through the stages one by one to reach maturity, and that is the process of growth. So, it's inevitable that a tree's life begins with a seed, then a sapling, a young tree and finally, a mature fruit-bearing tree. In our life, youth is the journey towards maturity. It is a time of great promise and potential. When I spend time with the youth it gives me a window into their buoyant hearts. When I hear their problems, which some time ago were my problems too, it deepens our kinship. When I listen to their ideas, I feel energized. When I see them drowned in meditation, I witness a new humanity awakening. These adolescents (tweens and teens) and young adults, are the agents of change in our world.

Youth hold the promise for the future. They are resilient by nature. Their hearts are brimming with inquisitiveness and there is ingenuity in their thinking. They are defiant in the face of odds. Their energy is indefatigable.

As parents, it's our duty to prepare children for youth by laying strong moral and emotional foundation. From an early age, if we introduce good habits, then when they grow up, they will have a well-tuned inner GPS guiding them. Throughout history, whenever the aspiration of youth was guided by the wisdom of the elders, they went on to change the world in amazing ways.

But guiding the youth is not an easy task. Saying 'This is how we do it' to young adults won't cut it because they push back on such blatant authority. One has to meet them at their level and engage them. Talking down to them or pandering to them doesn't work. It takes patience, empathy, authenticity and a good bit of humour to connect with them.

Once a group of twenty-year-olds, about ten of them, came to visit me at our meditation centre in Kanha Shanti Vanam, India. Kanha is a sanctuary of peace. Chiselled out of the igneous earth of the Deccan plateau, Kanha is home to thousands of trees that line the walkways leading to the world's largest meditation hall. Imagine meditating with 50,000 people from all over the world. Kanha is the Eden Gardens of meditation.

At the time the twenty-year-olds visited in 2017, the meditation hall was still being built. Several projects were underway, and 2000 people worked every day at the site. The youth were there for volunteer work. When one volunteers, be it laying bricks, planting trees, pulling cables or sweeping the floors, the heart becomes more open. Their hearts align with the vision, and they care for what is being done. The work ethic and habits they develop by doing volunteer work serve them well in all aspects of their lives.

I gave the youth a fact-finding mission. I asked them to observe the work and then report back to me with their findings. When we got together a few days later, they pulled out a list, almost two pages long. They identified problems related to shift hours for workers, on-site waste management, landscaping issues, worker safety, quality of cables and many other problems.

As a next step, I gave them a couple of days to brainstorm solutions to the problems they identified. When we next met, I asked them to present their ideas to the project team at Kanha. I also told them that I wouldn't be attending their meeting. I preferred that they have a free-ranging discussion, and I asked one of my associates to listen in. After the meeting was over, my associate told me that the meeting started well but quickly went off the rails.

Here's what happened that day. When the youth team presented their findings, the project team felt that they were calling their baby ugly. They also felt that the suggestions were half-baked and lacked proper context. The project team was defensive, and the youth team was aggressive. In the heat of the moment, neither team was mindful of the goal, which was how to make Kanha even better. I knew this would happen.

Over the years, I have seen how ego clashes ended up trumping enthusiasm. I wanted the project team to learn how to process feedback. I wanted them to grasp the proverbial wisdom of separating the wheat from the chaff. But, when emotions run high, one ends up collecting chaff from the wheat. I also wanted the youth team to learn how to offer feedback in a constructive way.

A few days after, when both teams had had some time to cool off, I called them over to my place. I used my weapon of choice, which hasn't failed me to date: warm masala chai and some finger-licking Gujarati savouries. No sooner than these weapons are fired, even the mightiest meekly surrender to the onslaught of sips and dips. Soon the teams started chatting again. This time around, I asked them to keep the big picture in mind, and having said that, I left for my walk.

I was later told that the conversation went well. This time around, the youth team understood the project team's viewpoint. They had a better appreciation of the sleepless nights and gruelling work the project team was putting in. The project team, for their part, appreciated the energy of the youth. They understood that not only were they offering solutions, but they would also work on implementing them. The meeting ended with a feeling of kinship and solidarity.

> Between seeing the glass *half full* or *half empty,* there is also the possibility of the glass being designed for *twice* the capacity.

There is an old engineer's lament, 'Between seeing the glass *half full* or *half empty* there is also the possibility of the glass being designed for *twice* the capacity.' When the energy of the youth is guided by the elders' wisdom, new perspectives emerge. Youth are not wild horses to be tamed by breaking them down. They need to be inspired and unleashed as a force for good.

The biggest strength of youth is their energy. Their energy is what makes them creative. There is no turning off the fire. There is no hibernating through this phase of life. When the youthful energies are guided in the right direction, such energy becomes creative energy. The energy of youth is not for rambunctiousness. It should be a period of vigorous activity with aspiration. What is this aspiration that should drive them? It should be how to become gentle, how to become loving, how to become wise. Volunteer work, meditation, mentoring by elders—all help the youth in their development.

Parenting Tip

Don't push them into finding a volunteer cause. In time, they will find a cause that appeals to them. When they do, support them and encourage them.

The Teenage Brain Is a Work in Progress

For all the promise and potential that youth have, elders often think of them, especially the teenagers, as raging hormones, rebels without a cause and reckless idiots. Why is this so? Why are the teenage years so turbulent? Some of the answers lie in the physiology of the human brain itself.

At the risk of simplifying neuroscience, I am sharing some insights that may help us understand what's happening with a teenager's brain. The brains of teenagers are still developing. By developing, I mean their brain is focused on finalizing what neural connections it needs to keep and which ones to prune. This process of synaptic pruning is a natural part of growth. When we are born, we have an excess of connections, and over time, the brain prunes away the excess connections.

Parenting Tip: Flexibility in Ideas

When children are between six to ten years old, their intuitive ability is active, and the reason for that is that their minds are flexible. Outside a tantrum here and there, children don't arrive at rigid conclusions and insist '*this is how it should be*'.

As they grow up, their worldview becomes more set. For example, it's easier to instil interests in little children. If the child doesn't like math, then through games and activities, math can be made fun. However, as children grow up, it becomes difficult to steer their interests. They have already made up their mind about their preferences. So as children grow up, parents need to get creative and have more patience.

How does the brain decide which connections to keep and which ones to prune away? The decision is based on the life experiences gathered till that time. For example, as a child, if you were into art, then when you become an adult the neural circuits that were formed will remain. This law is known as Hebbian Learning. When we learn something new, neurons in our brain connect with other neurons to form a neural network. The more these neurons fire, the stronger the connection becomes, and the action becomes increasingly intuitive. Hebb's Law has been summed up in a single phrase: 'The neurons that fire together wire together.'[1,2]

Besides pruning, something called myelination also takes place in the teen brain.[3] A fatty substance called myelin coats the tendrils (or axons) of the brain cells. Myelination connects various parts of the brain so that information moves much faster in the brain. Think of myelination as upgrading from muddy country roads to glasslike autobahns, so your car can zip through.

Myelination starts from the back of the brain and gradually makes its way forward. Now, at the back of the brain are the emotional and impulse centres. They are myelinated first. But the front of the brain, the prefrontal cortex is still on country roads, and it takes a few years for them to get upgraded. The front area of the brain is the voice of reason. Decision-making, self-control, rational thinking and faculties associated with maturity are in the prefrontal cortex. So, while happiness, sorrow, excitement, invincibility and other thrill-seeking impulses are travelling in the brain at warp speed, decision-making and self-control are moving slower. This explains why teenagers end up doing what seems incoherent to an adult. For a moment, think about your antics as a teenager. I'm sure many things will pop up that make you wonder, *What was I even thinking?* The physiological reason for teens behaving in illogical ways is a result of how their developing brain is processing the world.

One may think that myelination from back to front is a flaw. But it's in line with our evolution. As a hunter-gatherer, fight or flight impulse dominated our existence. Swift decisions on whether to run from the sabretooth tiger or fight back needed split-second emotional impulses. The development of the prefrontal cortex came much later, as human beings evolved and established themselves at the top of the food chain.

Parenting Tip: Meditate Together at Home

Meditation creates peace within. It helps us manage our emotional apparatus better. When parents meditate with their children, it helps their hearts come together. Across the globe, practitioners of Heartfulness, every day, at 9 p.m., local time, offer an intention of peace. For about 15 minutes, they close their eyes and meditate for universal love, brotherhood and peace. As you read these lines, it's 9 p.m. somewhere in the world, and someone is praying for you. This unbroken chain of silent peaceful intention has been going on since the early 1980s. It started from a quaint corner in India and today, across the globe, the silent intention creates ripples of peace. Adopt this practice in your family and see how it changes the environment at home.

Studies show that the teenage years are also a time of vulnerability. About 70 per cent of mental illnesses, including anxiety, eating and mood disorders and depression, appear first during the teen years and early adulthood. This is also the time when youth have the highest propensity to get hooked on drugs and develop addictive behaviours. The reward circuits of the brain are in full potency and if mental and emotional health are not good, then the teenager becomes vulnerable. Also, deficiencies in the development of the child's brain due to trauma (for example, exposure to neglect, violence, abuse, homelessness) are often revealed during the teenage years. For example, a traumatic childhood causes the brain circuits responding to stress to be well developed. As a result, the impulses to react and be aggressive are also well developed. But the compensatory circuits for self-control and composure may not be as well developed. So, it's possible that the child may need help and counselling during teen years to correct some of these tendencies.

Deficiencies in the development of the child's brain due to trauma, are often revealed during the teenage years.

With this understanding of the teenage brain, here are some suggestions about how to support your teenage children during these times of promise and pitfalls.

Recognize the Transition and Facilitate the Change

In cultures the world over, the transition to youth is formally recognized. Jewish people celebrate the bar or bat mitzvah. Parts of India celebrate the *Langa-Voni* and *Ritu Kala samskara*, Hispanics celebrate the *quinceañera and quinceañero*. Each culture has its own traditions and rituals which were designed such that the community came together and celebrated.

These rituals help the teenagers understand their responsibility in the community. The recognition by the elders also helps groom one's sense of self.

Today, even though we celebrate coming of age, in many cases we've forgotten the significance of these customs, and sometimes over-the-top celebrations overshadow the importance of the event. Coming of age is generally associated with rights. The right to drive, the right to vote, the right to drink and so on. However, we don't emphasize the duties that come with one's age. When rights and duties are both duly acknowledged, the transition from childhood to youth is smoother. If not, then adolescence is extended for a much longer period. In such cases, children may grow in age but not in maturity. If they don't take responsibility in their teenage years, it may become a pattern for the rest of their lives.

Use a Light Touch and Have Keen Eyes

When children are small, they aspire to be like their fathers and mothers. It's natural. But as children grow up and become teenagers, most of them stop feeling that way. Somewhere along the way, the respect they have for parents goes away. Your children, now teenagers, still love you, but parents need to start earning respect again. Parents need to evolve morally and spiritually to continue to earn their teenager's respect. They appreciate authenticity. They are idealistic and look up to people who are authentic. As a parent, share your successes *and* your failures with your teenager.

Once my boys came to me asking for some advice on a business clause. I reviewed the language and told them that in my days, I would sign contracts with much more lenient terms. I asked them to consult an investor friend of mine for some professional opinion. I also told them stories of the many ways in which I lost money in business. I could see that they liked the conversation, and I could also see how they both would muse about all my mistakes later on.

Our teenagers are not looking for perfection. They are looking for authenticity and love. As parents, when we embrace our vulnerabilities, acknowledge our errors and share life lessons, it will deepen the connection between our hearts. An honest conversation with them about what we may have done wrong in the past and how it affected our life will register much better than a lecture on what is right and wrong.

> As parents, when we embrace our vulnerabilities and share life lessons, it will elevate our position in the child's heart.

Who likes being corrected all the time? When our flaws are pointed out to us, it hurts. Youth are no exception. One approach I have seen work is to be very subtle with them. Find indirect ways to get your message across. For example, share stories with them—beautiful stories, inspiring stories. The problem is that we have stopped reading stories to them. Even when they are thirteen, fourteen, fifteen or eighteen, even when they are thirty, share a nice story. Share ideas that will make them think. When you read a profound philosophical message, share it with them with a lot of joy, 'My child, listen to this, how wonderful it is.' Just share it and leave it at that. Do not probe them after sharing and do not lecture them.

Use a *light touch* and have *keen eyes*.

Laugh together. Humour brings families closer. When was the last time you told your children a joke? When was the last time your children told you one?

Strict rules and constant nagging from parents frustrate teenagers. Over-cautiousness destroys the relationship with teenagers as much as neglect does. As parents, you need to be careful, but not show it. I know this can be difficult, when your teenager, whom you love so much, acts in the most incorrigible way. Do some breathing exercises, grind your teeth and hold it in. Your neurons have the myelin advantage.

Parenting Tip

If you know you are prone to lashing out, teenagers will match your decibel for decibel. Just as angelic newborns melt your heart, teenagers will make your heart humbler.

Conversation is important, and communication is crucial in the relationship. Laughter plays a key role in communication. It's a great way to normalize a situation and makes it easier to get the message across. Jokes that you used to share with little children don't have to stop as they become teenagers. Share a nice joke with them. Laugh together and laugh at the situation's life brings along. And remember dad jokes are always in season. Humour brings families closer.

How the Parents Give Feedback Matters a Lot

Mistakes are a part of any process of learning. Just as small children fall over many times when they are learning to walk, teenagers, too, trip at least a few times as they are learning the ropes of life.

How parents give feedback matters a lot. When your teenager makes a mistake, be sympathetic in an indirect way. Behave as though you don't know anything because their pride is riding high at that time. They don't want to show their mistakes to their parents whom they adore so much. The feeling of 'I don't want to let my parents down' is always there. Even though a teenager may be going haywire, this inner sense is always prevailing. That is why they lie. That is why they hide. Otherwise, if they were so proud of their actions, they would do them right in front of you. Their conscience is still active, still alive. They realize when they have made a mistake, and you can make it worse by reminding them, 'You see what you have done. I knew you were going to do this.' Then they rebel. The worst is reprimanding teenagers in front of their friends. Please avoid this. If you see something wrong, find a separate time and place to talk about it.

Parenting Tip: Ask this Question

When you meet other parents who have children much older than yours, ask them this simple question: 'What would you have done different when it comes to raising your children?'

Their answers will give insights into how you may want to approach your own parenting style and ideas.

When you watch them making a mistake and get into problematic situations, don't let them go too far. Educate them about the perils and offer positive feedback. One way to do this is by saying, 'I wish I had known. I would have helped you out, my child.' When you do this a few times, then they realize, 'My mother or my father told me that, but I didn't listen. They are more experienced than I am. Now it's time to listen.'

Of course, there are times when they are in harm's way. In that case, direct intervention is a must. But in general, be available, offer discreet guidance and ensure that children figure out solutions independently. This will help them grow in confidence.

In my experience when someone faces a problem, be it a child or a grown-up, they're looking for compassion. Listening with love to someone sharing their problem is enough. Most of the time, they don't need much more from us. When we listen with love, we give the person the safe space they need to express themselves and feel lighter.

When your child has a problem, walk with them, listen to them, make them feel comfortable and so loved that they feel you are with them. When children, especially adolescents can express their opinions at home and have an open dialogue, especially with their parents, those teenagers feel more confident when they step out of the home. They are mentally stronger and will do better at resisting bad habits and bad company. Giving your teenagers a safe space to vent gives them the confidence to share more with you.

For parents eager to play MacGyver (an 1980s action hero who can fix anything with WD40 and duct tape) to solve their child's problems, please slow down. Don't take over your children's problem and solve it for them. If they forgot the music notes at home despite your reminders, don't rush off to school to drop them off. Similarly, don't lend extra allowance because they mismanaged the budget. Let them learn to deal with their problems.

> For parents who are eager to play MacGyver and solve their children's' problems, please slow down. Do not take over their problem and solve it for them.

And then, there are times when your children do need your help. For example, your child has college applications due the next day, and the computer has crashed. While the blue screen of death is staring your child in the face, a parental lecture on cloud backups will be a tone-deaf approach. Now is the time to play Geek Squad to ensure that the college applications are submitted in time.

Youth are our future. Guide them, nurture them, correct them and love them, all the way to the moon and back.

Daily Dilemma:

Daaji, I heard your talk on 'Speaking with love'. I do try to speak with love as much as I can, and I feel that my teenagers do not even listen to what I am saying. They are not interested in what I say because I am not saying what they like to hear. I am a bit old-fashioned they say and the more I become soft and gentle and speak with love, the less they seem to listen to me! What to do?

Daaji: We don't speak with love because we want a certain outcome. We speak with love because that is the right thing to do. So, my suggestion is to speak with love with one and all, not just your children. Let this become a habit. Then it will add a different flavour to your relationship with your children.

About the lack of discipline that you are seeing at home, love and discipline are inseparable. They are like the poles of a magnet. Only one who loves will be bold enough to discipline both themselves and others. When the correctional ability is lost, love is also lost. It is because we love our children that we teach them. We correct them.

19

Experimentation, Thrill-Seeking and Friendships in Teen Years

Imagine this: you are watching *Mission Impossible 4* along with a group of teenagers. You've reached the scene where Ethan Hunt (played by Tom Cruise) is crawling down the windows of the Burj Khalifa like a spider with a death wish. Ethan is racing against time to intercept the enemy mole, and he jumps thirty floors, flailing in the air and somehow nails the landing into an open window. It's a riveting scene, and when Cruise jumps, you hold your breath and watch, but the teenagers who are already on the edge of their seats scream with more excitement than Tom Cruise himself.

The reason for this: the teenagers' brains served them a triple shot dopamine espresso.

Feel-good hormones like serotonin, dopamine, oxytocin and other endorphins are more potent during the teenage years. Research suggests that even though the dopamine levels in teens are lower than those of adults, the spikes of dopamine in response to experiences are higher in teens.[1]

The spikes of dopamine jolts them with a strong sense of being alive. But these spikes also drop fast, and before you know it, the *bored* eye-rolling teenager is back. A craving for the spikes drive teenagers to explore new areas, seek new experiences, enjoy new thrills and experiment with danger. This is why most habits like smoking, drinking and using mind-altering drugs take root in the teenage years.

'We cannot always build the future for our youth, but we can build our youth for the future.'

—Franklin Delano Roosevelt

The numbers prove this point. According to the CDC (The Centers for Disease Control and Prevention) in the USA, 37 per cent of high school students reported using marijuana in their lifetime, and 22 per cent reported use in the last 30 days.[2] The numbers are similar for teens who drink or smoke while in high school. Because these numbers are high does not mean this behaviour is acceptable or healthy. It also does not mean that making sure their child steers clear of drugs and alcohol is a lost cause, and parents should resign themselves to the fact that their child will also smoke and drink. What these numbers tell us is that our children are at risk. As parents, we need to educate them to make the right decisions. What they also tell us is that while teens may experiment, most of them also stay out of trouble and avoid becoming addicted. Otherwise, by now, we would have become a zombie society. With this understanding of the teenage psyche, let's focus on what parents can do to help their children make good choices.

Teach Your Child Decision-Making

Good decision-making is a skill that comes from making many decisions and learning from them. Young adults have to make some important decisions in their lives. Some of these decisions can have a significant long-term impact. So as parents, we need to train children early about mental models (frameworks for thinking) of making decisions. There are many good children's books dedicated to decision-making that I recommend parents read along with their children. Here, I can share with you some of the things I did with my children.

I often explained to my sons how I made decisions. I would sit down with them and tell them how I tackled a situation at work. For example, if I knew some associate was stealing at the Pharmacy I would explain to them how I would approach the situation. I explained how decisions turn into action. For example, I'd tell them that I said this to so and so because I knew he would react in this way and then do this thing. I would also let them listen in on my phone conversations so they learned how I managed the business.

My sons, who now manage a couple of businesses on their own tell me that these discussions helped them in understanding human behaviour.

Give Liberty and Build Trust

Give some level of liberty to your child. Smoking or drinking is not the end of the world. It is not that we are giving them the freedom to do anything they want, but at times we have to let children learn certain lessons on their own. When you come to know that your child is smoking, find some funny stories or movies depicting the negative effects of such habits and share them with your child. There is a lot of such information available on drugs, drinking, etc. Share it with them and let them think it over.

Also, rope in an elder cousin or a friend whom the child looks up to. Instead of speaking with your child yourself, have this person convey the importance of avoiding bad habits. Many tobacco cessation studies on teens have shown that if their peer group condemns such behaviour, it has a much better impact than parents saying, 'No. Don't do it.'[3] If your child still insists, go ahead, and give them the freedom. Tell him, 'I will buy you a carton of cigarettes. But see for yourself how it affects your studies and your physical well-being.' Show them the negative effects of such indulgence. This is, of course, an extreme example to make the point.

> Build trust with your children by allowing some mistakes to happen and then supporting them through those times.

Sometimes, children may also share to gauge your reaction. For example, they may share an incident about a friend drinking or smoking. How you react to this will send a message to your child. If you are understanding and suggest positive ideas to counsel your child's friend, you will make it easier for your child to confide in you. The idea is not about playing mind games with our children. As grown-ups, when we demonstrate the maturity to listen and understand them, children will recover from the mistakes they make and build resilience.

Once my younger son, who was in grade 8 in India at that time, got spanked by his schoolteacher. He was supposed to go to her for extra math lessons. Instead, he ran off with his friends to play basketball. I knew the teacher had a habit of spanking children. But this time around, she did hit my boy hard.

When my son came home that day, he saw my face and knew something was wrong. I called him over and in front of him, I called up his teacher. I apologized for my son's behaviour and also requested that she stop spanking children going forward. Not just my son, but all students. No more spanking. She understood where I was coming from, and the conversation ended cordially. After that, I went back to whatever I was doing. My son tip-toed out of the room. There was no point in chastising him more. He got the message. He also understood that 'Dad won't tolerate my bad behaviour, and Dad will always be there to watch my back.' The important thing is to build trust with your children and set clear boundaries.

The Power and Pressure of Friendships

When children become teenagers they shift their mental and emotional dependence from their parents to themselves. There is a streak of independence in their nature, and their social acceptance in their peer group is of immense importance. With today's lifestyle, independence and peer acceptance are important needs. Children leave home for school, and they need to make it on their own in a new environment. When they start their careers, they may need to move to a new city or even a new country. Building social connections with people outside one's family is an important life skill. During the teenage years, while friendships play an important role, those close friendships also come with peer pressure.

Statistics show that reckless behaviour in teenagers is largely a result of peer pressure. Most of them start smoking and drinking when they're in the company of friends. And the presence of teen passengers in a car increases the crash risk of unsupervised teen drivers. Moreover, this risk increases with each additional teen passenger.[4] As parents, the words 'peer pressure' make us cringe. The term conjures the image of a gullible teenager egged on by a brawly bunch of friends to do something reckless. But the story is more nuanced than this.

Professor Laurence Steinberg, distinguished university professor at Temple University, and his colleagues conducted extensive research in the area of peer pressure and they have coined the term 'peer effect'. What they mean by peer effect is that pressure is not necessary, mere presence is enough to have an effect on the behaviour of the teenager.[5] To prove how peer effect works, they gathered a group of adolescents, young adults and adults to play a car racing video game.[6] During the race, rewards were given for taking risks and those who finished fastest won the race. In one setting, the players sat alone and played the game. In another, the friends could watch the player from another room and give feedback through an intercom. The participants were connected to an fMRI machine to record the brain responses. What they found was remarkable.

The scientists observed that for the adolescents, the feedback from their peers on the intercom was like jet fuel for the impulse decision-making of the teens. The teens made 30 per cent more risky decisions and crashed 40 per cent more times than when they were playing alone! Just the presence of other teens was enough to provoke risk-taking behaviour.

Understanding the Benefits of Peer Effect

What do we take away from the studies conducted by Professor Steinberg and his team? Are friendships bad? Should we discourage group activities? Do parents need to hover above their children all the time? Even though the findings of the peer effect feel alarmist, there is a silver lining here, and it's a good one.

Think about This

What do we take away from the studies conducted by Professor Steinberg and his team? Are friendships bad? Do parents need to hover above their children all the time?

But before I get to that, I want to share a personal experience from my days in school. I studied pharmacy at the L.M. College in Ahmedabad, Gujarat, India. During my time there, I had a group of friends. We'd all get up at the crack of dawn and one of us would make tea. After a quick cold-water shower, and a cup of hot tea, we would meditate together. Over time, the word spread that a group of boys meditated together. We came to be known as the 'meditators group'. When we walked together on campus, people looked at us with admiration. Some of our professors were inspired by us and they also started meditating.

Our group did well in studies and most of us secured the top percentile in grades. We had a lot of fun too. Sometimes when we went to the movies, we would start with the first show at eight o'clock in the morning, watch the next one at eleven, then another at two in the afternoon and we'd end with a grand finale at six in the evening. By the time the day ended, I would remember the beginning of one movie, the middle of the eleven or two o'clock shows, and possibly the ending of the last one. It was a colossal mash-up of impressions, and I tell you, it was sublime fun.

Sometimes when a student in our college was struggling with their studies, the professors would suggest that they 'go and join Kamlesh's group for a few months. It will help you get better.' We would take the student under our wing, and he would start hanging out with us. Over time, the student's grades improved and as a bonus, they'd also developed the habit of meditation. All my friends who started meditating with me back then, meditate even today. They have all done well in life, and they have banked enough credits for the afterlife too.

Through research, Professor Steinberg and the team established that the *company we keep matters*.

The point here is not to hark about how good we were in our teenage years. The key takeaway is about the wisdom of my professors. They intuitively knew the power of peer effect and its benefits. They knew that to drive a change in behaviour, change in the environment was necessary. If a struggling student needed help, the correct approach was to nudge the student to choose better company. The benefit of the good company had a reinforcing effect on everyone.

The research on peer effect shows that it's neither positive nor negative. Instead, it depends on how it's used. Through research, Professor Steinberg and team proved the wisdom behind the idea that the *company we keep matters*. Isn't this what elders across cultures have said time and time again? Choose your friends carefully is one of the key messages from *Aesop's Fables,* the *Hitopadesha* and the *Panchatantra*. The fables, passed down from one generation to the next, teach us that we must be discerning about the friends we choose.

Parents are right to be concerned about who children spend their time with. We need to ensure that our children are friends with children having good values and behaviours. Doing so will set up a positive circle of influence for the children. They will motivate and watch out for one another. As parents, we are not our child's friend. We can be friendly with our children but our role as parents is to care, discipline and love.

Daily Dilemma:

My teenage girl has suddenly changed. She has gone very quiet and aloof. How do I approach a conversation with her?

Daaji: Most children undergo a transformation in their teenage years. They are coming to terms with their sense of self. They are in the process of shaping their identity and reflecting it through their personality and behaviour. Some children are vocal about the changes going on, while others are quieter.

If you notice an abrupt change in behaviour for no reason, it's important to have a sit down with your child and try to understand what is going on. Don't rush these conversations like an item on a checklist. If something is not right, your child may take some time to open up. Be patient.

After a few conversations, if you feel whatever your child is going through is a natural shift in personality, then it's okay. If you are still uneasy, reach out to a therapist.

Principle 8

Lifestyle Is an Expression of One's Attitudes

20

Sleep Cycles Are an Investment

In 1952, science-fiction writer Ray Bradbury published the short story 'A Sound of Thunder'[1] in which two hunters time travel back 66 million years to the Cretaceous period to hunt a T-Rex. The hunt goes terribly wrong and the hunters retreat to the present, where they notice significant changes. The words in the English language are both spoken and spelled differently, the elected leaders are different and even the air smells funny.

Perplexed, one of the hunters looks down to find a dead butterfly from the past stuck in the muddy soles of his shoes. The death of a flapping butterfly (that was not supposed to die yet) millions of years ago set off a series of events that ripple across time.

Ray Bradbury took '*butterfly effect*' from the textbooks of chaos theory and made it a part of English vernacular. In our bodies, sleep (deep or disturbed) sets off a butterfly effect that ripples across our physical, mental and spiritual selves.

> A good night's sleep can trigger a butterfly effect of positive benefits, including better brain health, improved memory, glowing skin, happier mood, better digestion, improved virility and so on.

A good night's sleep triggers a butterfly effect of positive benefits, including better brain health, improved memory, glowing skin, happier mood, better digestion, virility, fertility and the list goes on. When we sleep well, those around us also benefit. We are in better control of our emotions and are more friendly with family and friends. Our creativity improves and its easier for the brain to handle tougher cognitive challenges.

But night after night spent wrestling with the pillows unleashes a butterfly effect of problems. When we don't sleep well, our bodies are tired, leading to inflammation and aches. Our immunity drops and we age faster. Our gut microbiome is disturbed, and our digestion, heart and mental health also take a hit. Just a week of sleep deprivation increases the body's resistance to insulin and puts blood sugars on the pre-diabetic or diabetic spectrum.

When we don't sleep well the brain doesn't detox. Memory falters and we can't retain information the way we normally could. Disturbed sleep increases irritability, which spills over into interactions with family and co-workers. Sleep deprivation is among the leading causes of road accidents.[2]

Most human beings spend one-third of their life in sleep. How well we sleep determines the quality of the remaining two-thirds.

How Much Sleep Do We Need?

Age Group		Recommended Hours of Sleep Per Day
Age Group	0-3 months	14-17 hours (National Sleep Foundation) No recommendation (American Academy of Sleep Medicine)
Infant	4-12 months	12-16 hours per 24 hours (Including naps)
Toddler	1-2 years	11-14 hours per 24 hours (Including naps)
Preschool	3-5 years	10-13 hours per 24 hours (Including naps)
School Age	6-12 years	9-12 hours per 24 hours
Teen	13-18 years	8-10 hours per 24 hours
Adult	18-60 years	7 or more hours per 24 hours
	61-64 years	7-9 hours
	65 years and older	7-8 hours

Source: cdc.gov website

Basic Understanding of Sleep Cycles

Spoiler alert! This section can be read in two lines or two pages. The choice is yours. The two-line version is, 'Early to bed, early to rise makes you healthy and wise.' If you are convinced, then you can go to the next section 'Sleep, subtle bodies and the soul.'

If you are curious to know why sleep cycles are important, then two-page version helps. So here we go.

Our sleep switches between cycles of non-rapid eye movement (NREM) sleep, and rapid eye movement (REM) sleep through the night. We first experience NREM sleep, followed by a shorter period of REM sleep, and then the cycle repeats. Dreams typically happen during REM sleep.

Non-Rapid Eye Movement Sleep

NREM sleep (also called slow wave sleep) has three stages:[3]

Stage 1. In the first five to ten minutes of going to sleep, our waking consciousness is still active and it's easy for us to wake up. We feel drowsy in this state.

Stage 2. This is the light sleep stage. In light sleep, the heart rate slows down, and the body temperature drops a little. During light sleep, the brain begins putting out short bursts of activity, which scientists refer to as *sleep spindles*. These are like noise cancellation devices. They cancel out the external noises and protect sleep. The more sleep spindles, the better we sleep.

Stage 3. Once we enter the deep sleep stage, it is harder to wake up. Deep sleep is time for restoration and rejuvenation of the body. Deep sleep is also referred to as NREM sleep. Yogic science refers to deep sleep as *sushupti*.

* * *

NREM sleep is the deepest sleep of the night. The brain releases the growth hormone from the pituitary gland during deep sleep. Especially in children, this sleep helps in the development of muscles, organs and strengthens the immune system.

> Especially in children, NREM sleep helps with development of muscles, organs and strengthening the immune system.
> NREM sleep is also when the brain detoxes.

NREM sleep is also when the brain detoxes. During this phase of sleep, the cerebro-spinal fluid flows through the spaces between the brain and cleanses out all toxins that may have deposited during the day. Researchers have found a sophisticated plumbing mechanism in the brain that is activated during sleep and cleanses the brain and the neural pathways for the next day.[4] This cleansing protects the brain from unwanted protein build-up that may cause diseases such as Alzheimer's and dementia later in life.

One of the crucial tasks performed during NREM sleep is consolidation of memories. It fosters the saving of relevant memories and getting rid of those that are not considered important. It is a process of sorting and weeding out connections, called synaptic pruning (which we referred to earlier also).

Rapid Eye Movement Sleep

After a cycle of NREM that usually lasts for ninety minutes, the REM sleep cycle kicks in. In this cycle of sleep we dream, so it's also called dream state sleep. Yogic science refers to dream state sleep as *swapna*.

During active sleep, the body is still, but the brain is active, racing in fact. The eyes dart back and forth behind closed lids, blood pressure increases and the breathing pattern speeds up.

An electroencephalogram (EEG) of someone during REM sleep looks almost the same as the EEG of a person in the waking state, although one is still asleep and the body is still immobile.

REM sleep plays a vital role in harmonizing the experiences we have in the world outside. The impressions that were sorted and arranged during NREM sleep are *organized* and *integrated* during this cycle. This is a creative process, and REM sleep helps the brain decide which connections need to be strengthened. The overall model of the world, the experiences and understanding is improved during in REM sleep. Impaired memory, hallucinations, attention issues—all are a result of disturbed REM sleep.

Going to sleep late compromises the NREM phase of sleep, which affects physical health and cognitive health. If one wakes up too early or works a shift that disturbs the REM cycle, then that creates its own set of problems. A good night's sleep brings emotional stability and good health. It is crucial that we offer ourselves and our children the opportunity for enough sleep each day.

Sleep, Subtle Bodies and the Soul

Let's say you are out taking a walk and you see a tree. How do you know it's a tree? What happened in the interactions between your eyes and your mind that you could conclude that, yes, this is a tree? Here is a breakdown of the steps:

1. The sensory organs (in this case the eyes) receive the external inputs.
2. The optic nerves transfer the inputs to the brain.
3. Our *thinking* gathers the relevant memories.
4. The *intellect* receives the memories and thoughts. It now deliberates and decides.
5. The decision is submitted to the *ego*. The ego responds 'yes' or 'no'.

Steps 3, 4 and 5 are played out in the field of *consciousness*.

The soul remains a witness.

The soul is the life-force that powers the body. Think of the human brain as the hardware of a computer. There are many software programs installed on this computer. The four main programs are consciousness, ego, intellect and thinking. Combined, the four main programs are called the subtle bodies.

The soul is the electricity, the life-force. When we see a tree and recognize it as one, it is because of the interaction of the physical body and the subtle body. While intellect, ego and thinking are somewhat self-explanatory, some of you may be wondering what consciousness is.

Think of consciousness as a spectrum of awareness. Just as light has infrared, UV and visible, as three broad categories, consciousness also is divided into three main categories. These are subconscious, conscious and super conscious.

When we are awake, our consciousness is projected outward to what is going on around us. The thinking, intellect and ego are busy working with the senses to help us perform daily tasks.

But when we are in deep sleep (NREM), the subtle bodies are focused inward. They align in close resonance with the soul. It's as if the soul is the warm fire around which the subtle bodies bundle up and sleep. Just as the physical body grows and develops during sleep, the subtle bodies also recharge when we are in deep sleep.

Let the Sleeper Sleep

During my days with my Master, I observed that he *never* disturbed anyone who was asleep. I saw this happen many times. He would be preparing to conduct a meditation session, and if he saw someone asleep, he would gently tell those around the person, 'Let him sleep. Don't wake him up.' This wasn't cordial behaviour from a caring teacher. Beyond the human courtesy extended by my Master, there is spiritual significance to his actions. Through my observations of sleep patterns, I have concluded that one should let the sleeper sleep. Especially, when it comes to children, don't wake them up forcefully. Always allow children wake up on their own.

When we forcefully wake up a child their subtle bodies are tormented from such a shock.

The ego, which is active during waking hours, is inactive during sleep. In resonance with the soul, the ego lowers its barriers to any spiritual work that may happen during sleep. The intellect, too is active during the day. During sleep, the intellect is at rest, further allowing any spiritual work that may be happening. During sleep, thinking also subsides altogether. Our consciousness is also tuned inward towards the soul. So, during sleep, ego, thinking, intellect and consciousness are all drawn inward towards the soul and are in a state of rest and contentment.

Sleep offers an important window for spiritual work to happen. In most cultures there is a practice of offering prayer before going to sleep. The wisdom behind this practice is applying your intention to work on the subconscious mind. Before going to sleep when you offer prayer, you allow spiritual work to carry on all throughout the night. Thus, you use the time of sleep to not only benefit you physically and mentally, but it also serves a spiritual purpose.

When we wake a child forcefully, we yank the child out of many levels of work that may be happening. Forcefully waking up a child is the equivalent of tasing the child to wake them up.

Please adapt your lifestyle to give children a good amount of sleep, so that they wake up on their own. When they grow up, school, jobs and other commitments will anyway infringe on their sleep. So while you can, give them ample windows of sleep opportunity.

Yet, there are times when we have to wake them up. In such cases, do this: give yourself ten to fifteen minutes to wake your children. Gently call out to them. Do this in a soft, loving voice. Softly rub their feet and massage them. Do this for a few minutes and see if they wake up. If they don't after a few minutes massage their feet again and gently callout to them. Sleep is nature's state of contentment. Sleep is the anchor for the waking consciousness. Sleep is the time for rest and rejuvenation. Let the sleeper sleep.

Disturbing the Body Clock

All living creatures, including plants, animals and humans have evolved a rhythm that works on a fine-tuned body clock called the circadian rhythm (*circa* meaning *around,* and *dian* derived from *day*). The circadian rhythms have evolved over millennia.

The human body clock developed during our days as a hunter-gatherer and we're still on that same clock today. A few hours before we wake up, the body clock shuts down melatonin, the sleep hormone. Gradually, breathing becomes faster and the body temperature goes up a little, enabling us to wake up from sleep. During the day, our activities such as eating, digestion, respiration and excretion are governed by the body clock. At night, as the light dims, the body clock kicks in the sleep cycle to prepare us for a restful night.

For newborns, the circadian rhythms are not set into action. However, in just a few months, the circadian rhythms activate, and the baby develops a cycle of waking up, eating and sleeping. Light is a trigger for the circadian rhythm, and so is hunger. Light and hunger trigger the genes that put the body clock into action. Our discipline in maintaining the body clock helps in our health and well-being.

For this reason, the elders instituted discipline at home to regulate the timings for eating, sleeping and other activities. Conditioning the body from the outside by following a routine that cooperates with the inner rhythm helps us physically, mentally and emotionally. Such conditioning is akin to swimming with the current of water as opposed to against it, which is what happens when we don't stick with a proper routine.

However, the modern-day lifestyle has disrupted the rhythms, and the biggest culprit is the availability of light, on-demand. Before the invention of electricity, most non-natural light came from lanterns, and prior to that, from sitting around the fire pit. However, the invention of the light bulb changed the game. Lights from bulbs, screens and other electronic devices all have a detrimental effect on our natural circadian rhythm.

Dr Satchin Panda, an eminent researcher at the Salk Institute for Biological Studies, and his team made a remarkable discovery in 2002.[5] They found that inside the eyes, in the retina cells, is a protein called *melanopsin*, which is activated primarily by *blue light*. The melanopsin cells in the eyes then indicate to the brain that it's daytime, even though it's night and you are browsing on your tablet in bed.

Dr Panda and his teams are credited with the introduction of the blue light filter that we find today in most smartphones and devices. It inhibits the flow of blue light thus allowing for the circadian rhythms in the body to function well. He, like many other doctors, recommends avoiding using devices right before sleep.

Sleep Is an Investment

'Compound interest is the eighth wonder of the world. He who understands it earns it, he who doesn't, pays it.' This quote often attributed to Einstein is important because it explains that when you start early, invest regularly then over time, the returns are exponential.

Why do I talk about compound interest when discussing sleep? Sleep is the long game.

Sleep is the compound interest for your health. Every day that you sleep well is an investment. Start investing in your children's sleep and teach them good sleep habits early on. For all my young friends who think sleep is overrated or brag about how they can get away with just a few hours of sleep, think about compound interest and its wonders. When we sleep well, the body rejuvenates, the mind feels fresh and the soul is enlivened.

Finally, for my dear reader, if it's already late at night, and you feel like reading further, please don't. Put this book aside and get a good night's sleep.

Daily Dilemma:

My child of ten is addicted to video games, and continues to play well into the night. As a result, it is a struggle to wake him up for school in the morning and his concentration suffers too. What should I do?

Daaji: Would you allow your child to roam alone in a scary ghetto just because the child wants to? No parent would allow that. Today, children roam around in scary digital ghettos in the privacy of their rooms. It starts with playing games online or sharing videos on social platforms and soon things can get out of hand. Learn how parental controls work and put them in place. Parents can be friendly, but you are not their friend. You are the parent. Set boundaries and enforce them as needed.

21

Poverty and Prosperity Paradox

In April 1981, my Guru, Babuji, visited Ahmedabad for three days. Hundreds of people from nearby towns and villages travelled to Ahmedabad and joined him in meditation. Arrangements had to be made for transport, food, accommodation and other facilities. I was in pharmacy college back then and was one of the volunteers.

My task was to take care of transport. It meant ferrying people to and from the train station and the bus depot. As with any volunteer work, it also meant helping out with other tasks such as medicine runs for the elderly, milk runs for the children and last-minute logistics at the meditation venue.

On the final day of his visit, Babuji shared a parting message. It was a two-line message in the form of a couplet. I will share that couplet here in Urdu and then its translation:

'Raahein talab mein aise bekhabar ho gaye,
manzil pe aake manzil ko dhoondhete hain.'

'We are so engrossed with the path, that even when we reach the goal, we continue searching for it.'[1]

This couplet explains the problem of being engrossed in the details and losing sight of the goal. Parents can relate to this, especially regarding their child's grades. The goal of going to a school is to learn, and grades are a way to measure how well the student is learning.

But what ends up happening? Most of the time, getting top grades becomes the focus, and the children end up cramming before the exams to get good grades. In fact, most of them forget what they learned within days after the exams. Focusing on grades and losing sight of learning is a classic example of 'medium maximization'. We maximize focus on the grades (the medium) and lose sight of the goal, which is learning.

Medium maximization keeps us going in circles, and we lose track of the goal. A goal that we all pursue is happiness. And what's one common medium to pursue happiness? Its money. We all think that money will make us happy, and nothing wrong with it. Money does contribute to our happiness. Everything takes money. Even to read this book, you spent some money. But you will also agree that we often get stuck in medium maximization when it comes to money? So as elders how do we teach our children the role of money? How do we help them understand the value of money in the larger scheme of life? We will be covering these questions in the rest of the chapter.

Thinking about Money Differently

Can money buy happiness? A study of lottery winners shows that with all the money they win, at the end of two years, they are back to the same levels of happiness they had before the lottery. Does that mean we don't need money to be happy? Financial stress is among the top stressors for families. So, while money may not keep you happy all the time, it does eliminate some stress from life.

We need to think about money in a different way. Money by itself is neither good nor bad. Money is a *necessity*. Like petrol is a necessity for a car. Without it the car won't run. But just because it's a necessity you don't overfill the tank. You need money to take care of yourself and your loved ones. The body needs food, water, shelter and clothing, all of which need money.

I suggest you think of money as energy. Whether the energy is beneficial or harmful depends on how you use it. For example, fire keeps a person warm. However, the same fire can also burn down the house. Is fire good or bad? It's a rhetorical question. In the same way, whether money helps you raise a happy family or not depends on how you use it.

I often give the example of a bird flying in the sky. For a bird to soar, both the wings need to be strong and well-balanced. If either wing is weak, the bird goes around in circles. Likewise, human life also has two wings, the material and the spiritual.

Too much emphasis on the material, and one gets afflicted with *materialism*. But, on the other hand, running away from responsibilities and living life in jungles is *asceticism*. In either case, materialism or asceticism are examples of medium maximization, and life goes round in circles without making progress.

In today's time's parents are more concerned about materialism and how to protect children from its effects. Materialism is a value system that places importance on wealth, status, power, possessions and a display of these as symbols of superiority over the other human being. Materialism, when left unchecked, becomes an addiction where more of the drug is needed to get to the same high.

How Does Materialism Affect Us?

Materialism keeps you running on the treadmill without answering the question of how much is enough. It is a classic case of medium maximization of money to seek out happiness. Leo Tolstoy's story 'How Much Land Does a Man Need' exemplifies the extremes to which materialism can afflict one's psyche.[2]

In the story, a peasant named Pahom is very possessive of his land. He keeps buying and selling land, and his fortune keeps growing. Then, one day he is introduced to the Bashkirs, who are simple-minded people and own vast tracts of land.

Pahom goes to them to buy their land, and the Bashkirs' offer is very unusual. Pahom can walk starting at daybreak, on as much land as he can, marking his route with a spade along the way for a sum of 1000 rubles. All the land he covers will be his if he returns to his starting point by sunset that day. But if he doesn't reach the starting point, he loses the money and gets no land. A delighted Pahom runs like a possessed man and covers a lot of ground. Towards the end of the day, he realizes he is far from the starting point and runs back as fast as possible to the waiting Bashkirs. He finally arrives at the starting point just as the sun sets. The Bashkirs cheer his good fortune, but exhausted from the run, Pahom drops dead. His servant buries him in a grave six feet long, thus answering, 'How much land a man needs?'

Materialism glorifies things over people, and as a result, people lose sight of what's important in life.

> Materialism glorifies things over people and as a result, people become self-centred.

Berkeley psychologists Paul Piff and Dacher Keltner have done some insightful research about how money affects human behaviour. Through quizzes, online games and lab experiments, they showed that living high on the socioeconomic ladder (meaning lots of money) can colloquially speaking, dehumanize people.[3] It can make them less ethical, more selfish, more insular and less compassionate than other people. It can make them more likely, as Piff demonstrated in one of his experiments, 'to take candy from a bowl of sweets designated for children'.[4]

Keltner and his colleagues also conducted studies about how social class influences compassion towards people who are suffering. In a study, they asked participants to watch a video while having their heart rate monitored. They showed a video of children who have cancer. After watching the video, participants indicated how much compassion they felt while watching the video.

The study results showed that participants with less income and education were likelier to report feeling compassion while watching the video. But, more importantly, the research also showed 'how upper-class individuals are worse at recognizing the emotions of others and less likely to pay attention to people they are interacting with (e.g., by checking their cell phones or doodling)'.[5]

The idea behind sharing this research is not to label rich people as heartless and money as an evil force. What the research is showing us is that becoming wealthy may decrease one's compassion. Why does this happen? Having more should make one more generous. It should motivate one to pay it forward.

The answer from Piff and his team is *empowerment*. Money gives a feeling of freedom and independence from others. Money reduces one's reliance on others, so why does anyone need to care for that person? It makes one self-focused and puts one in a spiral of selfishness. The more one has, the more one wants. In the pursuit of more, we isolate ourselves from others.

Going back to our example of the bird with two wings, what helps the bird fly straight? It's the tail. The tail gives control of the flight. The tail is a metaphor for one's inner compass. To live an integrated life, where spirituality is infused into all our actions, we need to keep fine-tuning our inner compass.

Time and Love of the Parents Is Crucial

Our role as parents lies in instilling a strong foundation of character in children, so their inner compass is well calibrated. When parents lead an integrated life and channel higher purpose and meaning into their actions, children too pick up on this good habit.

Having money ensures parents can be good *providers* for their children. The best schools, excellent tutors, international vacations, the latest gadgets and whatnot. Providing for children makes parents feel good.

Especially for self-made parents who didn't have what they needed while growing up, being a good provider is a way to make up for that loss. Nothing wrong with it. But the challenge most parents face today is how to teach children the value of money. We are all too familiar with conversations that start like this: 'When I was your age, I had to walk a mile to get to school,' or 'The first time I had a good pair of shoes was when I was in sixth grade' and so on.

But such comparisons lose their impact over time. Children are not motivated by such examples, and there is a reason for this. While it's true that you or your father might have walked barefoot to school, or your parents may have grown up in extreme poverty, your child hasn't experienced it. When a child has grown up in abundance, parents need to address the area where scarcity exists. And that area is *togetherness*.

Research after research shows what our intuition already tells us. What children care about is the presence of their parents in their lives. The importance of money goes down after a certain amount, but the importance of parental love and presence in the child's life hardly diminishes. Children want more togetherness with their parents, not less. But the relative increase in wealth doesn't help after a certain limit. It's like the law of diminishing returns where after a certain amount of personal wealth, your quality of life doesn't change much. But when it comes to relationships, togetherness always helps.

Parents' presence in a child's life reassures them. They feel comfortable about sharing their challenges and issues with their parents. So, no matter how much time you spend with your child, increase it. It will only do good.

Ensure that family meals are a staple. In a research study to understand the relationship between family meals and the well-being of children, it was found that the frequency of family meals was inversely proportional to a child's tobacco, alcohol and marijuana use, low GPA, suicidal tendencies and depression.[6]

Families that eat together grow together. Families that pray together rise together.

Parents know most of the things that I am sharing. What they struggle with is time poverty. Stretched thin between jobs and making sure the bills get paid, most parents cannot give the time they want to. For single parents, everything is doubly difficult. I want to assure you that your children understand your struggles. They may not express it, but in their hearts, they know, 'Mama, Papa are working hard. They love me and care for me.'

For parents, who, for whatever reason, are taking their time away from children and prioritizing parties and social commitments, please rethink your time allocation. Prioritize your child's emotional needs. Parental supervision and support are important for the child. Togetherness in relationships are created with time and attention. Being a good provider is not the same as being a good parent.

A Personal Story

I had a friend who was from Fiji, and we studied pharmacy together in India. We moved to the US around the same time, and we both landed jobs as pharmacists in New York City. He came from a large family. His father, mother, two uncles, wives and children all lived together under one roof in Fiji. The patriarch of the family, my friend's grandfather, was still alive. He was a wise man, and he wished to see his family prosper. So, he sent some money to my friend in New York and asked him to start a hotel business in the US. My friend got to work, and for a few years, he worked two jobs, a pharmacist during the day and a hotelier by night.

It was a lot of elbow grease, and he put his everything into building the hotel. Over time, the business took off and he acquired one more hotel property. To support the growing business, more family members immigrated to the US, and my friend also gave up the pharmacy job and began working in the hotel business full time. To give you an idea of the scale of the business, imagine owning dozens of Marriott and Hilton hotels at prime locations across the US. The business was a bumper hit.

Besides investing money in the hotel business, my friend's grandfather also sent one of the sons to India with some money to start a salt business. That business also took off. In a few years, the salt business became a major supplier to India's big brands of salt makers.

As time went by, the grandfather passed away, and the brothers continued to live with their families in Fiji. There was growing unease, though. In the old man's time, there was an honour-bound contract that the family wealth would be equally distributed amongst the three brothers. Those were days when words held more sway than a paper contract. However, when the businesses were incorporated, for some reason, my friend's name was not on the paperwork.

With time, things began changing, and the familial bonds were not as cordial as before. My friend started feeling uneasy. As the business kept growing, so did his unease. One day he broached the subject of asset allocation with his uncles. He did not ask for his share or a split in the business. All he asked for was some paperwork that gave clarity on what he owned.

The elder uncle frostily balked, 'The hotels are mine. Thank you for your services. I can calculate a salary for your work and pay that off with interest. But, don't harbour any illusions of equity in the business. It was my share of the money that was invested, and the paperwork also says so.' That was it. In one statement, my friend was finished. He couldn't come to terms with the betrayal and took to drinking and started wasting away his life.

One day, he decided to travel to India and approach his other uncle, the salt mine owner and request him to share that business. It was a more cordial conversation with the uncle in India, but the result was the same. My friend was courteously shown the door. Distraught and defeated, he returned to the US and spent much time depressed. Finally, he fell back on his pharmacy license and started working as a pharmacist to make a living.

Why do I share this painful story?

As wealth grows in the family, ensure that values also grow. Ensure that wallet growth goes hand in hand with wisdom growth. Focus on the moral fabric and ensure that the spirit of unity in a family is emphasized.

As parents, keep your focus on helping children grow into outstanding human beings. What do I mean by outstanding when it comes to children? Outstanding children have developed a sense of 'self' that is authentic, capable, loving, creative, in control and moral.[7] These qualities may depend on money to some extent, but they do depend on the character foundation that has been laid in the child.

Teach Children Practically

Teach your children how to be clear and precise in dealings about money. Teach them to be careful and clear in financial transactions, especially with family members and friends. A candid and clear conversation, in the beginning, will avoid misunderstandings later on. Give children an understanding of how money works and how to manage money.

When my children were young, around eight or ten years old, I would show them the weekly reports from the pharmacies. These reports included weekly sales, prescription volume, inventory and other details. Then, I would ask them to fill up this information in excel sheets. Once they did this, I would have them consolidate data from all the pharmacies. They loved doing this work for me over the weekends.

After a few weeks of doing this, I taught them how to read the data. By looking at the numbers, I could tell which pharmacist was working hard and at which pharmacy theft was taking place. I taught them about human behaviour and being pragmatic in financial dealings. Some time ago, my younger son was having a chat with me. He said, 'Dad since you stopped monitoring the business, we never caught any theft in the store.' I think everyone is now honest (or my boys weren't paying attention when I was teaching them).

To Teach Responsibility, Give Responsibility

If we want our children to grow up into responsible adults, we need to give them *real* responsibilities early on in life. Give them responsibility and let them learn from their mistakes. At work and home, I give responsibility and trust the people to get the job done. For example, when my younger son was in medical school in India, I asked him to check out a nearby property. He took a few days to scout it and suggested that it was a good property.

A week later, I called him and said that I had bought the property and now he should build a house there. I could hear the shock in his voice. He understood that I trusted him so much that after one phone call, I bought the property. And now he needed to build a house. I wired the money and left everything else to him. I never asked him for any updates. He would share the progress, and I would listen. It took him a few years to complete the project. And he built a beautiful house. That experience of managing the project while studying in med school served him well later on in building his business as a young entrepreneur.

Family and friends often complain that I am too trusting. But my policy in life is that *people are good and want to do right*. Of course, sometimes mistakes happen, people may cheat too. But trust is the currency to build responsibility. Trust your children, keep an eye and allow them to grow.

Finally, understand that money and happiness are not related all the way. Happy people may be rich, rich people may be happy, but money does not buy happiness. The real wealth that you can shower on your child is your presence in the child's life. Being present to connect with them, listening to what they are going through, hearing their ideas and being there for them as a wall of support. Presence is the real challenge in parenting. See how you can adapt your lifestyle to create the time and connection with your child, the real wealth that they truly care about.

Daily Dilemma:

My daughter loves everything colourful and sparkly, and usually I am happy to indulge her demands. But lately I have noticed that her demands are more like orders and not requests, and that concerns me. What should I do?

Daaji: A few years ago, I was speaking to a girl. She was around ten at that time. It was back to school season, and I asked her what she bought for school. She told me that she had everything she needed, but she bought a box of crayons for her friend and a set of pencils for her brother. I was touched by this girl's generosity.

Instead of correcting your girl, ask her what she would like to buy for her friends. Let her widen the circle of thinking. This will be a good first step. Then I also suggest that you both do some volunteer work at a local orphanage or a senior centre. Once your daughter experiences the joys of sharing and caring, her demeanour will change.

22

Conscious Eating Habits

For most of my childhood, we didn't have electricity in our village. So the routine at home was in keeping with the sunrise and sunset. The elders woke at dawn and soon the house hummed with activity. By dusk, the routine at home also slowed down. After the evening prayers, we would all have dinner together and relax. During summers, the neighbours would get together in the courtyard, eat together and share the stories of the day. Food brought together the sense of community, not just while eating but also while making the food. The women of the households would get together and clean the grain, make pickles and prepare the breads.

My father who was an ayurvedic doctor kept an eye out for changing seasons and advised my mother about the foods that would help boost immunity. My mother took these suggestions and prepared food that was nutritious and tasty. In hindsight, I can see that the guiding principle in the family was to partake of food that honoured the body, the mind and the soul, and this principle was followed without much hoo-ha. There were no announcements of going on a diet or eating superfoods. It was a matter of general discipline and that's how our house functioned.

From my childhood days in my village, Kalla, until the time of this writing—almost sixty years now food habits in India have changed significantly. The food we eat today and the way we eat have changed—in some areas for the better, and in some for the worse. The supply chain of trucks and trains hauling food across the nation has reduced the inequity in access and affordability of food. The social programmes that focus on food for school children and expectant mothers are also the right steps towards a healthier nation.

While access to food has improved, the habits around food eating are a cause for much concern, especially in India. Specifically, eating junk food that's causing the epidemic of obesity, hypertension and diabetes. India is deemed to become the diabetes capital of the world.[1] Once thought of in India, as the rich man's disease, diabetes is growing fastest in the middle class and poorer strata of urban India.[2] Sedentary lifestyles, the availability of cheap processed foods and lack of diabetes testing combined with genetic propensity are the main reasons for the explosive growth of the disease.

Another contributor to poor eating habits is the expense of locally sourced and organic foods. Growing up in the village, life was different. All the food we ate was local. Farm-to-table was the way of life for us. Fresh homemade preserves and pickles were a staple and there was barely any processed food at home. Today, organic and locally sourced food is expensive, and most people can't afford it. The community feeling around food is also lost. To corral everyone at home for family dinners takes effort, and to make mealtimes screen-free takes even more.

It is crucial that we not only feed our children healthy diets but that we instil in them the importance of eating these foods. There are many books that explain the importance of a balanced diet and how to instil healthy eating habits in children. What's not discussed as much is the role of food in our spiritual development. With what attitude should we prepare and eat food? How can we teach the right attitudes to children? Knowing these answers parents can bring together the best of nutrition science and the spiritual importance of food.

Cooking: Community, Purity and Love

In Greek, the word for 'cook' is *mageiras,* which shares the etymology with the word 'magic'. Cooking is the magic that brings the family together. A home where cooking is respected forges deep connections and memories for the family and the loved ones. But this doesn't mean winding the clock back to where mothers and sisters were relegated to the kitchens. What it means is that, as a family, we need to give food and its preparation their due place in our day-to-day lives. As sentient beings, we need to ensure that the way we cook and the way we eat reflects an evolutionary outlook to our growth as human beings.

Squirrels store away acorns, bees collect the nectar and bears stash away meats, but it's only the human being that cooks. Cooking is a part of our collective learning. Through cooking, we create a sense of togetherness and community that we all cherish. Scan your own memories, and you might find that in most of the cherished ones, food plays a central role. Whether it's a birthday, a wedding, a campfire or a festival—cooking, community and eating together weaves the fabric of our shared humanity.

Food weaves a sacred thread through this fabric. The wafer of the Eucharist, sweets after puja, matzah during Passover and dates during Ramadan, are a few examples from across cultures that exemplify the idea of purity and the sacredness of food. Even customs that are secular today find their roots in cultural norms that held food as a sacred offering. For example, lighting candles on a birthday cake is said to have come from the ancient Greeks, who would make round cakes to honour Artemis, the goddess of the moon. The lit candles on the cake represented the glow of the moon, and the smoke from the blown-out candles carried the prayers and wishes of those at the ceremony to the goddess who lived in the heavens.

Outside of festivals and ceremonies, the idea of purity and food can be seen even in daily life. For example, in the traditional households of south India, it's common to see elderly women set aside clothing that they wear only when cooking. Usually, after taking a bath, they put on these clothes, offer their prayers and then begin cooking. While they cook, they also recite hymns or sing devotional songs. During meal preparation, the kitchen is treated as a sacred space and not a place for anyone to walk in willy-nilly.

Over time, though, the rituals of bathing and cleaning devolved into orthodoxy while the central idea of purity became more of a ritual. Even today the women of these households are slogging away in the kitchens while the real significance of purity has blurred away.

Any work becomes pure when it is infused with love. When we cook with love while staying connected in the heart with the Almighty, we raise ourselves to a higher vibration. The food cooked this way also carries a superior vibrational quality. The loving vibrations in our thoughts are infused into the prana (life) in the food and enlivens the food with divine vibrations. Such food, when consumed, purifies the physical and subtle bodies. So cooking with love benefits those who eat the food *and* those who cook it.

Often, I ask volunteers, especially boys in their early twenties who visit me in Kanha, to spend a few days working in the kitchen. A kitchen is an assembly line of emotions. There's such a sense of connection and joy that comes from creating a meal together. Everyone is in sync. They bond. Laugh. Food gets cooked, but what's really being served are the emotions of all the people working in the kitchen. I have seen how working in the kitchen opens these young peoples' hearts. They become more caring, accepting and loving.

Do This: Involve Children in Cooking

When children learn to cook early on, then they can help prepare meals at home. When they grow up, their eating habits will also be healthier. With processed foods proliferating the grocery aisles, cooking is an important life skill to give our children. Also, when we involve children in cooking, they understand the effort it takes and will appreciate the food more.

Cooking takes time, and parents, especially those in cities, are busy. So it's important to prioritize cooking by putting family prep days on the calendar. Here are some suggestions to get everyone involved:

1. Make a list of all the chores that go into making a meal like cutting veggies, cleaning the table, doing the dishes

and sweeping the floor. Allocate these tasks and swap them around the next time.

2. FaceTime grandma and have her share the recipe of the family's favourite curry.

3. Let the children create meal plans. Have a few recipes handy and allow the children to get creative.

4. At the grocery store, let the children pick the produce or other ingredients on your list. They will learn to estimate quantities, understand prices and learn to make decisions.

Eating with a Happy Disposition

Our bodies are a living ledger of our emotions and feelings. The growing wrinkle on our forehead, hair greying too soon and the aches in our joints are not signs of aging alone. They are the imprints of our emotions on the body. Fear, anger, jealousy, prejudice and other toxins start as emotions but end as scars on the body. In the same way, a face glowing with peace, the softness of being and a positive sense of self are the imprints of nutrients such as love, gratitude, contentment and kindness.

The disposition with which we eat has a direct effect on our well-being. If we eat while we are stressed, then the food stays undigested and we end up having issues like obesity, gut problems, diabetes and so on. Similarly, eating with a happy disposition, helps us enjoy the food and we also digest the food better.

A happy disposition is a relaxed state of mind. Let me explain. Take the example of two friends playing a game of chess. With furrowed eyebrows, they intently gaze at the board.

A child walks in and inadvertently hits a corner of the chess board and knocks over the pieces. The players' minds were in a flow state. When the board is disturbed, the result is irritation and anger.

Take another example. You are enjoying a quiet walk in the garden. The blooming daisies, chirping birds and the golden sun make for a serene setting. Out of nowhere a terrible noise of a heavy-duty lawnmower reverberates through the serene setting. The result again is a disturbed and, thus, unhappy mind.

In these two examples, the *flow* of the mind was settled, in one case on a game of chess, and in the other case on the serene garden setting. A steady, settled mind makes for a happy disposition. When the mind is disturbed, irritation and unhappiness result. When we sit down to eat and through the meal, we should ensure a steady and settled disposition.

Now, how to create and maintain such a state? It starts with the attitude and the environment. Try to avoid phones and tablets at the dinner table. Television, even if playing in the background, is a bad idea. Screens dissipate the flow of the mind into a separate channel and when we don't give food attention, we short-change the spiritual and energy giving benefits of food. Parents can lead by example in creating the environment. A loving and calm demeanour of parents will help the children develop a similar state while having a meal and, in the future, as they grow up and have their own families.

Before beginning a meal, a good way to centre oneself is through prayer. The reason many cultures propose offering a prayer of gratitude before eating food is to bring the mind and body into a state of flow. It's been scientifically proven that gratitude helps us form better bonds. It motivates us to connect with those around us and know them better.[3]

Besides creating an attitude of gratitude, prayer also creates a meditative state of mind. It's important to retain the meditative connection throughout the meal. Here is a visualisation you can practice for keeping the inner connection. When you sit down to eat, imagine you are joined at the head of the table by Lord Jesus or Lord Krishna or whomever your heart reveres. How would you eat at such a time? What thoughts would run through your mind? How would you pass the food at the table? What conversations would you engage in? If God is omnipresent, then there is no reason why God wouldn't join your family at the dinner table, if invited with love. Gratitude and prayer invoke a certain sacredness to mealtimes, and when families eat in such a setting, it creates togetherness and love.

For those partaking of the meal, when the sacred thought connects with the energy in the food, the divine energy is carried by the food and infused into the cells of the body. Spiritual diseases like jealousy, fault finding, prejudice and many other evils soon bid farewell, thanks to the spiritual superfood being consumed. Earlier in the book, I also mentioned how eating together helps ensure that children stay away from bad habits. Studies also show that students who do not regularly eat the main meal with their parents are significantly more likely to be absent from school.[4]

So far, I have shared about the attitudes beneficial for us while cooking and eating a meal. To round out this conversation, it's important to touch upon how to finish the meal. After you are done eating, close your eyes for half a minute and connect with your heart. Be grateful from the bottom of your heart for the meal, and for all those who served you (farmers, transportation, stores, cleaners, shoppers and cooks). It is an immensely powerful moment once you have finished eating to be grateful for everything and everyone who made it possible. If you are eating in a restaurant, be thankful to growers and so on, but also to the manager, cleaning staff, cooks and waiters. It is easy to give a tip, but it is rare to give prayerful blessings from the heart. It will touch them at some level (and yes, don't use prayer to go stingy on the tip).

My Preference Is Plant-Based Food

I'm often asked, 'Should we eat vegetarian food?', 'Is eating meat a bad thing?' and some other variants of these two questions.

From a health perspective, there is enough data that shows a plant-based diet is better for the body's overall health.

Novak Djokovic, Serena Williams, Sarah Stewart, Colin Kaepernick, Lewis Hamilton, Aarathi Swaminathan and Virat Kohli—what do these names have in common? They are all professional athletes with peak fitness. They are wildly successful in their sport. All of them are predominantly vegetarian, if not vegan.

These athletes shifted to a plant-based diet and achieved better results in their sport. Documentaries like *The Game Changers* or *Forks Over Knives* focus on the virtues of a plant-based diet. If your goal is long-term health for your child, a plant-based diet is my suggestion. I am also in favour of dairy, if there are no allergies or an intolerance of any kind in the body to dairy.

All food carries a vibrational quality. When we eat meat, fowl, fish and eggs, the vibrations of sentient beings are carried forward in the food. It affects our consciousness. The heaviness meat creates in the system is an obstacle to evolution of one's consciousness. Don't take my word for it. I would like you to experience this yourself. Most of my associates who ate meat at one time have now given it up. They often comment about the lightness and general well-being they experience after giving up meat.

Forget for a moment the spiritual or moral argument in favour of plant-based food. Let's look at it from the lens of aesthetics. In a previous chapter (Explore the World Together, See More), I mentioned the role that aesthetics play in creating the right environment for children. Aesthetic is that which pleases the heart and not just the senses. It includes in it a sense of flow, orderliness and harmony.

Consider the food you eat and its aesthetic or non-aesthetic nature. Consider the aesthetics of how the meat patties and nuggets on your table came to be. If you were in the slaughterhouse and saw a sentient life form beheaded to serve your hunger, how would that feeling weigh on you?

The farm-to-table aesthetic for peanuts, chickpeas and meat are vastly different.

Mind, Gut and Spirit

In the sinuous trackways of the gut (digestive system) lies a vast network of nerves that scientists call the enteric nervous system. The nerves, the neurons and the neurotransmitters in the enteric nervous system are the same as those in the central nervous system. In fact, the number of nerve cells in the gut (500 million) is only second to the brain (86 billion). For this reason, the gut is also called the 'second brain'.[5] There is constant communication between the two brains and their communication channel is called the gut-brain axis. The primary role of the gut is digestion. But there are many other functions that the gut performs to help with the well-being of the body.

First, the gut is the immunity powerhouse in the body. Seventy per cent of the immune cells in the body are in the gut.[6] Why do you think this is the case? It is to protect the body from anything that we may ingest that is not good for it. Along the lining of the gut, immune cells set up defences to take on any infection or bacteria that may be harmful to us.

Serotonin is a neurotransmitter associated with the brain, and nearly 95 per cent of the body's Serotonin is biosynthesized in the gut.[7] Serotonin plays a vital role in regulating sleep, appetite, mood, sensitivity and the feeling of well-being.

Finally, perhaps the most fascinating role the gut plays is in housing and nurturing the microbiome of the human body. It is estimated that more than 100 trillion microbes, or microorganisms, live in the human gut.[8] In comparison, the total number of cells in the human body is a mere 10 trillion.

The gut microbiome is an area where extensive research is being done. From what we know so far, the microbes in the gut help babies to digest breast milk (important for the gut biome), assimilate fibres, control the immune system, regulate moods and boost brain function.[9] Recent studies on newborns have shown that treating babies (especially in the first week of life) with antibiotics decreases the healthy bacteria and increases antimicrobial resistance. Experts now suggest that any over-prescription should be scrutinised, and special attention should be given to the need for antibiotics.[10]

Gut health, plant-based food, attitude with which we cook and eat these are all important for parents to learn and implement. Most important is to cultivate a happy disposition, especially while eating as a family.

The little miracles that we all seek, ones that fill a house with joy and grace, are to be found not in a pilgrimage or in sacrifices but in simple moments of togetherness and gratitude such as those found around the dinner table of a family partaking of a meal. In today's world, where everything is being rushed and hastened, pause for your meals. Relish them with loved ones and eat with an attitude that leaves joyful imprints on the body and the soul.

Daily Dilemma:

My two-year-old simply won't eat vegetables. What do I do?

Daaji: My granddaughter has the same problem. Let me know if you know of a fix. Usually, children's eating habits improve over time. There are books by therapists and nutritionists that may come in handy for some tips and tricks.

What has worked for me is what I call the 'Verify Method'. When I want my granddaughter to try something, I offer it to her and ask her, 'Please try it and let me know if it's good or bad for me. I need you to verify it for me. Should I eat this or not?'

The little one would try a little and say, 'It's good, Daada . . . it's good . . . you can eat it.'

Next time they make it, I eat it and ask her, 'I am eating it, why don't you also eat a little?' Then she laughs and understands the game. Most of the time she will eat it along with me.

Nowadays, the challenge parents face is there are simply too many options for children to choose from. It's difficult to teach the value of food in the midst of abundant options and variety.

Principle 9

Discipline Your Love, Not Love Your Discipline

23

Discipline and Guidance for Your Child

Discipline. The topic receives a lot of attention because, whether we like it or not, we realize its importance in our lives. *Discipline is our ability to do the high-value tasks, those that enrich our lives and avoid low-value distractions.* Setting goals and achieving them takes discipline. A successful career, good health and happy relationships all demand personal discipline.

And when you become a parent, the importance of discipline increases even more because you know that childhood is an opportune time to teach your children good habits. Being punctual, cleaning up the room, taking care of toys, respecting elders, eating vegetables—are a few items that fall under the discipline checklist of a parent. Whether your child is a toddler, a middle schooler or a teenager, there are excellent techniques and books available to help you. My focus in these three chapters on discipline is to offer you something deeper: a spiritual perspective about discipline and its significance in our life.

But before that, I'd like to point out a few common misgivings about discipline. The word 'discipline' conveys a feeling of sternness, some sort of tension and imposition. So discipline is commonly thought of as something enforced. And in some cases, it is. In the army, for example, on the frontlines of war, a soldier's discipline (or lack of) can be the difference between life and death for him and his fellow soldiers. And to instil the code of discipline, the training for a soldier is one of strict routine and punishment for mistakes. But when it comes to parenting, discipline is a lot more than enforcing rules.

What Is Discipline and Some Key Takeaways

The first thing to understand when it comes to discipline is it's not something one can instil from the outside. Instructions can be given from the outside. Guidance can be given from outside. Discipline is always from within oneself. In the Sanskrit language, the word for 'discipline' is *anushasanam.* It's a combination of two words, *anu* which means self and *shasanam* which means governance. In Sanskrit, discipline means self-governance. Parents should adopt ways and means to encourage children to grow in self-discipline. For some time, guidance from parents and elders is needed, but over time the external guidance should make way for guidance from within the child.

> Discipline is always from within oneself.

Second, discipline is for everyone, not just for children. In a family, children learn discipline from the elders and follow their example. Rigidity from elders creates resentment against discipline in children. Instead, explain to your children why something needs to be done a certain way. For example, for early bedtime to be followed, explain to your children how going to bed early makes them stronger. Explaining why we do what we do is a positive approach to discipline. Children may still grumble at times, but resentment is not there.

Third, consistency helps in developing discipline. Consistency helps children foster automatism in their habits. For example, if dinner time is 7.30 p.m. then everyone should know the time and follow the routine. If one week's dinner is at 7.30, the next it's an hour earlier, and on weekends the house becomes a late-night diner, such a routine is unsettling for everyone, especially children. They need to learn to internalize timing and it's easier to do this in childhood.

Consistency drives permanency.

Finally, the idea of discipline is not to create robots that have no freedom. Discipline does not curtail freedom; discipline creates freedom. For example, if we want financial freedom, we must practice financial discipline. If we want freedom from disease, we must be disciplined about our lifestyle. If we want leisure, then we must be disciplined about how we allocate our time. Discipline is the way to freedom.

To quickly summarize, here are four takeaways to remember about discipline:

- Discipline is from within.
- Discipline is for everyone at home.
- Consistency creates discipline.
- Discipline creates freedom.

With this basic understanding of discipline let's now dive deeper into the levels of discipline and how they help a child grow.

The Three Levels of Discipline

There are mainly three levels of discipline. The first level of discipline starts in the family, and it reflects the love of the family. This discipline can be called as guidance. It includes instructions and rules, laid out by the elders. Guidance helps the child build moral muscles. In the next section, I explain more about guidance and how to offer it to children.

We start with guidance, and it should trigger a mechanism inside children so they are self-guided. This is the second level of discipline, and it's called self-discipline. Starting around age eight the child starts developing self-discipline. The fruit of self-discipline is moderation.

The final and the highest level of discipline is very rare. It is instilled in us because we make ourselves deserving enough to receive it. This discipline is called instilled discipline. The fruit of instilled discipline is the merger of the individual self with the higher self.

Guidance, the First Level of Discipline: How and Why

What is the role of a traffic light? It helps with the flow of traffic and prevents accidents. It fosters orderliness and mutual understanding for the riders. In a family, guidance from the parents is meant to ensure order and safety for the children. Make your bed, no television while eating, pray before you sleep, don't talk to strangers are some examples of guidance.

Besides orderliness and safety, guidance helps in building the moral muscles of children. Let me explain. The word 'morality' is generally used to indicate right versus wrong or good versus

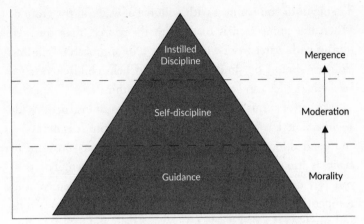

The three levels of discipline

bad. While this is fine, morality is more than discerning right from wrong. It also encompasses the idea of precision.

Morality is the capacity to be precise in our thoughts, words and actions. No waste, no indulgence and no exploitation of any of the faculties. Morality helps us in using our faculties for the purpose for which they were bestowed upon us.

Gorging on cake, binge-watching a series, mindless internet browsing, gossiping about a friend are all immoral acts because they indulge your senses excessively. Guidance which is the first level of discipline helps children in cultivating a keen sense of morality. But as anyone who has cared for a child knows that guidance needs to be repeated regularly. So, what's a good way to guide children? If we keep doling out instructions from morning until night, then our words become white noise. It also makes parenting laborious and dry. So, what should be our approach?

Let's say you are digging a well. Do you dig a few feet, then fill up the hole with buckets of water, and pronounce, 'Yes, now I have a well'? That's not how it works. Digging a well means digging until you connect with a source of water in the ground. When the connection is made with the source, then the well fills up with water from within itself. Our approach to guiding children should be similar. We should help children reach a level where they can get guidance from within.

To arrive at this level, parents need to repeat instructions for a while. There is nothing wrong with repetition. It is necessary and good things are worth being repeated. What you want to avoid is monotony in the way you guide children. For this, you can use all the tricks in the bag, including motivation, competition, giving bribes, reverse psychology, roping in friends and anything else that works for you and your children. Building moral muscles is important and your efforts in this direction will pay big dividends in the future.

Most of you are parents or parents-to-be. You are the role models for your children. Children do what their parents do. My Master used to say "Discipline, like rain, like grace, comes from above, in the sense that disciplined parents produce disciplined children. Loving parents create loving children". Remember, discipline with love is caring. Discipline without love is enforcing. Love without discipline is pampering. The right formula of all three is needed when you are raising children.

Just as a well fills up with refreshing water from within, in the same way, thanks to the efforts of the parents, there comes a time when the child finds guidance from within. Now at this stage, the second level of discipline, self-discipline, starts to kick in.

Daily Dilemma:

The school bus comes on time every day, but the children are always late. If we have to go somewhere, we never leave on time as the children have no awareness of time. How to instil a sense of awareness of surroundings, especially time?

Daaji: It's difficult. Children, especially the little ones who have just started school are not hardened with a consciousness of time. For them, life is a journey of wonder and discovery. You would have seen this on a walk with your child in the park. The children notice every little thing around them. To ease the stress of the morning, try to have things ready the previous evening.

As children begin middle school, instil a routine at home that everyone abides by. A regular routine, especially sticking with regular bedtimes will help in developing awareness of time and activity. By the way, your question is applicable to many adults too. So don't be too tough on the children.

24

Self-Discipline and the Magic Habit to Cultivate It

Self-discipline is the fuel for personal growth. This is the discipline we formulate for ourselves and obey ourselves. We're not subjugated to any authority. We're not obeying anyone else. *I obey myself, I discipline myself and I do this to grow.* The fruit of self-discipline is moderation. Moderation helps you stay balanced. It gives you the equanimity to enjoy the highs and cope with the lows of life.

When a child restrains from playing video games to practice his music lesson, it's a sign of self-discipline. When an athlete hits the track each morning before any of her teammates show up, it is her self-discipline that is pushing her. Self-discipline builds positive self-restraint. I restrain myself. Nobody asks me to do so.

Self-discipline reflects the interest people take in making themselves better. They are disciplined because their hearts say, 'Be disciplined.' They are disciplined because they are inspired and not because they are afraid. Above all, they know that only discipline will carry them on the path to success.

As parents, we help the child progressively develop self-discipline. Self-discipline moulds the character. It centres us. It shows itself in acts of courtesy—where you allow others to speak before you, you allow others at the table to eat before you, and so on. Such behaviour of putting the needs of others before oneself comes from self-discipline.

Is there a magic pill to ensure that children find a way to tap into their inner guidance? Is there a habit that guarantees self-discipline? The answer is yes: Follow your heart.

> Is there a magic pill to ensure that children will find a way to tap into their inner guidance? Is there a technique that will guarantee that the discipline becomes self-discipline?
>
> The answer is YES.

In the chapter 'Talk to Your Child', I suggested that if there is only one technique you take away from this book, let it be the Principles of Conversation. In the same vein, if there is *one habit* that you take away from this book, let it be this: Follow your heart.

Follow Your Heart

The gift of following the heart is self-discipline. The heart is the seat of the soul. All the wisdom and guidance comes from the heart. When parents teach children the habit of following the heart, then children's lives are guided by wisdom.

From the simple decisions (Should I eat cereal or pancakes for breakfast?) to the mind-bending ones that come later in life

(What subject should I study in college? Which job to take? Or whom to marry?), following the heart gives us the guidance in making the right decision. It is a habit one develops, and like most habits, it's easier to cultivate during childhood.

A good age to teach this habit to your children is when they are around eight years old. Right around this age, children start facing moral dilemmas. When your child asks you 'Can I watch more television?', 'Can I skip shower today?' and so on, ask your child, 'What does your heart say?' Your child may respond with something like, 'My heart says, "No, I should not watch more television," but I really want to. What do I do?' or 'I already played the video game for an hour, but I feel like playing longer.' What your child is saying is this, 'I *know* the right thing to do, but I don't *feel* like doing it.'

At such times, it's important to support your child's decision-making process. You could take an approach where you say, 'You're right, sweetie. Sometimes I feel like watching more television too. You know, it's wonderful that you can listen to your heart so clearly. Let's do this. Instead of watching television, why don't we read a story together or even better, play a board game? We can have fun and your heart will also be happy!' Something similar works for the shower too 'Why don't you take a quick two-minute shower, and I will have your favourite book ready for us to read together?' Such guidance from the parents shows the child the importance parents place on following one's heart.

The more children listen to their heart, the clearer they will be in making choices. Today it's a choice of watching more television or finishing homework. In the future it will be a choice between hitting the books or going out to a party with the wrong crowd.

As I mentioned earlier in the book, children truly care about what their parents value. When parents give importance to following the heart, children will do the same. Children, especially the little ones, face cute moral dilemmas such as, skipping homework, swiping away another cookie, plucking the flower in the garden and so on. Though they are cute dilemmas, they are real issues for the child. So, we must be respectful and not make light of the situation. Parents' support gives the child the confidence that 'Yes, when I share a problem, my parents listen.'

For parents, though, it means spending *more* time and energy. No doubt its more work but think of it this way: following the heart is the mother tincture of all that is good. It's a foundational investment that keeps on giving, and it's worth the effort.

The more children listen to their hearts, the clearer they will be in making choices. Today it's a choice between more television or finishing homework. In the future it will be a choice between hitting the books or partying with the wrong crowd. In the turbulent teenage years, clear inner guidance will help your child in choosing the correct path.

Who's Speaking? The Heart or the Mind?

Oftentimes I get this question 'How do I know if it's the heart or the mind that is speaking?' When things are happening naturally, the heart is silent. It's a witness. If things are not happening naturally, then the heart chimes in. Let me explain. If I am walking normally, my heart doesn't say, 'Hey Kamlesh, good job! Your legs are working well today.' But if I pull a muscle, the heart immediately signals, 'Kamlesh! Something is wrong.'

One more example. Someone asks you, 'What's your name?' and you answer, 'My name is Roger,' even though your name is Victor. Imagine how you feel inside. Right away, there is discomfort. There is a sense of unease. Some fear also develops. The inner voice says, 'You lied.'

But if you say, 'My name is Victor,' you'd feel no discomfort. The inner voice doesn't bother you. When we are natural and truthful, the heart is silent. When we sway from being natural, then the heart intervenes. The more we listen to the heart, the clearer its voice becomes.

> In the merger of the heart and the mind, there is total clarity of conscience. Now both logic and feeling convey the same thing.

The ideal state is when the logic of the mind and the feelings of the heart become one. In the merger of the heart and the mind, there is total clarity of conscience. Now both logic and feeling convey the same thing. So, the teenager facing a dilemma of partying or hitting the books knows that his heart and mind both are saying no. There is no conflict and doing the right thing becomes easier.

When children are trained from a young age to follow the heart, they grow up with a harmonized heart-mind field. The process of following the heart becomes so natural to them that they don't question if the guidance is from the heart or the mind. To them, they are one and the same. When children are old enough to meditate, usually fifteen and older in Heartfulness, then their meditation practice will further sensitize their awareness. Meditation will refine their thinking and make it easier for them to tap into their inner wisdom easily.

Some of you may have another question: 'What if the heart says yes and it turns out that it wasn't the right thing to do?' Let's take an example. Your child sees a pile of crayon boxes lying in the school library. He picks up a box and brings it home. When you ask him why he picked it up, he says, 'They were lying there, and I thought it was okay to take a box home.'

There could be many situations like this: 'I want to tease my friend because he teased me last time.' or 'I want to play more video games because my friend plays so much more.' Such moments are opportunities to calibrate the child's inner GPS. When such situations come up, teach your child to ask the question, 'What if everybody did the same?' Meaning, 'What if everybody at school took a box of crayons?', 'What if everybody teased their friend?' or 'What if everybody played more video games?' Through these questions, you are teaching the child the important lesson that what we *individually* think is right does not matter if it's not right *universally*.

Picking up a box of crayons is not a good idea because what would happen if all the children in the school did the same thing? Teasing your friend back is not cool because then all we do is tease one another and there won't be any time left to play cops and robbers. If everyone keeps playing video games, then we all miss out on running around in the park. In this way, you can guide the child.

Today, it's about the child not picking up a box of crayons. Tomorrow the same child, as a grown-up, will not add a few more dollars to an expense report, will promptly return any borrowed money, and will make good on commitments.

Self-disciplined people are disciplined because their heart says, 'Be disciplined.' They are disciplined because they love and not because they are afraid. They are disciplined above all because they know that it is only discipline that will carry them on the path to success.

Sometimes children may be worried about making mistakes while following their heart. They may be concerned about misunderstanding the heart's guidance. At such times, tell them, 'Heart or no heart, we all make mistakes. So it's okay. Early in life if you get into a habit of following the heart, then you have a longer window of time to tune in better to the inner guidance.'

The Opportunity to Learn Together

In our discussion about discipline, we touched on many ideas. The need for consistency, the importance of building moral muscles and the principle of following one's heart. These ideas share the spiritual wisdom behind the role of discipline in our life.

Some of you may have enjoyed these ideas. Some might want to revisit them. There are some who may feel uncomfortable teaching children something that they aren't following today. Such discomfort is a welcome sign.

There is an old Indian folklore of a young boy who kept nagging his mother for sweets. From morning to night, all the boy wanted was sweets. The mother was exasperated, and she did not know how to get rid of this habit. So, she took her boy and went to a saint in a nearby village. The saint listened to the problem and asked the mother and the child to come back after a week. When they came back, the saint lovingly looked into the child's eyes and said, 'Son, please stop eating too many sweets. It's not good for you.'

The mother was expecting some amulet or spell that would remove the habit. But the saint simply offered loving advice. She ended up asking, 'Sir, you could have given the same advice a week ago. I wonder why you asked us to wait.' The saint replied, 'Mother, I had to first give up my habit of eating sweets before I could ask this little one to do so. I kicked my habit last week and now I can suggest the same to the child.'

Becoming a parent gives you the opportunity to learn the lessons of life along with your children. Maybe some of you were not taught about discipline in a gentle, consistent manner. Maybe for some of you, discipline meant only canes, rubber belts and timeouts. Whatever the reason may be, if these ideas on discipline inspire you, please implement them in your life. This way, children will not only learn from you, but they will also see these principles put into action.

Daily Dilemma:

Children nowadays use lot of curse words. What happens when children use curse words? How to protect children from getting into this habit?

Daaji: We all have an inside voice, and it keeps on talking. It's a white noise of chatter that goes on in our heads. When children get into a habit of using curse words, then their inside voice imbibes this vocabulary. Then when they speak to themselves, they start becoming unkind to themselves. It hurts their sense of self and their outlook on life. So, it's important that you teach children early on the importance of civil language. As parents, you should lead by example. The way you talk, the shows you watch as a family and how you react to uncivil conversations all send a message.

When you can, visit a park or a playground where teenagers play. Listen to the language they are using. It wouldn't be pleasant. Your child hangs around children who may be similar, and sooner or later, your child may pick up some of these mannerisms.

I suggest you do a couple of things. Keep reminding your child about the importance of civil and polite language. Watch the company your child keeps and curate that company consciously. It's important that you ensure your child is in good company. Finally, once in a while, as a family, read aloud the Principles of Conversation and discuss your understanding.

In the Mahabharata, we find the mention of a rishi named Durvasa. And what was his claim to fame? He would get into fits of rage and curse people. Everyone feared his anger and the repercussions of annoying him. We don't want Durvasa's around us. We want to raise children who grow up to be humans who are loving, resilient and kind in thought, word and deed.

25

The Highest Discipline: A Gift from Above

The highest level of discipline, *instilled discipline*, is a mystery to most of us. When the barriers between the individual self and the higher self are dissolved then such discipline descends into our consciousness. Such discipline is instilled in us by the grace of God. The fruit of instilled discipline is merger.

At times, this chapter may seem more like an essay on spirituality than a chapter about parenting and discipline. But I felt that not sharing the deeper meaning of discipline would be cutting corners around the spiritual essence of discipline. So here we go.

The Beauty of Instilled Discipline

We may not know much about this type of discipline, but when we are in the company of people that have it, their presence touches us in a profound way. And if someone asks us to describe what we felt, we struggle to find the words. Most of the time, our response is a silent smile and moist eyes.

A person at this level of discipline is like a candle that gently illuminates everything around it. Such people have achieved what they needed to achieve in their life. Their inner transformation is complete. Love is their only discipline. Like the sun that shines for one and all, like the flower that releases its fragrance for the breeze to carry, such individuals are embodiments of love. Their love is no longer a verb. They don't love; they become love. In the company of such people, we forget our worries and are lifted into a state of bliss. Such a person is simplicity in action and purity in being.

When describing this level of discipline, my Master once said while speaking to a group of us, 'This is a level of discipline where no more shall you think of yourself. Your comforts are meaningless. Your hunger is meaningless. You don't exist anymore for yourself. You exist for the rest. And their welfare is your welfare. Their happiness is your happiness. And, in their growth, their fulfilment, lies the direction of human progress.'

Such souls consume themselves, give up themselves so others may grow, others may develop. They are not aware of their compassion, courtesy or love towards others. For them, it is their state of being. They are what they are. At this level of discipline, such a person's heart has expanded to embrace the whole world as one family. Instead of individual love and affection directed towards someone, their hearts have grown to embrace all in a spirit of universal love.

Such is the beauty of the highest level of discipline.

Inspirations for Parents from Instilled Discipline

Even though instilled discipline may seem like a lofty goal, one that's way beyond reach, nothing prevents us from trying. Our attempts in its direction will land us in a better place.

One remarkable trait of the people in whom instilled discipline is evoked is that their life is in tune with nature. Their lives are in harmony with nature's principles. Generally, living in tune with nature is thought of as leading a lifestyle with a low carbon footprint, buying earth-friendly products and if one can do it, then going off into the woods and living in a cabin by the lake.

But living in tune with nature means resonating with the principles of nature. When we study the lives of souls like Lord Jesus, Saint Therese, Buddha, Swami Vivekananda and Babuji, we can notice how they resonated with nature. I am sharing here some ideas that we as parents can discuss with our children.

Give Most While Taking the Least

When we look around in nature, we find that plants and animals take very little from their environment and give back so much more. For example, what does a mango tree require? Does it demand mango juice and caviar for its sustenance? It only needs sunlight, water, soil and a little manure every now and then. It takes only this much, and yet it produces the sweetest, juiciest mangoes. Then there is the humble coconut palm. In the Pacific Islands, entire communities rely on this one plant for food, shelter, clothing and medicines. But even though it gives so much to so many, its requirements like the mango tree are simple and few. It certainly doesn't demand coconut water for its growth. The same goes for livestock. A buffalo, which drinks water and eats grass, gives us nutritious milk in return. She does not demand milk in order to give back milk.

The key idea here is to *give our most while taking the least*.

In a human being, something that goes on increasing as one gives it away is love. As one gives away love, it only multiplies in one's heart. In day-to-day life, our love is a verb. We love, we give love, we receive love and so on. But by following the idea of giving our most, the field of our love begins to grow. From close family and friends, our heart expands to embrace everything around us with love.

When we practice giving away love, then the way we interact with the world changes. When you look at a homeless person, your pity is replaced with concern. Besides helping out with some pocket change, you catch yourself thinking about this person. How did he end up here? He must have had parents who loved him, birthday parties and gifts. How did this happen?

Likewise, when you are speaking with someone, you are mindful of your inner softness. You stay connected with the love flowing from the heart. Even when you are angry, the anger doesn't topple you off balance. You keep it in check, so it doesn't poison the love within.

The sublime lives of saints show us that when they practiced giving love away, they resonated with nature's principle of giving away the most. When we discuss this idea with our children, it will inspire them to cherish a loving heart that gives and gives.

Cooperation and Sacrifice

Building on the idea of living in tune with nature, here is one more idea you can share with your child. The mango tree doesn't compete with the coconut tree. The roses don't compete with the tulips. The bees don't try to one-up the butterflies. Nature is full of symbiotic relationships where each species cooperates with the other. Whatever predatory and parasitic behaviour we see in nature is driven by the instinct to survive and not by the desire to compete.

In a family when we look out for one another and don't compete with each other, there is harmony. Our children learn about cooperation. The Darwinian idea of survival of the fittest is a disastrous idea when applied to human society. Human evolution happens through kinship and unity. If we don't cooperate and take care of each other, we will become history, like dinosaurs. We evolve through cooperation and devolve through competition.

Children are gifted with compassion and cooperation. Most of us have seen videos of little children running a race and when one child falls behind the others slow down to help. The instinct to cooperate is innate to us. As parents, we need to nurture this instinct and allow it to grow in our children. We need to help our children exercise their compassion muscles.

When children are around eight or nine years old, get them to buy a pencil or a book for their friend. This way when they are getting something for themselves, they remember others too. Volunteer with your children at the local animal shelter or the soup kitchen. Train them in compassion and cooperation early on. They will grow up to become caring human beings and raise good families when their time comes.

The other principle we see in nature is altruism and sacrifice. In a forest, the evergreens act as windbreakers. Their swaying branches break the wind currents and protect the weaker trees. When a predator is near, the monkeys scream from the treetops and warn the deer. When a wolf sneaks up on a herd of sheep, the shepherd dog warns the sheep by barking and running circles. Often the dog ends up being killed by the wolf. These are acts of selfless altruism and sacrifice.

Practices observed in various religions like Lent, Ramadan, Ekadashi and Yom Kippur are observed to help us appreciate the importance of sacrifice. These practices help us understand how sacrifice cleanses our souls and helps us become better.

But beyond these rituals, the best example of selfless sacrifice that comes to my mind is the love of a mother for her newborn child. In the middle of the night, when the child wakes up multiple times to be fed and changed, a mother does all this naturally. Most of the days she feels like a zombie due to sleep deprivation. Her energy levels are low, and she barely gets a few minutes to herself. Her body aches, but her spirit keeps her going. And in all but a few months, she smiles about these testing times. Of course, fathers also help, but the selfless nature of the mother is something else.

And that brings me to the idea I mentioned earlier that people with instilled discipline have no awareness of their sacrifice. To others around them, their actions may seem like sacrifice, but to them, they act guided by their heart. Once in India, during the winter, some of us were sitting around Babuji. It was bitterly cold and those around him were all in sweaters and pullovers. He was sitting in a chair, wearing a sweater and a blanket covered his feet. Late into the night, a visitor showed up at his doorstep. He came in, and we saw that he wasn't dressed for the weather. Babuji immediately got up, took off his sweater and gave it to the visitor. Even before those sitting around him realized what just happened, he sat back in his chair and slipped back into his silence, seemingly unbothered by the cold.

To those around, the actions personified sacrifice, but he had lost all self-awareness of sacrifice. In our own small ways, when we show our children the means to arrive at compassion and care, they learn by association.

Giving most while taking the least, cooperating instead of competing, sacrificing selflessly—all are ennobling ideas that shape the character of a human being. These actions mould the heart to become a receptacle worthy of instilled discipline. I pray that you all aspire for such discipline and the grace of the Almighty grants us all this wonderful divine blessing.

Daily Dilemma:

My son, who used to be so kind and compassionate, is now twelve, and his compassion seems to have deserted him. The other day, I asked him if he'd help his cousin and me move my friend's bedroom from upstairs to downstairs. She's very ill and can no longer climb the stairs. 'Why?' he kept asking me. 'I don't know her.' I kept explaining that it was the kind and good thing to do, that she can't do it herself, but he couldn't see the logic in helping her. I'm sure his kindness will return, but in the meantime, how should I handle situations like these—and there are others!

Daaji: Each situation is unique, but from what I have seen, children, especially the tweens, like to help. They like being given responsibility. They want to be treated as grown-ups. I think your child's behaviour may be an indication of wanting more time with you. Are you spending enough time with your son? Did you have other plans for this weekend that had to be put aside? What you are seeing are the symptoms. The cause may be your child wanting more time with you.

Thank You for Your Time

I started writing this book in the throes of the pandemic. As I write the final chapter, we enter the third year in our battle with COVID-19. Globally, almost 6.5 million people have died. So far. While we have the vaccine to outlive the disease, to live out the grief needs the salve of time.

While we figure out what the new normal is, world over totalitarian regimes are on the rise, there is a growing lack of trust in institutions and rising economic disparities are fuelling unrest. Then there is the risk of an all-out war staring us in the face.

These worries get amplified when you look into the faces of your children and grandchildren, and you wonder what kind of world you are leaving behind for them. When this book started, I had one granddaughter. Today, I have two granddaughters and one grandson. As my farmer father would have said, 'It's a bumper harvest.' My grandson who is one and a half years old has this peculiar habit. When he sees someone whom he knows well, he will rush towards them and he expects them to pick him up and sway him around and hug him. If for some reason, you don't notice him running towards you, he slows down and slides into a corner. And then he sits there, slouched up and disappointed. It is so endearing to see him all puddled up and I love to pamper him at this time. For me, these micro-moments of joy add years to my life. I often wish I was fit enough to run around and play with them. I am sure your children and grandchildren have their own little quirks too.

Here, as we come to the end of the book, I want to leave you with a simple and important idea. Please take care of your Self. Your body, mind and spirit need care and nourishment. Usually, when we think of taking care of ourselves, we think of the body. But a healthy life doesn't mean the mere absence of physical disease. A healthy life is an integrated sense of well-being at a physical, mental and emotional level. While much is known about how to tend to the body and the mind, not much is known about how to care for one's spirit. The knowledge of your spiritual self and knowing how to tend to it, helps you tap into the strength and stability that comes from one's soul. In Yoga, this idea is expressed as *swasthya* meaning centred on one's Self.

Without this inner centeredness, the world outside can yank your energies all over. For a moment, if you put aside all the macro challenges we face in the world, just parenting itself can seem like navigating a labyrinth of contradictory advice. Let me give you a few examples. Should you co-sleep or put the child in a crib? Most Asian families I know will be up in-arms at the idea of having an infant sleep in a separate room. They point out examples from nature where no animal leaves her pups behind and goes elsewhere to sleep! But, when you look at Western societies, they have copious data and research that shows how it's safer for a child to sleep separately. How do you decide?

Or consider this example. Earlier in the book, I shared the Early Catastrophe case study that pointed out how a massive learning gap developed in children when parents didn't speak enough with them. Now, on the other hand, when scientists studied tribes in South America and Africa, they noticed that in some of the tribes, the parents barely spoke to their children. There were hardly any words exchanged and yet when these children grew up, they had no learning gaps. When the scientists studied this further, they observed one noticeable difference in the tribal societies. Here, the mother carried the child most of the day. The child was wrapped in a sack with skin-to-skin contact with an elder (usually the mother) from morning till night. The close contact gave the child reassurance and confidence and the child perhaps learned in a different non-verbal way. So, does this mean we get rid of the Britax and the Bugaboo? During my travels in Denmark, I often noticed baby carriages with little ones parked outside a restaurant while mom and dad were grabbing a meal. It's an accepted social norm there but try doing the same thing in Boston or New York City and you might get arrested.

There are no simple answers for 'How much cuddling is okay?', 'Should you let them cry it out or give in?', 'When to stop supporting the child financially?' and so on. The list of questions and contradictions will simply grow as you look across societies. There is no one formula to raising a happy family and resilient children.

But there is one magic ingredient that makes parenting a fulfilling journey. That magic ingredient is love. The highest wisdom in life is the wisdom to love. Give love and give it unconditionally. If there is one question you ask yourself at the end of each day, it is this: 'Did I pour enough love into my day today?'

Be love. Become love. This is the best way to take care of your Self. With this as my heartfelt prayer for you, I end this book, my dear parent.

Appendix

Brighter Minds for Your Child

Brighter Minds for children is a finely tuned system of tools and techniques informed by the latest advances in neuroscience. It helps children develop their cognitive abilities within a framework of science and support.

The brain is highly mouldable, especially in children—as they grow, the external stimuli they are continuously exposed to shapes their cognitive functioning. This phenomenon is called neuroplasticity. Research in neuroscience proves that just like we exercise different parts of our body, exercising different parts of the brain can enhance multiple aspects of cognitive function.

In Brighter Minds, the intellectual, emotional and social development that happens in every child seems nothing short of magical, but at the core of the programme and process is evidence-based science.

Neurons communicate through brainwaves or synchronized electrical activity. Brainwave frequency tends to align itself with the frequency of any external stimulus. This tendency is utilized in a process called brainwave entrainment where brainwave frequencies are adjusted or adapted to a desired external stimulus.

Every Brighter Minds programme is based on these twin concepts of neuroplasticity and entrainment. Appropriate tools and interventions in a conducive environment can stimulate neuroplasticity in the brain during childhood and beyond, enhancing every individual's capacity to learn throughout their life.

For more information, look up www.brighterminds.org

About Heartfulness

Heartfulness is a heart-centered approach to life, where you live life guided by the wisdom of the heart. It is to live naturally, in tune with the qualities of a heart enlightened through spiritual practice. These qualities include compassion, sincerity, contentment, truthfulness and forgiveness; attitudes such as generosity and acceptance; and the heart's fundamental nature, which is love.

To learn more, please look up www.heartfulness.org

To email Daaji, please write to daaji@heartfulness.org

Resources

Locate a Trainer Near You   Heartfulness Practices

Notes

Dear Parents

1 S.S. Luthar and C. Sexton, 'The high price of affluence' in *Advances in Child Development*, ed. R. Kail (San Diego, CA: Academic Press, 2005).

Principle 1: Raising a Child Still Takes a Village

Chapter 1: A Village Is the People, Not the Place

1 Matthew Sloan, 'The secret to happiness? Here's some advice from the longest-running study on happiness', *Harvard Health* (blog), 5 October 2017, https:// www.health.harvard.edu/blog/ the-secret-to-happiness-heres- some-advice-from-the-longest- running-study-on-happiness- 2017100512543#:~:text=The%20 Harvard%20Study%20 has%20found%20a%20strong%20 association,isolation%20 is%20a%20mood%20buster%2C%E2 %80%9D%20says%20 Dr.%20Waldinger.

2 'Every 7th doctor in US is Indian and they're working as soldiers, fighting COVID-19: AAPI president,' *The Economic Times* (New

York, USA), 27 April 2020, https://economictimes.indiatimes.
com/news/international/world-news/every-7th-doctor-in-us-is-
indian-and-theyre-working-as-soldiers-fighting-covid-19-aapi-
president/articleshow/75406158.cms?from=mdr.

3   Charlie Cooper and Rachel Pells, 'Most First-Time Parents
    Experience a Decline in Happiness, Research Shows,' *Independent,*
    5   August,   2015,   https://www.independent.co.uk/life-style/
    health-and-families/health-news/most-first-time-parents-
    experience-decline-happiness-after-initial-excitement-research-
    says-10441201.html.

4   AARP Research, *Loneliness and Social Connections: A National
    Survey of Adults 25 and Older,* (Washington DC: AARP
    Foundation, 2018), https://www. aarp.org/content/dam/aarp/
    research/surveys_statistics/life-   leisure/2018/loneliness-social-
    connections-2018.doi.10.26419- 2Fres.00246.001.pdf.

5   Cigna and Ipsos, *2018: Cigna U.S. Loneliness Index,* (Bloomfield:
    Cigna,   2018),   https://www.multivu.com/players/English/
    8294451-cigna-us-loneliness- survey/docs/IndexReport_
    1524069371598-173525450.pdf.

Chapter 2: Halo Parenting: Rebuilding the Village

1   Carol Sue Carte, *Attachment and Bonding: A New Synthesis*
    (Cambridge: MIT Press, 2005), 359.

2   Stephanie Coontz, *The Way We Never Were: American Families
    and the Nostalgia Trap* (New York: Basic Books, 2016), 306.

3   S.J. Spieker and L. Bensley, 'Roles of living arrangements and
    grandmother social support in adolescent mothering and infant
    attachment,' *Developmental Psychology,* 30, no. 1 (1994): 102–
    111, https://doi.org/10.1037/0012-1649.30.1.102

4   Sarah Blaffer Hrdy, *Mothers and Others – The Evolutionary Origins
    of Mutual Understanding* (Cambridge: Harvard University Press,
    2011).

Principle 2: Be Guided by Wisdom. Seek It. Cultivate It. Share It.

Chapter 3: Wayfinders, Shamans and Grand Parents: The Wisdom Bridge

1   J.F. O'Connell, et al., 'Grandmothering and the evolution of *Homo erectus*,' *Journal of Human Evolution* 36, no. 5 (May 1999): 461–485, https://doi.org/10.1006/jhev.1998.0285.

2   Ibid.

3   Sophie Foster and James Francis West, 'Pacific Islands,' *Encyclopedia Britannica*, 17 November 2020, https://www.britannica.com/place/Pacific-Islands.

4   Captain James Cook, *The Journals of Captain Cook* (London: Penguin Books, 2003), 537.

5   Earl R. Hinz, *Landfalls of Paradise: Cruising Guide to the Pacific Islands* (Honolulu, University of Hawai'i Press, 1999), 47.

6   Christina Thompson, 'The Enduring Mysteries of How Polynesia was Settled,' Interview by Jamie Bologna and Walter Wuthmann, *Fresh Air*, NPR, updated 29 March 2019, https://www.wbur. org/radioboston/2019/03/29/mysteries-polynesia-settled.

7   Mark Plotkin, 'What the people of the Amazon know that you don't,' 2014, TED.com, 0.35, https://www.ted.com/talks/mark_plotkin_what_the_people_of_the_amazon_know_that_you_don_t?language=en.

8   'Drug Development Costs Jump to \$2.6 Billion,' *Cancer Discovery* 5, no. 2 (1 February 2015), DOI: 10.1158/2159-8290. CD-NB2014-188.

9   'About New Therapeutic Uses,' National Center for Advancing Translational Sciences (NIH), Accessed January 4, 2022, https://ncats.nih.gov/ntu/about.

10 Susan Moore and Doreen Rosenthal, *Grandparenting: Contemporary Perspectives* (Oxfordshire: Routledge, 2016).

Chapter 4: We All Pay the Price for Lost Wisdom

1 Scott Ard, 'Google's 300-year plan,' *CNET,* 30 June 2005, https://www.cnet.com/news/googles-300-year-plan.

2 'How the Ancient Greeks Proved the Earth Was Round More Than 2,000 years ago,' *Independent,* 28 December 2017, https://www.independent.co.uk/life-style/history/ancient-greeks-proved-earth-round-eratosthenes-alexandria-syene-summer-solstice-a8131376.html.

3 John Willis Clark, *The Care of Books: An Essay on the Development of Libraries and Their Fittings, from the Earliest Times to the End of the Eighteenth Century* (Cambridge: Cambridge University Press, 2009), 21.

Principle 3: Preparation Begins Long before the Children Arrive

Chapter 5: Becoming a Parent: Approach and Attitude

1 World Economic Forum, *Global Gender Gap Report 2021*, (Switzerland: World Economic Forum, 2021), https://www.weforum.org/reports/global-gender-gap-report-2021/.

2 'My Cousin Vinny', Her Biological Clock (1992) HD, 4 August 2015, YouTube, https://www.youtube. com/watch?v=Dh0210A-VZo.

3 Yash S. Khandwala, et al., 'Association of paternal age with perinatal outcomes between 2007 and 2016 in the United States: population based cohort study,' *BMJ* 208, no. 363 (31 October 2018), doi: https://doi.org/10.1136/bmj.k4372.

4   Ibid.

5   'Guidelines for sperm donation,' *Fertility and Sterility* 77, no.
     5, (1 June 2002): 2–5, https://www.fertstert.org/article/S0015-
     0282(02)03181-3/fulltext.

6   Sarah Berger, 'Building a career is more of a priority than having
     kids, say single American Women,' *Make* It, 22 June 2018, https://
     www.cnbc.com/2018/06/25/study-single-american- women-say-
     career-is-priority-over-having-kids.html.

7   Payscale Research, *2021 State of the Race and Gender Pay Gap
     Report,* https://www.payscale.com/research-and-insights/gender-
     pay-gap.

8   'What You Need to Consider Before Having Kids, *PsychCentral,*
     Med Review 2016, accessed 15 January 2022, https://
     psychcentral.com/lib/what-you-need-to-consider-before-having-
     kids#7.

9   Korrel Kanoy, 'Marital relationship and individual psychological
     characteristics that predict physical punishment of children,'
     Journal of Family Psychology 17, no.1 (March 17, 2003): 20–28,
     https://doi.org. 10.1037//0893-3200.17.1.20.

Chapter 6: All Parents Are Adopted

1   Rollin McCraty, *Science of the Heart: Exploring the Role of
     the Heart in Human Performance,* Volume 2 (Boulder Creek:
     HeartMath Institute, 2015), 36, https://www.heartmath.org/
     research/science-of-the-heart/energetic-communication/.

2   Sonja Lyubomirsky, 'Pursuing Happiness: The Architecture of
     Sustainable Change', *Review of General Psychology,* Vol 9, No.2,
     (2015): 111-131.

3   Robert T. Muller, 'Children Born of Rape Face a Painful Legacy,'
     The Trauma & Mental Health Report, 22 January 2016, https://
     trauma.blog.yorku.ca/2016/01/children-born-of-rape-face-a-
     painful-legacy.

Principle 4: Happy Mothers Make Happy Families

Chapter 7: D-Day, Dutch Hunger Winter and Epigenetics

1   'For Chinese Moms, Birth Means 30 Days In Pajamas,' *NPR*, heard on *All Things Considered*, 20 July 2011, https://www.npr. org/2011/07/20/138536998/for-chinese-moms-birth-means-30-days-in-pajamas.

2   Robert S. Sholte, et al., 'Long-Run Effects of Gestation during the Dutch Hunger Winter Famine on Labor Market and Hospitalization Outcomes,' *Journal of Health Economics* 39 (January 2015): 17–30, https://doi.org/10.1016/j.jhealeco.2014. 10.002.

3   'What is Epigenetics?', Center for Disease Control and Prevention, 18 May 2022, https://www.cdc.gov/genomics/ disease/epigenetics. htm.

4   Priya Vat Sharma, 'Garbhini Vyakarana,' *Caraka Samhita*, 4 vols. (Sanskrit and English edition), (Delhi: Chaukhambha Orientalia, 2000).

5   Meeta Jhala and Sushma Shankar, 'Post Conception Care Through Ayurveda', *International Ayurvedic Medical Journal*, ISSN: 2320 5091, http://www.iamj.in/posts/2018/images/ upload/1800_1805.pdf.

6   Margaret Mead, *Coming of Age in Samoa: A Psychological Study of Primitive Youth for Western Civilisation* (Boston: Mariner Books, 2016).

7   David Murphey, et al., 'The Health of Parents and Their Children: A Two-Generational Inquiry', *Child Trends*, 4 October 2018, https://www.childtrends.org/publications/the-health-of-parents-and-their-children-a-two-generation-inquiry.

Chapter 8: Ashtavakra, Abhimanyu and the Scientific Theory of Foetal Origins

1   Annie Murphy Paul, *Origins: How the Nine Months Before Birth Shape the Rest of Our Lives* (New York: Free Press, 2011), 21.

2   Annie Murphy Paul, 'What we learn before we're born,' July 2011, audio-video: 6:00–6:30, TEDGlobal 2011, https:// www. ted.com/talks/annie_murphy_paul_what_we_learn_ before_we_ re_born?language=en.

3   D.J. Barker, et al., 'Weight in Infancy and Death from Ischaemic Heart Disease,' *The Lancet* 334, no. 8663 (9 September 1989): 557–580, https://www.thelancet.com/journals/lancet/article/PIIS0140-6736(89)90710-1/fulltext.

4   Lei Cao, et al., 'Prenatal Maternal Stress and Epigenetics: Review of the Human Research,' *Current Molecular Biology Reports* 2 (17 February 2016): 16–25, https://doi.org/ 10.1007/s40610- 016-0030-x.

5   Terry A. Gordon, 'Today's Saber Tooth Tiger', *Psychology Today*, 25 January 2013, https://www.psychologytoday.com/us/blog/transforming-suffering/201301/todays-saber-tooth-tiger.

6   Janell Ross and National Journal, 'Epigenetics: The Controversial Science Behind Racial and Ethnic Health Disparities,' *The Atlantic*, 20 March 2014, https://www.theatlantic.com/politics/archive/2014/03/epigenetics-the-controversial-science-behind-racial-and-ethnic-health-disparities/430749.

7   Birthe R. Dahlerup, et. al., 'Maternal stress and placental function, a study using questionnaires and biomarkers at birth,' *Plos One* 13, no. 11 (15 November 2018), https://doi.org/ 10.1371/ journal. pone.0207184.

8   Psychology Today, *Burnout*, https://www.psychologytoday. com/ us/basics/burnout.

9   Desai K, Gupta P, Parikh P, Desai A, 'Impact of Virtual Heartfulness Meditation Program on Stress, Quality of Sleep, and Psychological Wellbeing during the COVID-19 Pandemic: A Mixed-Method Study', *Int J Environ Res Public Health*, 18(21), (2021):11114.

10   Jayaram Thimmapuram, et al., 'Effect of heartfulness meditation on burnout, emotional wellness, and telomere length in healthcare professionals,' *Journal of Community Hospital Internal Medicine Perspectives* 7, no. 1 (31 March 2017): 21–27, https://doi: 10.1080/20009666.2016.1270806.

Chapter 9: Japanese Fishing Village, Oxytocin and Mother–Child Bonding

1   Dr Terry Brazelton, *Learning to Listen: A Life Caring for Children, Chapter Touchpoints* (Boston: Da Capo Press, 2013), 142.

2   Dr Terry Brazelton, 'On Guiding Parents and Learning to Listen,' interview by Jacki Lyden, *NPR News,* NPR, 16 June 2013, https://www.npr.org/transcripts/191695052.

3   Ibid.

4   Katie Silver, 'Romania's lost generation: Inside the Iron Curtain's orphanages,' *All in the Mind with Sana Qadar,* ABC, 7 July 2014, https://www.abc.net.au/radionational/programs/allinthemind/inside-the-iron-curtain%E2%80%99s-orphanages/5543388.

5   Robert Karen, *First Relationships and How They Shape Our Capacity to Love, reprint edition* (Oxford: Oxford University Press, 1998), Chapter 23.

6   Robert Karen, *Becoming Attached: First Relationships and How They Shape Our Capacity to Love*, (Cambridge: Oxford University Press, 1998), 23.

7   Kendra Cherry, 'What Is Attachment Theory: The Importance of Early Emotional Bonds', *Verywell Mind*, updated 2 May 2022, https://www.verywellmind.com/what-is-attachment-theory-2795337.

8   Ruth Feldman, 'Oxytocin and social affiliation in humans,'
    Hormones and Behavior 61, no. 3 (March 2012), https://
    ruthfeldmanlab.com/wp-content/uploads/2019/06/OT-and-
    social-affiliation.HB2012.pdf.

9   Tobias Esch and George B. Stefano, 'The Neurobiology of
    Love,' *Neuro Endocrinology Letters* 26, no. 3 (June 2005): 175–
    19, https://www.researchgate.net/publication/7752806_The_
    Neurobiology_of_Love.

10 Ilanit Gordon, PhD, 'What is Synchrony and Why is it Important?'
    Psychology Today, 12 June 2020, https://www.psychologytoday.
    com/us/blog/the-biology-bonding/202006/what-is-synchrony-
    and-why-is-it-important#.

11 Ruth Feldman, 'The Biology of Love: Synchrony and the Human
    Affiliative Brain in Health and Psychopathology,' 27 February
    2020, video 6:27, YouTube, https://www.youtube. com/
    watch?v=IzPC-h0xLBQ.

Principle 5: Early Childhood Is the Foundation

Chapter 10: Early Childhood: The Neural Goldrush and the Art of Relaxed Efforts

1   'Eagleman on the Colbert Report,' In 2011, David visited The
    Colbert Report to talk about his new bestseller, Incognito: The
    Secret Lives of the Brain. Video, 1:05 https://www.cc.com/
    video/9catel/the-colbert-report-david-eagleman

2   Elizabeth Howell, 'How Many Stars Are in the Milky Way?'
    Space, 9 June 2021, https://www.space.com/25959-how-many-
    stars-are-in-the-milky-way.html.

3   Frederico AC Azevedo, et al., 'Equal numbers of neuronal and
    nonneuronal cells make the human brain an isometrically scaled-
    up primate brain,' *Journal of Comparative Neurology* 513, no. 5
    (10 April 2009): 532–541, https://doi.org/10.1002/cne.21974.

4   Mary Gauvain and Michael Cole, *Readings on the Development of Children,* 5th ed. (Fort Worth: Worth Publishers, 2008).

5   Harvard University, 'Brain Architecture,' *Center on the Developing Child,* accessed 12 July 2022, https://developingchild.harvard.edu/science/key-concepts/brain-architecture/.

6   Mary Gauvain and Michael Cole, *Readings on the Development of Children,* (Broadway: Worth Publishers Ltd, 2008).

7   National Research Council (US) and Institute of Medicine (US) Committee on Integrating the Science of Early Childhood Development, JP Shonkoff and DA Phillips, eds., *From Neurons to Neighborhoods: The Science of Early Childhood Development* (Washington DC: National Academies Press, 2000), Chapter 8.

8   Duke University, 'Humans don't use as much brainpower as we like to think: Animals had energy-hungry brains long before we did,' *ScienceDaily,* 31 October 2017, https://www.sciencedaily.com/releases/2017/10/171031143717.htm.

9   Rebecca L. Gómez and Jamie O. Edgin, 'Sleep as a window into early neural development: Shifts in sleep-dependent learning effects across early childhood,' *Child Development Perspectives* 9, no. 3 (2015): 183–189, https://doi.org/10.1111/cdep.12130.

Chapter 11: I Once Asked a Three-Year-Old Her Favourite Colour. Her Answer Still Makes Me Smile.

1   Maxwell King, *The Good Neighbor: The Life and Works of Fred Rogers, Part III,* (New York: Abrams Press, 2018), 182–184.

2   Betty Hart and Todd R. Risley, 'The early catastrophe: The 30 million word gap by age 3,' American Educator 27, no. 1 (1995): 4–9, http://www.aft.org/pubs-reports/american_educator/spring2003/catastrophe.html.

3   Kathy Hirsh-Patek, et al., 'The Contribution of Early Communication Quality to Low-Income Children's Language

Success,' *Psychological Science* 26, no. 7 (July 2015): 1073–1083, https://doi.org/10.1177/0956797615581493.

4   Rachel R. Romeo, et al., 'Beyond the 30-Million-Word Gap: Children's Conversational Exposure Is Associated with Language-Related Brain Function,' *Psychological Science* 29, no. 5 (14 February 2018), https://doi.org/10.1177/0956797617742725.

5   Jessa Reed, et al., 'Learning on hold: Cell phones sidetrack parent-child interactions,' *Developmental Psychology* 53, no. 8 (August 2017): 1428–1436, https://doi.org/10.1037/dev0000292.

6   Naja Ferjan Ramirez, 'Why the baby brain can learn two languages at the same time,' *The Conversation* (15 April 2016), https://theconversation.com/why-the-baby-brain-can-learn-two-languages-at-the-same-time-57470.

7   Connor P. Williams, 'The Dual Immersion Solution,' *Edutopia*, 14 November 2018, https://www.edutopia.org/article/dual-immersion-solution.

8   'Culture influences young people's self-esteem: Fulfillment of value priorities of other individuals important to youth,' *Science Daily* (24 February 2014), https://www.sciencedaily.com/releases/2014/02/140224081027.htm.

9   Susan Goldin-Meadow, 'How gesture promotes learning through childhood,' *Child Development Perspectives* 3, no. 2 (1 August 2009): 106–111, https://doi.org/10.1111/j.1750-8606.2009.00088.x.

10   Ram Chandra of Fatehgarh, *Complete Works of Ram Chandra, (Lalaji), vol. 4*, 'The Principles of Conversation,' (Shri Ram Chandra Mission, India, 2018).

Chapter 12: East Meets West, Massage Meets Research: The Story of Touch

1   Sam Stein, 'How a Failed Experiment on Rats Sparked a Billion Dollar Infant-Care Breakthrough', *Huffington Post*, https://www.huffpost.com/entry/major-science- breakthrough_n_5840036

2   '2014: Rat and Infant Massage', *Golden Goose Award*, https://
     www.goldengooseaward. org/01awardees/rat-and-infant-massage.

3   Nehad Nasef, 'Effect of Tactile/Kinaesthetic Massage Therapy on
     DXA Parameter of Preterm Infants,' *ClinicalTrials.gov*, 3 April
     2018, https://clinicaltrials.gov/ct2/show/NCT03412578.

4   'Born Too Soon: The Global Action Report on Preterm Birth,'
     The Partnership for Maternal, Newborn & Child Health, Accessed
     14 January 2022, https://www.who.int/pmnch/knowledge/
     publications/preterm_birth_report/en/index3.html.

5   Tiffany Field, et al., 'Preterm infant massage therapy research: A
     review,' *Infant Behavior and Development* 33, no. 2 (April 2010):
     115–124, https://doi.org/10.1016/j.infbeh.2009.12.004.

6   Tiffany Field, 'Touch in the time of social distancing,' interview
     by Uday Kumar, *Heartfulness Magazine,* 28 February 2021,
     https://www.heartfulnessmagazine.com/touch-in-the-   time-of-
     social-distancing/.

7   Cesár Ernesto Abadía-Barrero, 'Kangaroo Mother Care in
     Columbia: A Subaltern Health Innovation against For-profit
     Biomedicine,' *Medical Anthropology Quarterly*, (24 January 2018):
     384–403, https://doi.org/10.1111/maq.12430.

8   'Losing Touch: Another Drawback of the COVID-19 Pandemic',
     The Scientist Magazine, https:// www.the-scientist.com/news-
     opinion/losing-touch-another- drawback-of-the-COVID19-
     pandemic-67542.

9   Tiffany Field, et al., 'Massage therapy reduces anxiety and
     enhances EEG pattern of alertness and math computations',
     PubMed, https://pubmed.ncbi.nlm.nih.gov/8884390/.

10   Heartfulness, 'Hearfulness Relaxation,' 14 August 2020,
     YouTube, https://www.youtube.com/watch?v=PrYt0Iew8WM.

Chapter 13: Explore the World Together, See More

1   Laura Sanders, 'The Brain Set Free,' *Science News*, 27 July 2012,
     https://www.sciencenews.org/article/brain-set-free.

2 'David Hubel, Nobel-Winning Scientist, Dies at 87', *The New York Times,* https://www.nytimes.com/2013/09/25/ science/ david-hubel-nobel-winning-scientist-dies-at-87.html.

3 Statistica Research Department, 'Forecast on connected devices per person worldwide 2003–2020,' *Statistica,* 30 November 2013, https://www.statista.com/statistics/678739/forecast-on-connected-devices-per-person.

4 Paul Virilio, *Politics of the Very Worst* (New York: Semiotext(e), 1999), 89.

5 'American Academy of Pediatrics Announces New Recommendations for Children's Media Use,' *American Academy of Pediatrics,* 21 October 2015, https://www.aap. org/ en/news-room/news-releases/aap/2016/aap-announces-new-recommendations-for-media-use/.

6 WHO, *Guidelines on Physical Activity, Sedentary Behaviour, and Sleep for Children under 5 Years of Age,* (Geneva, Switzerland: World Health Organization, 2019), https://apps.who.int/ iris/bitstream/handle/10665/311664/9789241550536-eng. pdf?sequence=1&isAllowed=y.https://apps.who.int/iris/ bitstream/handle/10665/311664/9789241550536-eng. pdf? sequence=1&isAllowed=y.

7 Ryan Jaslow, 'Background television at home may be harming U.S. kids' development,' *CBS News,* 2 October 2012, https:// www.cbsnews.com/news/background-television-at-home-may-be-harming-us-kids-development.

8 Rebekah A. Richert, PhD; et al., 'Word Learning from Baby Videos,' *JAMA Network,* 164, no. 5 (May 3, 2010): 432–437, https://doi.org/10.1001/archpediatrics.2010.24.

9 Stephanie Pappas, 'What do we really know about kids and screens?' *American Psychological Association* 51, no. 3 (1 April 2020): 42, https://www.apa.org/monitor/2020/04/cover-kids- screens.

10 Plato, Edith Hamilton, ed, *The Collected Dialogues of Plato: Including the Letters* (Bollingen Series LXXI) (Princeton: Princeton University Press, 2005), 520.

11   Adrian F. Ward, et al., 'Brain Drain: The Mere Presence of One's
     Own Smartphone Reduces Available Cognitive Capacity,' *Journal
     of the Association for Consumer* Research 2, no, 2 (2017), https://
     www.journals.uchicago.edu/doi/abs/10.1086/691462.

12   Gopi Kallayil, *The Internet to the Inner-net: Five Ways to Reset Your
     Connection and Live a Conscious Life* (New York: Hay House,
     2016), 82.

13   University of Bristol, 'Getting Dirty May Lift Your Mood,'
     ScienceDaily, 10 April 2007, www.sciencedaily.com/releases/
     2007/04/070402102001.htm.

Principle 6: Character Builds Personality

Chapter 14: Character Is the Foundation of Life: The Role of Parents in Laying the Foundation

1   'The Mask of Tragedy,' *Memento,* 17 July 2018, http://www.
     diptyqueparis-memento.com/en/the-mask-of-tragedy/

2   Jean M Twenge and W.Keith Campbell, *The Narcissism Epidemic:
     Living in the Age of Entitlement,* (Simon & Schuster, 2009), 2.

3   Jacob Dirnhuber, 'Children turn backs on traditional careers
     in favour of internet fame, study finds', *The Sun,* 22 May
     2017, https://www.thesun.co.uk/news/3617062/children-turn-
     backs-on-traditional-careers-in-favour-of-internet-fame-study-
     finds/#:~:text=Hide%20the%20menu-,Children%20turn%20
     backs%20on%20traditional%20careers,of%20internet%20
     fame%2C%20study%20finds&text=FORGET%20driving%20
     a%20train%20or,teaching%20or%20being%20a%20doctor.

Chapter 15: As You Do, So They Learn: The Story of Mirror Neurons

1   Richard Roche, *Pioneering Studies in Cognitive Neuroscience*
     (Maidenhead, Berkshire, UK: Open University Press, 2009), 41.

2   Sandra Blakeslee, 'Cells That Read Minds,' *The New York Times,* 10 January 2006, https://www.nytimes.com/2006/01/10/science/cells-that-read-minds.html.

3   Giacomo Rizzolatti, 'Initial Reaction,' *GoCognitive*, YouTube, 26 March 2011, https://www.youtube.com/watch?v=fFR2J4ECPMk.

4   'The neurons that shaped civilization'. TEDIndia 2009, November 2009, https://www.ted.com/talks/vilayanur_ramachandran_the_neurons_that_shaped_civilization?language=en Timestamp: 6:58

5   John Mark Taylor, 'Mirror Neurons After a Quarter Century: New light, new cracks,' *Science in the News* blog, Harvard University, 25 July 2016, https://sitn.hms.harvard.edu/flash/2016/mirror-neurons-quarter-century-new-light-new-cracks.

Chapter 16: Interest and Observation Are Twins

1   Maria Montessori, *The Absorbent Mind* (New York: Start Publishing, 2013), 62.

2   Vicki G. Morwitz, *et al.,* 'Does Measuring Intent Change Behavior?' *Journal of Consumer Research* 20, no. 1 (1993): 46–61, https://www.jstor.org/stable/2489199?seq=1.

3   Gaston Godin, *et al.,* 'Asking questions changes behavior: mere measurement effects on frequency of blood donation,' *Health Psychology Journal* 27, no. 2 (March 2008): 179–184), https://doi.org/10.1037/0278-6133.27.2.179.

Chapter 17: The Strength of Humility

1   *The Bhagavad Gita*, 13:08, (Gorakhpur, Gita Press).

2   Mitchell, Stephen and Lao Tzu, *Tao Te Ching: A New English Version*, (New York, NY: Harper Perennial Modern Classics; Reprint edition, 2006).

Principle 7: Youth Are the Future. Guide Them, Don't Break Them.

Chapter 18: Youth: A Time of Promise and Potential

1   Donald Hebb, *The Organization of Behavior* 99th *ed.* (London: Psychology Press, 2005), Kindle.

2   C.J. Shatz, 'The Developing Brain,' *Scientific American* 267, no. 3 (September 1992): 60–67, https://doi.org/10.1038/scientificamerican0992-60.

3   Linda Patia Spear, 'Adolescent Neurodevelopment,' *Journal of Adolescent Health*, 52, no. 2 Supple 2 (February 2013): s7–13, https://doi.org/10.1016/j.jadohealth.2012.05.006.

Chapter 19: Experimentation, Thrill-Seeking and Friendships in Teen Years

1   Daniel J. Siegel, M.D, *Brainstorm: The Power and Purpose of the Teenage Brain*, (New York: TarcherPerigee, 2014), 67.

2   Jones CM, et al., 'Prescription Opioid Misuse and Use of Alcohol and Other Substances Among High School Students—Youth Risk Behavior Survey, United States, 2019' *Morbidity and Mortality Weekly Report* 69, Suppl-1 (21 August 2020): 38–46, http://dx.doi.org/10.15585/mmwr.su6901a5external icon.

3   Francesca Scalici and Peter J. Schulz, James G. Scott, ed., 'Influence of Perceived Parent and Peer Endorsement on Adolescent Smoking Intentions: Parents Have More Say, But Their Influence Wanes as Kids Get Older,' *PLOS One* 9, no. 7, . (3 July 2014), https://doi.org/10.1371/journal.pone.0101275.

4   'Teen Drivers: Get the Facts,' *CDC*, accessed on 31 January 2022, https://www.cdc.gov/transportationsafety/teen_drivers/teendrivers_factsheet.html.

5 Lydia Denworth, 'Friendship Is Crucial to the Adolescent Brain,' *The Atlantic*, 28 January 2020, https://www.theatlantic.com/family/archive/2020/01/friendship-crucial-adolescent-brain/605638.

6 Jason Chien, et al., 'Peers increase adolescent risk taking by enhancing activity in the brain's reward circuitry,' *Developmental Science* 14, no. 2 (March 2011): F1–F10, https://doi.org/10.1111/j.1467-7687.2010.01035.x.

Principle 8: Lifestyle Is an Expression of One's Attitudes

Chapter 20: Sleep Cycles Are an Investment

1 Ray Bradbury, 'A Sound of Thunder', *Colliers*, 28 June 1952.

2 Oxford University Press USA, 'Sleep deprived people more likely to have car crashes,' *ScienceDaily*, 18 September 2018, www.sciencedaily.com/releases/2018/09/180918082041.htm.

3 'A deeply refreshing sleep,' *Heartfulness*, 3 April 2018, https://www.heartfulnessmagazine.com/a-deeply-refreshing-sleep.

4 Jeffrey Illiff, 'One more reason to get a good night's sleep,' filmed at TEDMED 2014, video, https://www.tedmed.com/talks/show?id=293015.

5 Satchidananda Panda, et al., 'Melanopsin (Opn4) requirement for normal light-induced circadian phase shifting,' *Science* (13 December 2002): 2213–6, https://doi.org/ 10.1126/science.1076848.

Chapter 21: Poverty and Prosperity Paradox

1 Kamlesh D. Patel, 'Create happiness now,' *Heartfulness*, 28 February 2022, https://www.heartfulnessmagazine.com/create-happiness-now.

2   Leo Tolstoy, Louise Maude and Aylmer Maude, trans., *What Men Live By and Other Tales*, (Maryland: Wildside Press, 2004), 34, Kindle.

3   Paul K. Piff, et al., 'Higher Social Class Predicts Increased Unethical Behavior,' *Proceedings of the National Academy of Sciences* 109, no. 11 (February 2012): 4086–4089, https://doi.org/ 10.1073/pnas.1118373109.

4   Paul K. Piff, et al., 'Higher Social Class Predicts Increased Unethical Behavior,' https://www.pnas.org/content/109/11/4086? phpMyAdmin= cfc2644bd9c947213a0141747c2608b0.

5   Ibid.

6   Marla E. Eisenberg, et al., 'Correlations Between Family Meals and Psychosocial Well-being among Adolescents,' *Journal of the American Medical Association* 158, no. 8, (August 2004): 792–796, https://doi.org/ 10.1001/archpedi.158.8.792.

7   Madeline Levine, PhD., *The Price of Privilege: How Parental Pressure and Material Advantage Are Creating a Generation of Disconnected and Unhappy Kids* (New York, Harper Perennial; Reprint edition, 2008), 66.

Chapter 22: Conscious Eating Habits

1   Dr Peet Kaur, 'Undiagnosed Uncontrolled Reason Why India Is Diabetes Capital of World,' *Businessworld*, October 2019, https://www.businessworld.in/article/Undiagnosed-Uncontrolled-Reason-Why-India-Is-Diabetes-Capital-Of-World/12-10-2019-177424.

2   Ranjit Mohan Anjana, MD, et al., 'References in Prevalence of diabetes and prediabetes in 15 states of India: results from the ICMR-INDIAB population-based cross-sectional study,' *The Lancet Diabetes & Endocrinology*, 5, no. 8 (1 August 2017): 585-596, https://www.thelancet.com/journals/landia/article/PIIS2213-8587(17)30174-2/fulltext.

3   Sara B. Algoe, et al., 'It's the little things: Everyday gratitude as a
    booster shot for romantic relationships,' *Wiley Online Library*, 21
    May 2010, https://onlinelibrary.wiley.com/doi/10.1111/ j.1475-
    6811.2010.01273.x.

4   OECD, 'Who Are the School Truants?', *PISA in Focus 35*, (1
    January 2014), https://doi.org/10.1787/5jzb019jwmd5-en.

5   Heather Gerrie, 'Our second brain: More than a gut feeling,'
    University of British Columbia Graduate Program in Neuroscience,
    accessed 28 February 2022, https://neuroscience.ubc.ca/our-
    second-brain- more-than-a-gut-feeling.

6   G. Vighi, et al., 'Allergy and the gastrointestinal system,' *Clinical
    and Experimental Immunology* 153, no. 1 (21 July 2008): 3–6,
    https://doi.org/10.1111/j.1365-2249.2008.03713.x.

7   Jessica Stoller-Conrad, 'Microbes Help Produce Serotonin in
    Gut,' *Caltech*, 9 April 2015, accessed 28 February 2022, https://
    www.caltech.edu/about/news/microbes-help-produce-serotonin-
    gut-46495.

8   Rachael Rettner, '5 Ways Gut Bacteria Affect Your Health,' *Live
    Science*, 5 September 2013, https://www.livescience.com/39444-
    gut-bacteria-health.html.

9   Ruairi Robertson, PhD, 'Why the Gut Microbiome Is Crucial
    for Your Health,' *Healthline*, last updated 27 June 2017, https://
    www.healthline.com/nutrition/gut-microbiome-and-health.

10 Uzan-Yulzari, A., Turta, O., Belogolovski, A. et al., 'Neonatal
    antibiotic exposure impairs child growth during the first six
    years of life by perturbing intestinal microbial colonization.' *Nat
    Commun* 12, 443 (2021). https://doi.org/10.1038/s41467-020-
    20495-4.